Questions
— of—
Character

Questions
— of —
Character

The Presidency of
Donald J. Trump

Robert C. Smith

LYNNE
RIENNER
PUBLISHERS

BOULDER
LONDON

Published in the United States of America in 2022 by
Lynne Rienner Publishers, Inc.
1800 30th Street, Suite 314, Boulder, Colorado 80301
www.rienner.com

and in the United Kingdom by
Lynne Rienner Publishers, Inc.
Gray's Inn House, 127 Clerkenwell Road, London EC1 5DB
www.eurospanbookstore.com/rienner

Library of Congress Cataloging-in-Publication Data
Names: Smith, Robert C. (Robert Charles), 1947– author.
Title: Questions of character : the presidency of Donald J. Trump / Robert C.
  Smith.
Description: Boulder, Colorado : Lynne Rienner Publishers, Inc., 2022. |
  Includes bibliographical references and index. | Summary: "A comprehensive
  exploration of the consequences of Trump's character—personal, presidential,
  and democratic—in the period leading up to, during, and immediately after
  his term in office."— Provided by publisher.
Identifiers: LCCN 2021030416 | ISBN 9781955055086 (hardcover) | ISBN
  9781955055093 (paperback)
Subjects: LCSH: Trump, Donald, 1946– | Trump, Donald, 1946– —Psychology. |
  Character—Political aspects—United States. | Decision
  making—Psychological aspects. | Presidents—United States—Biography. |
  United States—Politics and government—Decision making. | United
  States—Politics and government—2017–2021.
Classification: LCC E913 .S625 2022 | DDC 973.933092 [B]—dc23/eng/20211018
LC record available at https://lccn.loc.gov/2021030416

British Cataloguing in Publication Data
A Cataloguing in Publication record for this book
is available from the British Library.

Printed and bound in the United States of America

∞   The paper used in this publication meets the requirements
    of the American National Standard for Permanence of
    Paper for Printed Library Materials Z39.48-1992.

5   4   3   2   1

Contents

Acknowledgments

I THANK MY WIFE, SCOTTIE, FOR HER LOVE AND CARE, and for her help in preparing the manuscript for this book. Without her assistance, it could not have been done. I appreciate Sally Glover at Lynne Rienner Publishers for her early interest in and encouragement of the project. I have multiple thanks for Lynne herself. First, for her support of the study. Second, for the selection of learned, discerning, and careful reviewers. And finally, for her meticulous comments, criticisms, and suggestions, substantively, editorially, and stylistically. Without her, this would have been a much lesser book. All scholars yearn for a publisher and editor with the character of Lynne. I am grateful for her work.

The three anonymous reviewers were astute and perceptive. Their familiarity with the literature on character and the presidency, and about President Trump, was evident in their useful comments, criticisms, and suggestions. One of the three was especially sagacious, identifying gaps in my theorizing and data, pointing to sources I had overlooked, and providing detailed chapter-by-chapter marginal comments. I wish I knew his or her name so that I could personally express my appreciation.

I can thank by name Wilbur Rich, emeritus professor of political science at Wellesley, who on short notice and within several days provided a detailed chapter-by-chapter critique of the manuscript with bountiful theoretical, empirical, and occasionally normative suggestions that improved both the inferences and interpretations.

Wilbur also urged that I take care to be fair and balanced in my treatment of the controversial forty-fifth president and not be unduly influenced by the political science consensus. I did not incorporate all of Wilbur's substantive and stylistic suggestions, but the many I did improved each chapter. As with a good publisher and editor, one yearns for colleagues with the alacrity and thoroughness of a Wilbur Rich.

I have authored multiple papers, articles, and books with my former Howard University colleague Richard Seltzer, including *Polarization and the Presidency: From FDR to Barack Obama,* which I draw on to some extent in this work. A methodologist, Rick's keen eye for data and detail identified sources I had overlooked, and he clarified inferences and interpretations. My mentor John R. Howard of the State University of New York and my San Francisco State colleague David Tabb offered useful comments and suggestions. John, a lawyer and sociologist, encouraged me to make the book accessible to those not familiar with the political science literature and the intricacies of the various theories of character and the presidency. Without compromising the integrity of the scholarship, I endeavored to do this—I hope with some success.

The excellent copyediting improved the clarity and consistency of the manuscript, for which I am grateful to Shena Redmond and her colleagues. There may be errors of fact and interpretation in this work. If there are, I alone am responsible. President Trump is a controversial and likely consequential president. I have tried to examine him in a detached, professional, and objective manner. Whether I have succeeded is for readers to judge.

1

The Trump Presidency: Examining Coolly in a Hot Time

AT THE END OF PRESIDENT DONALD J. TRUMP'S FIRST year in office, the Presidents and Executive Politics Section of the American Political Science Association—the foremost organization of political science experts on the presidency—conducted one of its periodic Presidential Greatness Surveys, asking respondents to rate or rank each of the forty-four persons who occupied the office.[1] President Trump made his debut on the survey as the worst president in US history. His average rating of 12.34 was nearly three points lower than James Buchanan's, who previously occupied the position of worst president.[2] The 12.7 percent of respondents who were Republican and the 17.4 percent who identified as conservative were a bit more favorable to Trump, ranking him fortieth instead of forty-fourth (ahead of William Henry Harrison, Franklin Pierce, Buchanan, and Andrew Johnson). Thus, at the end of the first year of the Trump presidency there was a near consensus among scholars the Trump was the worst president in the history of the republic.

Reviewing the early political science literature on the Trump election and presidency, I found, not surprisingly perhaps, that Trump was viewed as a most unusual president. Jon Herbert, Trevor McCrisken, and Andrew Wroe write that Trump is "a deeply flawed character wholly unsuited for the job of president—mendacious, narcissistic, quickly bored, misogynistic and ethnocentric, thin skinned and easily provoked, stunningly ill-informed and yet utterly convinced of his own brilliance and intelligence."[3] Michael Genovese argues that

Donald Trump represents a distinctly American version of illiberal democracy. We have had demagogues in our past, but none has ever gotten close to becoming president. Donald Trump is thus an American first! His brash, bombastic attack style, his bold promises and manifest lack of knowledge, his rapid-fire insults and misogynistic utterances and racist rants and bulling ways. . . . Trump won the presidency when no one in their right mind thought it possible.[4]

James Pfiffner observes the lies of Donald Trump have "undermined enlightenment epistemology and corroded the premises of liberal democracy."[5] E. J. Dionne, Norman Ornstein, and Thomas Mann—after labeling the president a "narcissistic politician," "demagogue," "charlatan," and a "nihilist"—write that "our purpose is to make clear that Trump is not a normal president, that he lacks the self-restraint democracy requires of leaders, and his ethical conduct raises systematic doubts about his capacity to govern in the public interest."[6] George Edwards concludes,

Both the tone and substance of Trump's public utterances are beyond the norms of the presidency. His willingness to demean his opponents, mislead the public about the nature of threats, prevaricate about people, issues, nations, policies, and accomplishments, employ racially charged language, and challenge the rule of law add a unique-disturbing-element to American political life.[7]

In the most widely discussed political science book on the Trump election and presidency, Steven Levitsky and Daniel Ziblatt write,

When extremist demagogues emerge in 'healthy democracies,' the first test is whether political leaders, especially political parties, work to prevent them from gaining power in the first place by keeping them off mainstream party tickets, refusing to endorse them, and when necessary making common cause with rivals in support of democratic candidates. . . . America failed this first test in 2016, when we elected a president with dubious allegiance to democratic norms. Donald Trump's surprise victory was made possible not only by public disaffection but also by the Republican Party's failure to keep an extremist demagogue within its own ranks from gaining the nomination.[8]

Finally, Zachary Callen and Philip Rocco, editors of *American Political Development and the Trump Presidency,* write Trump's "actions in office have sparked credible fears about the future of democracy. . . . Trump is a figure untethered to republican virtues, who refers to the media as 'the enemy of the people' and dehumanizes minorities, immigrants and anyone who opposes him."[9]

What distinguishes the forty-fifth president from his predecessors—such that this early consensus could exist about his fitness for the office—is character, which is the dominant focus of this study. Given the controversial nature of Trump and the negative assessments of most political scientists, in this work I want to be consciously, scrupulously objective; to perform professional empirical analysis; and to be ever alert to the possibility of bias. The character analysis should discipline data collection, analysis, and interpretation, which I hope allows me, to paraphrase the great presidency scholar Clinton Rossiter, to "examine coolly in a hot time."[10]

The core of the book is a study of the president's character—personal, presidential, and constitutional. Mainly I use James David Barber's "much praised and much maligned" theory of the presidential character to explain Trump's behavior as candidate and president.[11] For analysis of his personal character, I rely on James Pfiffner's studies, and for constitutional character Dennis Thompson's article "Constitutional Character."[12]

In terms of character, Trump is sui generis. But with respect to ideology, he has been a chameleon for much of his career, changing views on issues and party affiliations multiple times. His extraordinary and unexpected election in 2016 is rooted in the polarization of contemporary American politics that started with the election and presidency of Ronald Reagan and the growth in the Republican electorate of the influence of paleoconservatism, a political philosophy that stresses American nationalism, Christian values, and traditional conservatism. The Reagan polarization, as Richard Seltzer and I show in *Polarization and the Presidency: From FDR to Barack Obama,* has its origins as a reaction to the presidency of Franklin Roosevelt, issues of taxes, the welfare state (particularly health insurance), and after 1964, race and racism.[13] The modern polarized polity is also rooted to some extent in the White nationalist and paleoconservative ideas advanced by Patrick Buchanan in his writings and presidential campaigns.[14] At the end of the Obama administration, the party system was highly polarized (Obama was the most polarizing president prior to Trump) and the Republican Party had already been Trumped. As Thomas Mann and Norman Ornstein highlight in 2012, "However awkward it may be for the traditional press and nonpartisan analysts to acknowledge, one of the two major parties, the Republican Party, has become an insurgent outlier—ideologically extreme, contemptuous of the inherited social and economic regimes; scornful of compromise; unpersuaded by science; and dismissive of the legitimacy of its political opposition."[15]

In Chapter 2 I analyze the 2016 election. There are multiple, complementary theories of the nomination and election of Trump. Some view the election as the maturing of trends since the late 1960s toward authoritarianism among Republican voters, accelerated by demographic and economic changes, "which activated authoritarian tendencies, leading many Americans to seek out a strong leader who would preserve the status-quo under threat and impose order on a world they perceive as increasingly alien."[16] Others view it as a populist revolt by the "heartland" against "coastal elites" by those who believe the system is stacked against them.[17] Trump's election is viewed by some as rooted in old-fashioned racism or racial resentment,[18] and others view the election of Trump as an expression of emergent White nationalism or White identity politics.[19] As I indicated, the various theories of the Trump election are complementary; I shall emphasize White nationalism, fueled by economic anxieties and racial resentment, as a comprehensive theory of the nomination and election of the president.

A number of political scientists and other students of the Trump campaign and presidency have casually labeled Trump a demagogue. *Demagogue* is a contested concept in social science, but I shall attempt to show that Trump's rhetoric and behavior fit the definition and many of the indicators of a demagogue. Similarly, *charisma* is a contested concept, but in Chapter 2 I present analysis to show there is a charismatic relationship between Trump and his core constituents.

In Chapter 3 I review the literature on personality and political leadership, starting with Harold Lasswell's seminal work. I then present in detail Barber's theory of the presidential character, highlighting both its strengths and weaknesses in explaining presidential leadership behavior as discussed in the extensive literature on his work.

In Chapter 4 I examine the development of Trump's personality and character using James David Barber's theory as the organizing framework, focusing on his family, adolescence and first business success, showing, as Barber theorizes, how his style as a business executive anticipates his behavior as president.

In Chapter 5 I study the presidential character of Trump in terms of Barber's theory, focusing on how he organized the White House staff and his decisionmaking process, the extent to which he did his "homework," his personal relations with staff, the cabinet, and leaders of Congress. This chapter also looks at Trump's prioritization of the rhetorical dimension of the work of the president.

In Chapters 6 and 7 I deal with the domestic and foreign policies of the administration including in the domestic chapter how Trump handled the two major crises of his tenure, the Covid-19 pandemic and the nationwide uprising after the police murder of George Floyd. In both domestic and foreign policy, I am interested in the part played by character in the decisionmaking processes as compared to ideology, party, the political context, or the climate of expectations.

In Chapter 8 I am concerned with Trump's personal as well as his democratic and constitutional character. For personal character I use Pfiffner's three indicators: lying, marital fidelity, and keeping campaign promises. Democratic and constitutional character are analyzed in terms of adherence to the norms of democracy, for examples the integrity of the election process, respect for the role of press, the limits of executive power, the separation of powers, and ethnic and religious tolerance.

Consistent with the political science consensus discussed previously, this book that concludes President Trump, beginning with the 2016 campaign and continuing through the last days of his presidency, exhibited multiple character deficits, displayed most egregiously in his refusal to accept the outcome of the 2020 election, which resulted in the violent assault on the Capitol and his impeachment for a second time. In Chapter 9 I ask, how did it happen? How did a person with such manifest character deficits win the presidency and run a competitive race for reelection? First, it is suggested that many in the White majority who voted for Trump likely had reservations about his character, but nevertheless viewed him as an effective tribune to advance their values and interests as an aggrieved shrinking majority. Second, in the 1960s and 1970s, political science advanced the theory that democratic values were secured from the threat of a Trump-like character not by the behavior of the public but by the commitment of elites to democratic norms, which came to be known as the theory of democratic elitism. The fallacy of this theory is another explanation of what happened.

I briefly summarize in Chapter 10 the findings of this study with respect to each character dimension—presidential, personal, democratic, and constitutional—and then explore in detail Trump's refusal to accept his defeat in the 2020 election and his pattern of behavior that resulted in the most violent transfer of power in the history of the American democracy.

In the concluding chapter I raise questions about the long-term significance of the election and presidency of Trump for the Republican Party, conservatism, and the democracy in the United States.

Notes

1. Brandon Rottingham and Justin Vaughn, "Official Results of the 2018 Presidents and Executive Politics Presidential Greatness Survey" (Washington: American Political Science Association, 2018), https://www.boisestate.edu/sps-politicalscience/files/2018/02/Greatness.pdf. The survey was conducted online from December 22, 2017, to January 2018. Over 300 respondents were asked to participate; 170 useable responses were returned for a response rate of 53 percent.

2. Respondents were asked to rate each president on a scale of 0–100, with 0 = failure, 50 = average, and 100 = great. The rating for each president was tallied and then ranked from the highest to the lowest.

3. Jon Herbert, Trevor McCrisken, and Andrew Wroe, *The Ordinary Presidency of Donald Trump* (New York: Palgrave, 2019), 2.

4. Michael Genovese, *How Trump Governs: An Assessment and Prognosis* (Amherst, NY: Cambria Press, 2017), 245.

5. James Pfiffner, "The Lies of Donald Trump: A Taxonomy," in Charles Lamb and Jacob Neiheisel, eds., *Presidential Leadership and the Trump Presidency* (New York: Palgrave Macmillan, 2020), 18.

6. E. J. Dionne, Norman Ornstein, and Thomas Mann, *One Nation After Trump: A Guide to the Perplexed, the Disillusioned, the Desperate, and the Not-Yet Deported* (New York: St. Martin's, 2017), 2, 6.

7. George Edwards, "The Bully in the Pulpit: The Impact of Donald Trump's Public Discourse," paper presented at the annual meeting of the American Political Science Association, Washington, September 2019.

8. Steven Levitsky and Daniel Ziblatt, *How Democracies Die* (New York: Broadway, 2018), 7, 9. Reflecting this unease, the theme of the 2020 meeting of the American Political Science Association—democracy and destabilization—was developed in order to focus the discipline's attention on the threats authoritarianism and illiberal tendencies pose to democracy, as symbolized in "Trump's momentous election." The association devoted a special issue of one of its journals to understanding Trump's election and presidency (the call for papers received over 100 submissions). The editors noted that Trump was "an unprecedented figure in American politics [whose] lack of concern for how government works, his impatience to accomplish things, and what some regard as his clear disdain for the Constitution's contraints on executive power, has led many to fear he constitutes a threat to democracy." See Michael Bernhard and Daniel O'Neil, "Trump: Causes and Consequences," *Perspectives on Politics* 17 (2019): 317.

9. Zachary Callen and Philip Rocco, eds., *American Political Development and the Trump Presidency* (Philadelphia: University of Pennsylvania Press, 2020), 1–2.

10. Clinton Rossiter, "The Powers of the Presidency," in Harry Bailey, ed., *Classics of the American Presidency* (Oak Park, IL: Moore, 1980), 71.

11. The quote is from Michael Lyons, "Presidential Character Revisited," *Political Psychology* 18 (1997): 790.

12. James Pfiffner, "Judging Presidential Character," *Public Integrity* 5 (2002): 7–24, and his *The Character Factor: How We Judge America's Presidents* (College Station: Texas A & M University Press, 2004); and Dennis Thompson, "Constitutional Character: Virtues and Vices of Presidential Leadership," *Presidential Studies Quarterly* 40 (2010): 23–37.

13. Robert C. Smith and Richard Seltzer, *Polarization and the Presidency: From FDR to Barack Obama* (Boulder, CO: Lynne Rienner, 2015).

14. Patrick Buchanan's paleoconservative ideas are best advanced in his *Suicide of a Superpower: Will America Survive to 2025?* (New York: Thomas Dunne, 2011). Buchanan's biographer writes that Buchanan views himself as an "intelligent alternative to the racism and white supremacy of David Duke." See Timothy Stanley, *The Crusader: The Life and Tumultuous Times of Pat Buchanan* (New York: Thomas Dunne, 2012), 182.

15. Thomas Mann and Norman Ornstein, *It's Worse Than It Looks: How the American Constitutional System Collided with the New Politics of Extremism* (New York: Basic Books, 2012), xiv.

16. Amanda Taub, "The Rise of American Authoritarianism," *Vox,* March 1, 2016, https://www.vox.com/2016/3/1/11127424/trump-authoritarianism. See also Marc Hetherington and Jonathan Weiler, *Authoritarianism and Polarization in American Politics* (New York: Cambridge University Press, 2009).

17. Ron Fournier, "The Populist Revolt," *The Atlantic,* February 10, 2016; Victor David Hansen, *The Case for Donald Trump* (New York: Basic Books, 2019); Eric Oliver and Wendy Rahn, "The Rise of the Trumpenvolk: Populism in the 2016 Election," *Annals of the American Academy of Political and Social Science* 667 (2016): 189–206; and Stanley Renshon, *The Real Psychology of the Trump Presidency* (New York: Palgrave Macmillan, 2020): 80–89.

18. Michael Tesler, "The Return of Old-Fashioned Racism to White Americans' Partisan Preferences in the Early Obama Era," *Journal of Politics* 75 (2013): 110–123; and Alan Abramowitz, *The Great Realignment: Race, Party, and the Rise of Donald Trump* (New Haven: Yale University Press, 2018).

19. Ronald Walters is the pioneering scholar on the emergence of White nationalism in American politics. See his *White Nationalism, Black Interests: Conservative Public Policy and the Black Community* (Detroit: Wayne State University Press, 2003); and Robert C. Smith, "Understanding White Nationalism in America: The Contribution of Ronald Walters," *National Review of Black Politics* 2 (2021): 53–62. See also "White Racial Consciousness in the U.S.," 2016 ANES Pilot Study Proposal, Ann Arbor, University of Michigan, n.d.; Ashley Jardina, *White Identity Politics* (New York: Cambridge University Press, 2019); Alex Altman, "The Billionaire and the Bigots: How Trump's Campaign Brought White Nationalists Out of the Shadows," *Time,* April 25, 2016; and John Sides, Michael Tesler, and Lynn Vavreck, *Identity Crisis: The 2016 Presidential Campaign and the Battle for the Meaning of America* (Princeton: Princeton University Press, 2019).

2

The Context of the
2016 Presidential Election

FROM THE NEW DEAL UNTIL 1968, THE DEMOCRATIC
Party was the majority party in the United States, commanding the
allegiance of most of the electorate, winning the presidency in all but
two elections, holding the majority in both houses of Congress
except for two two-year intervals, and generally occupying most
state and local offices. Since the partisan dealignment that began in
1968, there has been no majority party in the United States. In the
2016 election exit polls, the electorate identified as 36 percent Democratic, 33 percent Republican, and 31 percent independent. In the
2018 election, the Pew Research Center found that when the partisan leanings of independents were taken into consideration, 50 percent of the electorate was Democratic and 42 percent Republican,
which represented a shift from 2016 when the party balance was 48
percent Democrat and 44 percent Republican when party-leaning
independents were included.[1] Party identification tends to fluctuate,
so the best judgment is that the parties are evenly balanced, with a
relatively small percentage of true independents.

The Democratic Party demographically is a broad coalition,
reflecting the diversity of the American people, while the Republicans are a narrow, White, Christian party. In the 2016 exit poll the
Democratic electorate was disproportionately urban, constituted by
26 percent minorities (20 percent Black, 6 percent Hispanics), Jews,
persons with no religion, and members of the LGBTQ community.
The Republicans were 89 percent White, disproportionately rural,

and Christian. Regionally the Democrats tend to live on the coasts, while the Republicans are anchored in the south, the plains, and the mountain west. The parties therefore tend to be divided racially, regionally, and religiously. Increasingly, there is also an education divide as the Democratic Party is becoming the home of the well-educated (college and especially postgraduates), while the Republicans are disproportionately those without postsecondary education.

Ideology

Political science research on ideology has consistently shown that Americans tend to be ideological innocents, without clear understanding or identification with the labels *liberal* and *conservative* as they are used by political elites; neither do they clearly identify with the policies or issues. In the 2016 exit poll, 26 percent of respondents identified as liberal, 35 percent conservative, and 39 percent moderate. We know, however, that the selection of these labels does not necessarily predict the issue or policy positions of respondents, and the polls exclude the large number of respondents who choose none of the three labels.[2]

Liberalism in the United States until Franklin Delano Roosevelt "captured" the label was conservatism.[3] This "classical" liberalism, as distinct from FDR's "modern" liberalism, celebrated individualism, limited government, the primacy of property rights, local autonomy, and states' rights. This "conservative liberalism" also celebrated the negative state, where the proper functions of government were to protect private property, enforce contracts, exercise the police power, provide for the national defense, and then leave free people alone. Roosevelt changed all of this by redefining liberalism to mean that the proper functions of government included regulation of the economy and the provision of a welfare state in the form of employment, health insurance, housing, and retirement income. Although the traditional liberals resented the appropriation of the term and resisted Roosevelt's use of the liberal label, by the 1940s they had resigned themselves to the fact and began to call themselves conservatives, and to argue that conservatism was superior to liberalism because it reflected traditional values of liberty, individualism, and limited government. It is not clear, however, that respondents in polls in the 1940s or thereafter understood the issue content of these ideological labels.

The first systematic study of the issue, or policy, content of the conservative and liberal labels for the mass public was conducted in 1964. It found that at an abstract level most Americans identified with conservatism, but at the operational level or in terms of specific policies most Americans were New Deal liberals. Among those who identified as conservative, only a third were operationally conservative, and 40 percent were liberals. This discrepancy between abstract principles and concrete policies was so large that the authors described it as "almost schizoid."[4] More recent studies confirm this central finding. Morris Fiorina writes, "The Americans who classify themselves as liberals tend to be liberal in the sense we understand the term on both economic and social issues. . . . By contrast, only 20 percent of conservatives are conservative on both social and economic issues, about 25 percent are social conservatives only, 15 percent economic conservatives only and about one-third are conservative on neither economic or social issues."[5] Similarly, Christopher Ellis and James Stimson found that about 30 percent of Americans are "consistent liberals," self-identifying as liberals and favoring liberal policies, while only 15 percent of conservatives are consistent conservatives.[6] Overall, the consensus in political science is that the American electorate remains almost ideologically contradictory, conservative at the abstract level of ideology while mostly liberal in terms of specific policies.[7]

The issue that most frequently organized the thinking of the mass White electorate in 2016 is the same issue that most frequently organized and structured it in the 1950s and early 1960s: race. In his study of the belief system of the public, Phillip Converse argued, "For the bulk of the mass public the object with the highest centrality is the visible, familiar population grouping (Negroes) rather than relations among parts of government and the like."[8] More than thirty years later Donald Kinder and Lynn Sanders conclude, "Compared with opinions on other matters, opinions on race are coherent, more tenaciously held and more difficult to alter. . . . [White] Americans know what they think on matters of race."[9] These coherent and tenaciously held opinions on race as much as any other factor shaped the outcome of the 2016 election, as they have shaped the outcome of most Republican triumphs since 1968.

Along with the consensus in political science about the general ideological innocence of the public, there is a consensus that beginning with the nomination of Barry Goldwater in 1964, the engaged, attentive public and party activists have become polarized on both ideology and issues.[10] Donald Kinder and Nathan Kalmore summarize this consensus: "The well-informed are more likely to display consistency in their partisanship and ideological identification than are the poorly informed—additional evidence . . . of the vital importance for ideology between those who are engaged in political life from those who are not."[11] Related to this polarization of the politically attentive and party activists is the emergence of ideological-partisan sorting, or fusion, whereby the engaged and the activists—reinforced by a partisan media—ideologically polarize the parties and the polity.[12]

Polarization as a result of this partisan-ideological sorting is not, however, purely an activist-elite development. At the mass level, using differences in presidential approval between White Democrats and Republicans and White liberals and conservatives, Richard Seltzer and I show the mass public has become highly polarized since the election of Reagan. From Truman to Carter the average White partisan difference score in presidential approval was 33 and the average White ideological difference was 15, but between Reagan and Obama the average White partisan difference in presidential approval increased to 54 and the ideological to 40.[13] Obama's partisan and ideological difference scores among Whites for his eight years were 71 and 61 respectively.[14] Trump's partisan and ideological scores both averaged in the low 80s during his term in office. Thus, paradoxically, an ideologically innocent public, cued by partisan activists and media, are polarized or sorted into distinct base voting blocs.

Looking at the partisan, polarizing elites and their base voting blocs, one finds there tends to be more divisions in the Democratic Party than the Republican. More ideologically cohesive than the Democrats, the Republicans have been described as America's first ideological party.[15] As late as the Reagan presidency, there was an influential liberal faction in the party, but by the George W. Bush presidency, it was no more. In 2016 it was a thoroughly conservative formation.

However, within contemporary US conservatism one finds differences on domestic and foreign policies between the traditional Goldwater-Reagan conservatives, a small libertarian faction, and neoconservatives and paleoconservatives. The paleoconservatives emerged mainly as reaction to the globalist, interventionist, militaristic foreign policy of the neoconservatives, but they also tend to oppose immigration from non-White countries and support protectionism. Unlike the neoconservatives who generally accepted the New Deal welfare state while opposing much of the Great Society, the paleoconservatives, like the traditional conservatives, are hostile, favoring abolition of as much of the welfare state as possible.[16] Patrick Buchanan in his writings and presidential campaigns is representative of this faction of paleoconservatives, although his biographer says he hates the term.[17] Buchanan is discussed in some detail below, because although Trump is an ideological chameleon, in his campaign and to an extent his presidency, he embraced key elements of the paleoconservative ideology.

The Democratic Party at the mass level is less ideologically schizoid than the Republican Party; persons who identify with the liberal label tend to be liberal on the issues. But the party is more demographically and ideologically diverse at both the elite and mass levels including, unlike the Republican, a sizeable moderate faction. The dominant liberal and progressive factions (those who identify as liberal or very liberal), which are about two-thirds White and 25 percent Black, tend to support, for example, universal single-payer health insurance (Medicare for All), including coverage for undocumented persons; liberal immigration policies, including citizenship for the undocumented; and universal free college access.[18] The moderate-conservative faction is disproportionately constituted by Blacks and Latinos (52 percent), tends to favor preservation of private insurance rather than a single-payer system and more restrictive immigration policies, and is somewhat more conservative on the social-moral issues.

In the 2016 primary election the progressives probably represented a quarter of the Democratic vote, the liberals another quarter, and the moderates and conservatives about half. (In the 2016 presidential election exit poll, 46 percent of Democrats identified as liberal, 39 percent moderate, and 14 percent conservative.) In the 2016 Democratic primaries the progressive faction was represented by Bernie Sanders and the liberal-moderate factions by Hillary Clinton. In the 2020 primaries Sanders and Elizabeth Warren represented the progressives, and former vice president Joseph Biden, among others, represented the liberals and moderates. Perhaps in reaction to Trump and perhaps also a result of the Sanders insurgency, the Democratic Party after 2016 moved more to the left, especially on issues of culture and race.[19] However, this did not prevent the liberal-moderate faction from easily winning the presidential nomination in 2020 as it did in 2016.

The Nominating Process

"Ever since the founding," Donald Robinson writes, "a determination to democratize the selection of presidents gradually cast aside every impediment."[20] The nominees for the presidency at first were selected by party caucuses in Congress. This impediment was removed in the 1830s as part of the "Jacksonian" democratizing "revolution," replacing the congressional caucuses with conventions of state party leaders. The conventions in the early twentieth century were supplemented by primaries in some states, but these primaries were referred to as "beauty contests" because they were not binding on the selection of candidates by the state's delegates. Rather, they were used by prospective candidates to demonstrate their political prowess (John F. Kennedy in 1960 ran in several contested primaries in order to show he could win in Protestant parts of the country). But the primaries (or caucuses in some states) after the 1972 McGovern reforms became the dominant process of choosing party nominees, although Robinson avers "they are clearly unfit."[21] Unfit because they prioritize personalized, well-financed television spectacles, and the "relative influence of states is so capricious that the results are an unreliable guide even to a candidate's popularity, much less his fitness for the nation's most demanding job."[22]

Most scholars of US parties do not accept Robinson's harsh assessment of the primaries as unfit for the selection of nominees, but there is agreement that party leaders have lost their dominant role in the selection process, and the role of the media has been enhanced.[23] William Crotty summarizes this agreement: "The new party system has witnessed a collapse in party control over its own nomination politics. . . . The new power center is media, especially television."[24] In order to restore some of the party's role in the nominating process, the Democrats created "super delegates"—members of Congress, governors, and state and national party leaders—who are seated at the convention and can vote for any candidate they wish.[25] In 2016 these delegates voted overwhelmingly for Hillary Clinton. She won a majority of primaries and caucuses and pledged delegates, but most of the super delegates seemed poised to vote for her even if she had won less than a majority in order to block the nomination of the insurgent democratic socialist Sanders. (In order to assuage the concerns of disaffected Sanders's forces about this possible use of super delegates, the party changed the rules to permit super delegates to vote only after the first ballot in future conventions.)

However, the notion that the parties have lost control of the nominating process is challenged by Marty Cohen and his colleagues in *The Party Decides:*

> We argue in this book that the demise of parties has been exaggerated. . . . Parties remain major players. They scrutinize and winnow the field before voters get involved, attempt to build coalitions behind a single preferred candidate, sway voters to ratify that choice. In the past quarter century, the Democratic and Republican parties have always influenced and often controlled the choice of presidential nominees.[26]

Alas, then comes Donald Trump in 2016.

It is clear that most Republican leaders, if the party had super delegates, would have been inclined to block Trump's nomination. For years Trump had taken positions against party orthodoxy—pro-choice, pro–universal health care, against the North American Free Trade Agreements (NAFTA)—so from the day Trump announced his candidacy, "Republican party leaders had privately plotted against him."[27] After the release of the Hollywood Access tapes on which Trump was heard bragging about sexually assaulting women, the Republican Party chair polled party leaders and found they wished to replace Trump with vice presidential designee Mike Pence and Condoleezza Rice as the new vice presidential nominee.[28] Aware from the outset of the party establishment's opposition, Trump repeatedly refused to say he would not run as an independent if he did not get the Republican nomination. In Trump's case, the party did not decide. This adds another extraordinary dimension to his extraordinary ascent to the presidency: he is the first person in the modern era to win a major party nomination against the wishes of the party. It is fair to say in this sense that in 2016 Trump hijacked the nomination.

The Partisan Media

The national news media, that is, the corporate media—constituted by the *New York Times, Washington Post,* and *Wall Street Journal*; the network news shown on ABC, CBS, and NBC; National Public Radio; and cable channels CNN, MSNBC, and Fox News—in the breadth, scope, tone, and style of their reporting play a major role in setting the daily agenda for discussion of issues, events, and persons. And they play an important role in the nominating process and in the general election in terms of the amount and content of their coverage of candidates. In 2016 the media, particularly television, inadvertently played a major role in advancing Trump's nomination through extensive coverage of his speeches and rallies. Fiorina, however, points out most Americans do not subscribe to or hear or see national media, therefore, its influence is at best limited, as he argues was the case in 2016.[29] Fiorina's analysis of the limited influence of the national media is part of his overall argument that the mass public is not polarized.[30] However, it is again not the mass public but rather the engaged public and party activists that consume and are influenced by the national media's agenda-setting, particularly the partisan-ideological media. Yet, even in the case of the mass public and the mainstream media there is evidence of partisan polarization in terms of consumption and trust of the national media. For example, nearly two-thirds of Democrats indicated "trust" in ABC and CBS as sources of political news, but less than a third of Republicans indicated the same trust. Meanwhile, 67 percent of Democrats trust left-leaning CNN and 65 percent of Republicans the right-leaning Fox News Channel.[31]

In 1996 Fox and MSNBC debuted as explicitly partisan, ideological media. The polity was polarized before there were ideological media. Its emergence therefore is consequence not cause of the phenomenon. They reflect, refract, and reinforce the polarized politics that brought them into existence and provide reassurance to their audience base. That audience base is small, estimated at about 3 million households or only a few percent of the adult population.[32] This 3 percent, as expected, is "more interested and engaged in politics, more strongly partisan and more polarized relative to the rest of the public."[33] Thus, the partisan media polarizes the polity not by moving the electorate toward the ideological left or right but by reinforcing those already ideologically committed.[34] Fox, MSNBC, and related radio and print media make their consumers more confident of their views, less willing to compromise, and more willing to question the legitimacy of the other side.[35] Finally, in helping to shape the discourse in the mainstream media, the consequences of the partisan media "are felt throughout the political system, so all citizens—even those who never watch partisan outlets—feel the effects of partisan media. Even with a relatively limited audience, partisan media have large and consequential impacts, especially with the amplifying effects of social media, on American parties in the twenty-first century."[36]

The Political Odyssey of Donald Trump

Donald Trump had his first major career success with the construction of the Grand Hyatt Hotel in Manhattan in 1980 when he was thirty-three. As I discuss in Chapter 4, that experience shaped the character he brought to his campaign and the presidency. In the 1980s Gallup ranked him the seventh-most admired man of the decade.[37] By the 1990s he was a successful businessman, a staple of the New York City tabloids, a celebrity who appeared frequently on radio and television talk shows and made cameo appearances on television shows and the movies. This made him one of the best-known persons in the nation. In 2004 he started the popular television program *The Apprentice,* which further enhanced his celebrity status, and in 2011 he became a weekly contributor on a Fox morning news program. Moreover, because of his decades of multiple business deals—hotels, casinos, golf courses—multiple corporate bankruptcies, and highly publicized marriages and divorces, he was a fixture, a star in America's celebrity culture.

In 1998 Trump began toying with the idea of using his celebrity status as a springboard to influence the national political debate and possibly run for political office. A man without settled political convictions, he changed his party affiliation multiple times between 1999 and 2012; he often contributed to both Democratic and Republican candidates and was a supporter of Hillary Clinton in her New York Senate campaign.[38] He also supported Bill Clinton during the Monica Lewinsky scandal and impeachment, writing that Clinton "should have refused to discuss his sex life. If the Clinton affair proved anything it is that the American people don't care about the private lives and personal affairs of our political leaders so long as they are doing the job."[39] Ideologically, Trump has veered from liberalism to conservatism, from traditional conservatism to aspects of paleoconservatism. In 2004 when he was considering challenging George W. Bush, he told CNN, "You'd be shocked, in many cases I probably identify as a Democrat."[40] In his 2000 book *The America We Deserve*, he supported abortion, a single-payer health insurance program, and a one-time wealth tax on income over $10 million in order to stabilize Social Security and pay off the national debt.[41] He also promised to select Oprah Winfrey or "someone like her" as his running mate. However, in his 2011 book, clearly written in anticipation of a possible run for the Republican nomination, Trump embraced traditional conservative orthodoxy, except on trade and immigration. He began the book, *Time to Get Tough: Make America Great Again,* by declaring "the country I love is a total economic disaster" due to the "incompetent community organizer-in-chief."[42] Often invoking Reagan, he proposed cutting taxes, deregulation, and aggressive exploitation of US energy sources. Echoing Reagan's attacks on "welfare queens," Trump charged that people were using welfare debit cards to pull money from ATMs at strip clubs, inveighed against "Obama's food stamp crime wave," and railed about the "welfare mentality that says individuals are entitled to live off taxpayers."[43] In order to address the problem, he proposed mandatory work requirements and drug testing for all welfare recipients.[44] Meanwhile, he broke with the Republican orthodoxy in its proposed cuts in Social Security and Medicare, arguing these were not entitlements but "honoring a deal."[45]

On immigration, trade, and foreign policy, Trump was more a Buchanan paleoconservative than a Reagan conservative. Both parties, he claimed, had turned a "blind eye" to these issues, and he proposed "getting tough at the border" and building a "serious 200-foot border wall." He also proposed tariffs on China, "taking Iraq's oil" to pay for the war, requiring US allies to pay for US troops stationed in their countries, and while proposing increased defense spending, he declared the United States should not be "the world's policeman."[46]

Trump also attacked the "dishonest press," and throughout the book he expresses ill-will and disdain for Obama: "In my opinion, our president is totally overrated as a person and a campaigner. The press has given a false impression of him as a brilliant student (which he was not), a brilliant leader (which he was not), and a campaigner the likes of which we have not seen in many years."[47] He subsequently became a leader of the "birtherism" campaign, the discredited idea that Obama was not born in the United States. Starting in 2011, he began to appear on television questioning Obama's birth certificate. He claimed he had sent investigators to Hawaii to look into Obama's birth and repeatedly asserted, "They cannot believe what they are finding."[48] Although he probably never sent investigators to Hawaii, Trump's repeated questions about the legitimacy of Obama's birth certificate increased his standing in the early 2012 preference polls for the Republican nomination.[49] This is because the idea that Obama was foreign born and thus an illegitimate president was believed by nearly half (43 percent) of Republicans.[50] Trump ultimately decided not to be a candidate in 2012, endorsing Mitt Romney. If he had run, he likely would have had considerable support. Early polls showed him running second behind Romney and first among Tea Party adherents, the conservative insurgency that emerged as an effective mobilization against the Obama administration.[51]

In 2014 Trump briefly considered challenging New York governor Andrew Cuomo, but when polls showed him losing badly, he decided not to run. He nevertheless tweeted, "While I will not be running for governor of New York, a race I could have won, I have much bigger plans in mind-stay-tuned-will happen."[52]

Earlier in 1999 Trump ran for the Reform Party nomination, in which his major opponent was Pat Buchanan.[53] Buchanan easily defeated Trump. In the course of the contest, Trump went on the *Tonight Show* and called Buchanan "a Hitler lover, anti-Semite. He doesn't like the blacks; he doesn't like the gays. It's incredible that anybody could embrace this guy. Maybe he'll get 4 or 5 percent of the vote and it really will be the staunch right-wing wackos."[54] In 2011, thinking about running for president, Trump did something he rarely does, something inconsistent with his character: he called Buchanan and apologized.[55] Once Trump was elected, Buchanan became one of his staunchest supporters and defenders. Buchanan views himself as offering "an intelligent alternative to the racism and white supremacy of David Duke."[56] He, however, clearly believes in the "superiority of the Christian faith and English culture and civilization," and believes they are under attack "by those who embrace ideas about the innate equality of all cultures and seek to overthrow traditional Christian morality, and through homosexuality, abortion, purges of Christian symbols and practices seek to dechristianize and secularize America."[57] In his 1992 "culture war" speech at the Republican Convention Buchanan unapologetically and militantly articulated these ideas, and he called on the party to join him in defending Western Christian values against the barbarians at the gate.[58] He has advanced these White nationalist ideas on television, in newspaper columns, and in several books.

Buchanan served loyally in the Richard Nixon and Ronald Reagan administrations, but he passionately disagreed with major parts of both their domestic and foreign policies. He accused both presidents of pursuing policies that continued the "socialization" of America, and mused about "scrapping the entire federal welfare and income support structure . . . Medicaid, food stamps, unemployment insurance and workers compensation."[59] Buchanan said he was "horrified" by Nixon's opening to China, and described Reagan's outreach to the Soviet Union as based on "illusions, inertia and nostalgia."[60] After the fall of the Soviet Union and the end of the Cold War, he called for a neo-isolationist foreign policy based on US national interests, protective tariffs to preserve US manufacturing, and withdrawal from policing the world. He opposed NAFTA and other trade agreements, and attacked the US invasion of Iraq as "Israel's war fostered by Jews in the administration who were asking Gentiles to die on their behalf."[61] On immigration, he wrote the United States should turn back the "invasion" from non-White countries, expel the intruders, build a wall, and secure the border.[62]

Buchanan's policy recommendations were Trumpian, or rather Trump's policies were Buchananian. On trade, immigration, and foreign policy, Trump campaigned and to an extent governed in Buchanan's shadow; a Buchanan slogan was "Putting America First." Buchanan is also akin to Trump in his use of the media. His biographer notes that to attract media attention, favorable or unfavorable, Buchanan's speeches were crafted to have at least "one outrage a day."[63] In *The Art of the Deal,* Trump writes, "One thing I have learned about the press is that they are always hungry for a good story, and the more sensational the better. It's in the nature of the job, and I understood it. The point is that if you are a little different, or a little outrageous or you do things controversial, the press is going to write about you. . . . Sometimes they write positively and sometimes they write negatively . . . the benefits of being written about outweigh the negatives."[64]

But perhaps the most definitive way Buchanan was Trump's precursor was in his strategy of deliberately not attempting to broaden the party's base by reaching out to Latinos. A strategy of reaching out to this rapidly growing group among Republicans goes back to Nixon and was pursued by Reagan and the Bushes, especially George W. Bush. In 2012 Romney—with his rhetoric about "self-deporting" undocumented persons—did not pursue the strategy, and some party leaders blamed his defeat partly on his alienation of Hispanic voters. After the election, the chair of the Republican National Committee commissioned a study of the party's loss. The study, "The Growth and Opportunity Project: Post-Election Progress Report," concluded, "We need to campaign among Hispanic, Black, Asian and Gay Americans and demonstrate we care about them."[65] It specifically rejected Romney's anti-immigrant stance and called for comprehensive immigration reform.

In Chapter 9, "White Party," of his 2011 book, *Suicide of a Superpower: Will America Survive to 2025?,* Buchanan argued it was a mistake for the Republicans to rely on outreach to minorities—African Americans, Latinos, Jews—in order to win the presidency. Instead, he contended Whites and White Christians outnumbered these minorities, constituting from three-fifths to three-fourths of the population, and their mobilization was key to Republican victory in national elections. Reviving the Goldwater trope from the 1964 campaign, Buchanan suggested the party should go "hunting where the ducks were" by increasing the size of the White and White Christian vote because this is where the "GOP will find victory or defeat."[66] A modest increase, he contended, in the size and share of the White vote for Republicans was worth more than doubling the vote of any minority group, Jews, Blacks, or Latinos. As an example, he used the Black vote: increasing the White vote from 55 to 58 percent would have the same effect as increasing the party's share of the Black vote from 4 to 21 percent.[67] How does the party accomplish this objective? Focus on issues of concern to Christians, such as abortion and same-sex marriage. Focus on "issues of concern to the white middle and working class, such as affirmative action, illegal immigrants and NAFTA. . . . What the above points to is a strategy, from which Republicans will recoil, a strategy to increase the share of the white Christian vote and increase the turnout of that vote by specific appeals to social, cultural and moral issues, and for equal justice for the emerging white minority. . . . Why should Republicans be ashamed to represent the progeny of the men who founded, built and defended America since her birth as a nation?"[68]

In 2016, Trump was not ashamed, although he may have got the idea from Steve Bannon, the editor of the far-right Breitbart News service, rather than Buchanan.[69] Bannon, who served as a Trump campaign manager and briefly as chief White House strategist, "had long been searching for a vessel for his populist-nationalist ideas. . . . Trump wasn't a serious candidate. . . . But Bannon soon discovered that Trump's great personal force could knock down barriers that impeded other politicians. . . . Bannon didn't make Trump the president the way Rove did for George W. Bush—but Trump wouldn't be president if it weren't for Bannon."[70]

I am not convinced Rove made Bush president or that Trump would not have become president without Bannon. I am arguing that Buchanan, the best-known White nationalist intellectual in the country, is a precursor of Trump's White nationalist politics. But whether Bannon or Buchanan is the source or whether the ideas emerged from Trump's worldview or some combination, he mainstreamed White nationalist politics and successfully mobilized Buchanan's White "working-class and middle-class Protestants and Catholics, small town and rural, often unionized, middle age and seniors, surviving on less than $50,000 a year. . . . The voters most loyal to the GOP—white folks without college degrees—[a] shrinking part of the electorate."[71]

Celebrity, Demagoguery, and Charisma

By the time Trump announced his candidacy for president in 2016, he had for decades been a bona-fide celebrity. American culture is perhaps—I am not aware of comparative studies—the most celebrity-driven culture in the world. It is not unusual for persons in the United States to use their celebrity status as a resource or base of power to successfully win elected office, from the actor Ronald Reagan to the wrestler Jesse Ventura, elected governor of Minnesota in 1998. Celebrity is an irrational force in politics. Richard Schickel observes large numbers of Americans place "thoughtless value on it," and "it is a corruption of the rational communication on which a democratic order must be based."[72] And it is not just the mass public that places thoughtless value on celebrities. In the 1950s C. Wright Mills observed the power elite's infatuation with celebrity was "carried to the point where a man who can knock a small ball in a series of holes in the ground with more efficiency and skill than anyone else thereby gains access to the President of the United States. . . . To the point where a chattering radio and television entertainer becomes the hunting chum of leading industrial executives, cabinet members and the higher military."[73]

Undoubtedly Trump's celebrity status was a base of power he had at the outset of the campaign, which was equal to or greater than the status of Jeb Bush, the former governor of a major state, and the son and brother of former presidents. It may have been the equal of the millions of dollars Bush raised and spent during his short-lived quest for the nomination.

Aside from Trump's decades of systematic cultivation of the media, he was the host and producer of *The Apprentice,* a top-rated weekly television show on NBC. The show made him one of the most recognized and popular people in America. The show also provided potential entry into the Black community; it was very popular with Blacks and Hispanics, partly because they appeared on the show in large numbers in nonstereotypical roles. As a result, he was more popular among Blacks and Latinos than among Whites."[74] As Joshua Green observes, "Viewed through the lens of politics, Trump had achieved by 2010 what Republican politicians had struggled, without success, to accomplish for more than fifty years. He had made himself extremely popular with a broad segment of blacks and Hispanics."[75] Although for sure "Trump was no racial innocent,"[76] he also was not viewed by the Black public or leadership as racist or as hostile. For example, he supported Jesse Jackson's Wall Street Project, the program to enhance Black access to capital and business opportunities, and provided office space in one of his buildings.[77] Jackson recalls, "He seemed like a decent guy to me. We went to fights together, and he seemed like a liberal Republican."[78] Yet, when he decided to seek the Republican nomination in 2016, he sacrificed the approbation and potential support of Blacks by embracing a deliberately provocative, racially charged campaign strategy, beginning with his birtherism ploy and including his vituperative attacks on the Black president. The effect was immediate; not only did his approval sharply decline among Blacks and Hispanics, but among Whites as well.[79]

Trump followed the Buchanan playbook, apparently making a deliberate strategic decision to appeal to racially resentful Whites rather than reaching out to minorities. Green summarizes what happened: "As someone possessed of perhaps the best raw political instincts of any Republican of his generation, Trump intuited, correctly, that a racist attack targeting a black president was the surest way to ingratiate himself with grassroots voters. And so, without batting an eye, proceeded to destroy the goodwill he had built up with minority voters in order to appeal to a new audience."[80]

I classify Trump as a charismatic demagogue, a classification not easy to make; nor is it easy to gather systematic data to support. Of demagoguery, James Ceaser writes, "Modern scholars of the presidency are reluctant to invoke the word. . . . Qualitative words like demagoguery . . . seem too normative. After all, one man's statesman is another's demagogue."[81] In addition, making the classification may often be shaped by ideology; whether the scholar is predisposed to ideologically agree or disagree with the subject. FDR is sometimes cited as an example of this ideological bias. Some might conclude that FDR at least occasionally, in some of his rhetorical assaults on the "economic royalists" on behalf of the "forgotten man" engaged in demagoguery, or that in 2016 and 2020 Bernie Sanders sometimes crossed the line from passionate rhetoric into demagoguery. Yet, liberal scholars are reluctant to apply the word to these progressives.

A fair point, perhaps. Yet, while both FDR and Sanders may have occasionally rhetorically crossed the line into demagoguery, it is probably fair to say neither were demagogues.

But it is difficult to identify objectively, let alone precisely, properties of demagogic behavior in political leaders. Yet the concept, however normative and slippery, captures an important phenomenon in politics, and to the extent it does we cannot abandon it when it seems appropriate. It seems clearly appropriate in Trump's case; if he is not a demagogue then there is no such thing.

Ceaser identifies ten relatively discrete indicators of demagogic leadership: (1) wins political influence through rhetoric or oratory and "position taking," (2) identifies a potential wave of opinion and uses it as far as he can, (3) where possible foments a wave by exploiting latent divisions and wedge issues, (4) invokes the forgotten people—the little guy—being exploited by powerful elites, (5) insecure in relation to rivals, he uses extreme, flamboyant, abusive language, (6) he breaks existing norms or rules that protect propriety, (7) appeals to the prejudices of the community, (8) claims to protect traditions, mores, and values of the community against individuals and groups perceived to be undermining them, (9) relies on fear and anger to arouse the passions of those who feel the "ancient way of life" is being threatened, and in such instances focuses on those who are different or alien, and (10) uses extreme rhetoric to encourage divisions among people in order to build and maintain his constituency.[82]

Even a casual observer of the Trump campaign and presidency could easily find evidence of each of these indicators in Trump's behavior. The now relatively extensive journalism record sustains the case, as does much of the relevant political science research. I referred to some of this research in Chapter 1 and will return to more in Chapter 5. To conclude here, notwithstanding problems in conceptual ambiguity and objectivity, there is sufficient evidence to show that Trump is the first unambiguous demagogue elected president, with the possible exception of Andrew Jackson, Trump's favorite president.[83]

Charisma is another important, but problematic, contested concept in the study of political leadership. I classify Trump as charismatic because he appears to have the capacity, as Ann Ruth Willner says of charisma, "to arouse and maintain belief in himself as sources of legitimacy."[84] In his typical braggadocio Trump asserted his possession of this power in relationship to his followers by saying, "I could stand in the middle of Fifth Avenue and shoot somebody, and wouldn't lose any voters."[85] During the campaign it appeared this might be an exaggeration that revealed a truth. As soon as he announced, he began to attract large enthusiastic crowds at rallies and established a following of 35–40 percent of the electorate that never wavered in its support. This is in spite of the fact that, according to the *Washington Post,* Trump said "twenty-three things that would have doomed another candidate."[86] The things that he said according to the *Post* included calling Mexican immigrants rapists, alluding to a newswoman's menstruation, alluding to the size of his penis, insulting the looks of his female opponent, claiming George W. Bush was involved in the 9/11 attacks, mocking a disabled reporter, falsely claiming thousands of Muslims in New Jersey celebrated the 9/11 attack, proposing to ban all Muslims from the United States, encouraging violence at his rallies, attacking the pope, and declining to immediately disavow the support of the leader of the Ku Klux Klan. Major newspapers ran stories and columns suggesting he was a fascist and a racist.[87] Mitt Romney labeled Trump a vulgar racist and misogynist.[88] His major opponent in the primaries, Texas senator Ted Cruz called Trump an "utterly immoral pathological liar" and a "serial philander."[89]

Yet, none of this appeared to alter the support of his core followers. Indeed, the charges may have reinforced their loyalty to their leader. This is so because, as Willner writes, followers of charismatic leaders "believe statements and ideas advanced by their leader simply because it is *he* who has made the statement or advanced the idea. It is not necessary for them to weigh or test the truth of the statement or the plausibility of the idea. For *he* knows and it is therefore enough for them that *he* has said it. If he has said it, it is unquestionably true, and may be right."[90]

For a segment of the electorate, Trump as an individual, as well as his substantive messages and rhetoric, appear to resonate culturally, making his perceived faults unimportant or irrelevant. He speaks forcefully to their values, fears, and hopes. Thus, although he was a billionaire playboy (he appeared on the cover of *Playboy,* March 1998, with a "playmate" apparently clothed only in his top coat), a serial adulterer, with marginal knowledge or attachment to religion, his core or base supporters are self-identified White evangelical Christians. They ostensibly prioritize personal character or morality in leaders. Yet, for *their* leader they radically and rapidly changed their view. In 2011 the Public Religion Research Institute asked the question: Do you think a public official who commits an immoral act in private life can still behave morally in public life? Two-thirds of White evangelicals responded no in the 2011 survey. In 2016 in the midst of Trump's campaign, 72 percent responded yes. Although the opinion of all religious groups moved in this direction, the change was most striking among White evangelicals, who went from the religious group least likely to say yes to the one most likely to say yes.[91]

Trump's "charisma" seems to cast a spell on his followers who view him as forthrightly and unapologetically defending their interests and values, which many believe are under siege. As long as he appears to do this, he can do no wrong.[92] This is the essence of the charismatic leader-follower relationship. This relationship carried over from the campaign to the presidency. Almost from the start of his tenure, there were multiple investigations of Trump involving his businesses, taxes, payoffs to women who claimed to have had sex with him, and possible collusion with Russia in its interference in the 2016 election. Eventually he stood trial and was acquitted in the Senate after the House twice impeached him, first for abuse of power and obstruction of its investigation into allegations that he tried to coerce Ukraine's president into providing personal, political benefits in exchange for US foreign assistance, and second for "inciting insurrection" after the 2020 election. Throughout these multiple investigations, Trump's approval among Republicans was always near 80 percent. This extraordinary level of support for a Republican president among his partisans is matched only by Dwight D. Eisenhower.

Trump's charismatic relationship with his followers may explain why the overwhelming majority of them believed him when *he* said, contrary to all available credible evidence, that the 2020 election was stolen and he won in a landslide (see Chapter 10).

Charisma, like demagoguery, is an elusive phenomenon that is often difficult to identify. The argument here about Trump's charismatic leadership is less about his personality or character, and more about his followers and their extraordinary attachment to him, as well as their disenchantment with the political system.[93]

The Election of 2016

As the 2016 election approached its end, most political commentators concluded that Trump would lose, and most formal political science forecasting models gave Clinton at least a small margin of victory.[94] Although formal modeling of the primary elections is not possible, most commentators at the outset dismissed Trump's chances of winning the Republican nomination.

The 2016 field of competitors for the Republican nomination was the largest and most diverse in the party's history. It included five incumbent US senators; two incumbent governors; four former governors (including Jeb Bush); Benjamin Carson, an acclaimed African American surgeon; Carly Fiorina, a former corporate executive; two candidates of Hispanic origin; and Louisiana governor, Bobby Jindal, the son of immigrants from India. This large field fairly quickly narrowed to a contest between Trump and Senator Ted Cruz.

Elected to the Senate in 2012, Cruz was one of the two candidates of Hispanic origin along with Florida senator Marco Rubio, although both downplayed their Cuban backgrounds. If Trump was a political changeling, Cruz was the opposite—a radical ideological conservative of convictions whose issue positions placed him further to the right than any candidate since Barry Goldwater. His proposals included replacing the progressive income tax with a 10 percent flat tax; adding a value-added tax; completely eliminating the estate tax, the Internal Revenue Service, and four cabinet departments; massively cutting food stamps, Medicaid, and other low-income support programs; rejecting programs to address climate change; overturning laws permitting abortion and same-sex marriage; denying legal status to undocumented persons; eliminating the constitutional guarantee of birthright citizenship; and constructing a southern border wall. These Buchanan-like proposals, and Cruz's strategy to mobilize White Christian America in many ways were a more reasoned, less inflammatory version of Trump's program and strategy. But in some ways Cruz, less bombastic and demagogic than Trump, was a more polarizing candidate, and his rhetoric was often as radical as his ideas, portraying the nation as in "horrible shape and only a return to an imagined pre–New Deal era of small government and state sovereignty" could save it.[95]

That the Republican Party's two top candidates were so alike in their policies and rhetoric is evidence that substantively Trump is not an aberration, but rather is within the mainstream of the evolving Republican Party.

Although Cruz had a more professional staff and was much better financed than Trump, as were Jeb Bush and Marco Rubio,[96] Trump decisively defeated his credentialed opponents. Overall, Trump won 44.9 percent of the primary vote, forty-one primaries and caucuses and 1,441 delegates, compared to Cruz's 26 percent of the votes, eleven primaries and caucuses, nearly 8 million votes and 551 delegates. Trump and Cruz were both appealing to the White identity and the nationalist faction of the Republican electorate, while the other candidates were dividing the remaining vote. Survey data show that White identity and nationalist beliefs are associated with voter support for Trump in the primaries. Those Whites, for example, who said their identity as Whites was "extremely important" to them, were 30 points more likely to vote for Trump; those who perceived a great deal of discrimination against Whites were 40 points more likely; and those who thought it was "extremely likely that many whites were unable to find a job because employers were hiring minorities" were 50 points more likely.[97] Moreover, his supporters were more likely to report they were economically struggling and that Whites were "losing out" because of preferences for Blacks and Latinos.[98]

Trump's signature issue during the campaign was immigration from Mexico, which he exploited from the day he announced his candidacy until the final days of the campaign. We know that immigration and affirmative action are the two issues that animate the White nationalist faction of the electorate.[99] Why Trump chose to focus on immigration and not affirmative action, or perhaps both, is not clear, particularly since affirmative action is far more unpopular among all parts of the White electorate.[100] For example, National Opinion Research Center (NORC) data for 2016 show that among all Whites, support for affirmative action in the form of racial preferences for Blacks in hiring and promotions was just 18 percent, and among conservatives and Republicans 9 and 8 percent respectively.[101] To allude to the Goldwater-Buchanan metaphor, there were more ducks to hunt in affirmative action than immigration. Yet, Trump completely ignored the issue during the campaign and, for the most part, during his presidency. Again, I have not encountered an explanation for this decision on the part of Trump or his campaign strategists.[102]

At the Republican convention, Senator Cruz in his address pointedly refused to endorse Trump; Ohio governor John Kasich, the host governor of the Cleveland convention and one of the 2016 contenders, boycotted; South Carolina senator Lindsey Graham, also a 2016 contender, announced he would not vote for Trump; both former presidents Bush declined to attend, as did Mitt Romney, the 2012 nominee. Trump's acceptance speech was dystopic, invoking a nation on the brink of a disaster that he alone could fix, setting the stage for one of the most acrimonious elections in modern history.

After Hillary Clinton's narrow loss of the Democratic nomination to Obama in 2008, followed by her service as Obama's first-term secretary of state, and Vice President Biden's decision not to run, party leaders assumed the former first lady and two term senator was the presumptive, probably uncontested, 2016 Democratic nominee. And then Bernie Sanders, the independent democratic socialist senator from Vermont, decided to enter the primaries and ran a surprisingly competitive race. Clinton, in a postcampaign memoir, writes, "I admit I didn't expect Bernie to catch on as much as he did. Nothing in my experience in politics suggested that a socialist from Vermont could mount a credible campaign for president."[103] Most commentators likely agreed, given what we know about the stigma attached to socialism in the American tradition and political culture.[104] At the height of the near collapse of capitalism during the Great Depression, only 1 or 2 percent of the public supported socialism or socialist candidates.[105] A 2015 Gallup Poll found that more than 90 percent of Americans would vote for a woman, Catholic, African American, Latino, or Jew for president; 81 percent for a Muslim; 74 percent for a homosexual; 58 percent for an atheist; but only 47 percent for a socialist.[106] Liberals, young people, Blacks, and Latinos were somewhat more favorable toward a socialist candidate, which provided potential constituencies for a Sanders campaign.

Sanders's major campaign theme was the need to address the growing income inequality in the United States. Although a declared socialist, he did not propose classic socialist policies, such as nationalization of industries or confiscatory taxes on the wealthy. Instead, he advanced traditional liberal or progressive ideas such as single-payer universal health insurance, increased taxes on corporations and wealth, free college tuition, paid family leave, and a substantial increase in the minimum wage. He advocated a less interventionist, militaristic US foreign policy and emphasized his opposition, unlike Clinton, to the Iraq war. The media initially ignored Sanders's campaign, but after he raised substantial money in small contributions and began to attract large crowds at rallies the media provided extensive, largely positive coverage, while the coverage of Clinton tended to be negative, focusing on so-called scandals involving her email and the killing of a US ambassador at a consulate in Benghazi, Libya.[107] Nevertheless, with the overwhelming support of African Americans and older voters, Clinton easily won, with Sanders winning a majority only among young voters (aged eighteen to twenty-nine).

At the end of both national conventions, the parties had nominated candidates disliked and distrusted by the electorate. Indeed, Trump and Clinton had the highest "very" unfavorable ratings of any candidates in modern history; Clinton at 37 percent and Trump 53 percent.[108] By

September, the Clinton-Trump campaign was vitriolic, vituperative, and dispiriting, with each accusing the other of corruption, racism, and bigotry in personal attacks that became increasingly shrill. The American Psychological Association in mid-October released a study that concluded half the electorate was suffering from "election stress disorder," including headaches, stomachaches, and loss of sleep.[109]

In a historically unprecedented upset, Trump became the fifth person to win the presidency while losing the majority of the popular vote (foreshadowing his behavior after he lost the 2020 election, Trump said he won the popular vote, falsely claiming there had been widespread fraud and millions of votes had been cast illegally for Clinton). Clinton won 48 percent of the vote (66 million) to Trump's 46 percent (63 million), but Trump won thirty states to Clinton's twenty plus the District of Columbia and 304 electoral votes to Clinton's 227.[110] Trump's victory was all the more remarkable since he was a novice candidate, and Clinton had a clear advantage in money, outspending Trump on everything from television ads and staffing to field offices. Her campaign organization was more professional and technologically sophisticated, and the polls indicated she won each of the three debates.

One advantage Trump had, however, was more extensive media coverage, especially on cable television. The media was taken in by Trump's media strategy of saying things outrageously controversial to attract coverage. A Harvard Kennedy School study of media coverage of the campaign concludes, "Trump [was] arguably the first bona fide media created nominee. . . . Journalists are attracted to the new, the unusual and sensational. Trump fit that need as no other candidate in recent memory."[111] In a report on media coverage of the early months of campaign, the *New York Times* estimated in the early months Trump received close to $2 billion in free media coverage, twice the amount received by Clinton.[112]

White Nationalism as a Theory of the Election

As discussed in Chapter 1, there are multiple theories on the Trump election, however, White nationalism seems to offer the most comprehensive explanation. Earlier in this chapter the role that White nationalism played in Trump's victory in the Republican primaries was analyzed. But that analysis was based on limited data, confined to Republican voters. On the general election, there are more extensive studies documenting its role in Trump's triumph.

Longtime Howard University professor Ronald Walters, as I noted in Chapter 1, is the pioneering scholar in the study of the emergence of White nationalism as a new phenomenon in American politics. In his 2003 book *White Nationalism, Black Interests: Conservative Public Policy and the Black Community,* Walters contends that the 1960s conservative resistance to the civil rights movement, the war on poverty, and affirmative action had by 1980 grown into a movement whose "dominant tendencies within the white majority conform[ed] to the criteria of nationalism."[113] These tendencies include (1) a sense of race consciousness and solidarity that defines Whites as a distinctive group; (2) a cultural notion of Whiteness that results in a strikingly unified self-perception of White, and negative stereotypes toward Blacks;[114] (3) the practice of racial separatism or segregation, involving the mass movement away from Black populations in cities, resulting in the creation of many thoroughly White or mostly White areas; and (4) control over the principal institutions of American society through dominance of numbers and through subordination of Blacks and non-White minorities.

Walters attributes the activation of these nationalist tendencies to three developments. First, White resentment of perceived Black social, economic, and political advancement at their expense. Although Blacks have not achieved parity or equality, many "whites resent the fact that blacks are accorded access to resources or that they appear to have achieved equal status."[115] Second, beginning in the 1970s and accelerating in the 1980s, economic inequality increased among the White working and middle classes. And "the slowly emerging, often unarticulated message of stagnation of white economic status is matched by whites' perception of a government-led black renaissance."[116] The result is the third development in the mobilization of White nationalist sentiments: the perception of a loss of resources to Blacks, which, Walters writes, "produced growing anxiety among whites, especially males."[117]

Although not necessarily racist, the ultimate aim of White nationalists in terms of public policy, according to Walters, was the transfer of resources from the Black to the White community, a process that began, he contends, with the tax and spending policies of the Reagan administration. The 1981 Reagan tax cut, one of the largest in history, was tilted toward the wealthy and resulted in the transfer of money from the Treasury to disproportionately wealthy Whites and corporations, while the budget cuts were to programs disproportionately benefiting African Americans. The president was unwilling to cut Social Security, the largest domestic spending program. Social Security is viewed as a program for Whites, thus nearly 70 percent of the cuts were in programs for poor people (for example, Aid to Families with Dependent Children, food stamps, job training, and housing assistance), which are viewed as programs for African Americans.[118] "The White majority," Walters concludes, "is proceeding to concentrate economic and social power in its own group, using its control over political institutions to punish presumptive enemies. The targets of this punishment have been Blacks, Hispanics and other minorities," manifesting "the classic symptoms of White nationalism such as resentment based on the belief that Blacks are more advantaged by affirmative action and other programs, and willingness to support radical—even punitive—measures to reverse the flow of public financial resources and other benefits to them."[119]

The interest of Republicans in advancing the interests of Whites was not limited to the Reagan administration or the presidency. Corey Cook in an analysis of the sponsorship and co-sponsorship of "white interest" legislation from the 102nd through the 105th Congress (1991–1998) found that in each Congress, "southern, white and Republican members were substantially more likely than northern, nonwhite and Democratic colleagues to vote consistently in accordance with white racial interests all else equal. The evidence of racial interest politics is overwhelming."[120]

In 2010 political science began to pay attention to White nationalist or identity politics when the American National Election Study (ANES) sponsored a pilot study on "White Racial Consciousness in the U.S."[121] Walters's pioneering work is not acknowledged in the proposal or in the subsequent research on the subject, but there is now a small but robust body of research on White nationalist politics that confirms his major propositions, which in American presidential elections are first systematically documented in Trump's victory in the Republican primaries, and subsequently in the general election.[122] This research is reported in the greatest detail in books by Ashley Jardina and John Sides and his colleagues, and a related work focusing on racial resentment by Alan Abramowitz.[123] The early commentary on Trump's election suggested it was fueled by White working-class anxiety caused by the loss of jobs, wage stagnation, and growing inequality in the United States. The research that points to White identity or nationalism as the principal theory of Trump's election does not dismiss economic factors but contends that they must be filtered through race and White identity. Sides and his colleagues call this "racialized economics": "The evidence for economic anxiety's influence in 2016 is thus much weaker than the evidence for the influence of attitudes related to race and ethnicity. . . . To downplay the role of economic anxiety is not to deny its existence. But when economic concerns are politically potent, the prism of identity is often present."[124] Of this relationship, Jardina notes that there is some indication that "whites high on racial consciousness do feel somewhat more financially troubled."[125] Abramowitz found that the key to Trump's victory was his support among the growing group of Republicans who express racial resentment:

> While Trump was not the first candidate to appeal to white resentment, the content of his appeal was more explicit. . . . His campaign slogan 'make America great again' . . . clearly implied more than bringing back manufacturing jobs. It also signaled that a President Trump would turn back the clock to a time when white people enjoyed a dominant position in American society.[126]

As Walters posits, maintaining White advantage is a central concern of White nationalists. Jardina confirming, writes that White identifiers, while not racists, seek "to protect whites' collective interests by opposing immigration and supporting welfare policies that disproportionately benefit their group."[127] Thus, while distinguishable from racists, their policy prescriptions and consequences are nearly identical.

These nationalist trends in conservative White voting began in the Reagan administration (Walters calls Reagan the first "modern nationalist"). The genial, avuncular Reagan cast his nationalist appeal in less inflammatory language than the crude and coarse Trump. But Trump's White nationalist appeal is evidence that his election reflects a maturation of trends long at work in the Republican Party. Race—the issue the Republicans have exploited since 1968—in 2016 trumped taxes and the welfare state as the dominant issue in the election of Trump.[128] But as Lilliana Mason writes, it is more than this:

> The election of Donald Trump is the culmination of a process by which the American electorate has become deeply divided along partisan lines. As the parties have grown racially, religiously, and socially distant from one another, a new kind of social discord has been growing. . . . The norms of racial, religious, and cultural respect have deteriorated. . . . In this environment, a candidate who picks up the banner of 'us versus them' and 'winning versus losing' is almost guaranteed to tap into a current of resentment and anger across racial, religious, and cultural lines, which have recently divided neatly by party.[129]

Notes

1. "Trends in Party Affiliation Among Demographic Groups," Pew Research Center, 2018. In the 2020 CNN exit poll, 37 percent of respondents identified as Democrats, 36 percent Republican, and 26 percent independent.

2. Between 1972 and 2012, Donald Kinder and Nathan Kalmore report many respondents refused to identify with any ideology—liberal, moderate, or conservative—and the moderate label "seems a refuge for the innocent and confused." See *Neither Liberal or Conservative: Ideological Innocence in the American Public* (Chicago: University of Chicago Press, 2017), 54, 71.

3. Ronald Rotunda, "The 'Liberal' Label: Roosevelt's Capture of a Symbol," *Public Policy* 17 (1968): 337–348.

4. Lloyd Free and Hadley Cantril, *The Political Beliefs of Americans: A Study of Public Opinion* (New Brunswick, NJ: Rutgers University Press, 1967), 37.

5. Morris Fiorina, with Samuel Adams, *Disconnect: The Breakdown of Representation in American Politics* (Norman: University of Oklahoma Press, 2009).

6. Christopher Ellis and James Stimson, *Ideology in America* (New York: Cambridge University Press, 2012).

7. Matt Grossmann and David Hopkins, *Asymmetric Politics: Ideological Republicans and Group Interest Democrats* (New York: Oxford University Press, 2016), 67–69.

8. Phillip Converse, "The Nature of Belief Systems in Mass Publics," in David Apter, ed., *Ideology and Discontent* (New York: Free Press, 1964), 238.

9. Donald Kinder and Lynn Sanders, *Divided by Color: Racial Politics and American Democracy* (Chicago: University of Chicago Press, 1996), 14. See also Vincent Hutchings and Nicholas Valentino, "The Centrality of Race in American Politics," *Annual Review of Political Science* 7 (2004): 383–408.

10. Norman Nie, Sidney Verba, and John Petrocik, *The Changing American Voter* (Cambridge: Harvard University Press, 1976), 200–209; and Alan Abramowitz, *The Disappearing Center: Engaged Citizens, Polarization, and American Democracy* (New Haven: Yale University Press, 2010).

11. Kinder and Kalmore, *Neither Liberal or Conservative*, 89.

12. Matthew Levendusky, *The Partisan Sort: How Liberals Became Democrats and Conservatives Became Republicans* (Chicago: University of Chicago Press, 2009).

13. Robert C. Smith and Richard Seltzer, *Polarization and the Presidency: From FDR to Barack Obama* (Boulder, CO: Lynne Rienner, 2015), 293.

14. Ibid., 265.

15. Nies Gilman, "What the Rise of Republicans as America's First Ideological Party Means for the Democrats," *Forum* 2 (2004): 1–4. Gilman writes, "In the last decades, the Republicans have adopted a new tack. Instead of just pandering to local interests, they have decided they want to recast the country in a radically different mold according to a well- articulated ideological vision. . . . As a result, they have started to act like a traditional, European political party, maintaining strict party formation in all voting, viciously punishing internal dissenters from the party and scotching the traditional congressional rules which were designed to keep the entire process tactical rather

than strategic" (2). The substance of the ideology, he contends, is rolling back the New Deal welfare-regulatory state and the social and cultural changes initiated in the 1960s. Meanwhile, Gilman argues the Democrats remained an interest group party "lacking ideological coherence." See also Jo Freeman, "The Political Culture of the Democratic and Republican Parties," *Political Science Quarterly* 101 (1986): 327–356; and Grossmann and Hopkins, *Asymmetric Politics: Ideological Republicans and Group Interests Democrats.* Partly as a result of the increasing presence of liberals in the party and Bernie Sanders's insurgent campaigns, the Democrats also appear to be tending toward becoming a more ideological party.

16. On the neoconservatives see Mark Gerson, *The Neoconservative Vision: From the Cold War to Cultural Wars* (New York: Madison Books, 1996). On the paleoconservatives see Joseph Scotchie, *Paleoconservatism: New Voices of the Old Right* (New York: Routledge, 1999).

17. Timothy Stanley, *The Crusader: The Life and Tumultuous Times of Pat Buchanan* (New York: Thomas Dunne, 2012), 141.

18. Thomas Edsall, "The Democratic Party Is Actually Three Parties," *New York Times,* July 7, 2019.

19. Thomas Edsall, "The Democrats' Left Turn Is Not an Illusion," *New York Times,* October 11, 2018.

20. Donald Robinson, *To the Best of My Ability: The Presidency and the Constitution* (New York: Norton, 1987), 167.

21. Ibid.

22. Ibid.

23. Nelson Polsby, *Consequences of Party Reform* (Berkeley: University of California, Institute of Governmental Studies, 1983); and Byron Shafer, *Bifurcated Politics: Evolution and Reform in National Party Conventions* (Cambridge: Harvard, 1988).

24. William Crotty, *The Party Game* (New York: Norton, 1985), 129.

25. Richard Herrera, "Are Super Delegates Super?" *Political Behavior* 16 (1994): 79–92.

26. Marty Cohen, David Karol, and John Zaller, *The Party Decides: Presidential Nominations After Reform* (Chicago: University of Chicago Press, 2008), 3.

27. Tim Alberta, *American Carnage: On the Front Lines of the Republican Civil War and the Rise of Donald Trump* (New York: Harper Collins, 2019), 243.

28. Ibid., 273. See also Jonathan Karl, *Front Row at the Trump Show* (New York: Dutton, 2020), 63–66.

29. Morris Fiorina, "The Meaning of the 2016 Election Has Been Exaggerated," *Real Clear Politics,* January 10, 2018.

30. Fiorina, *Disconnect.*

31. Mark Jurkowitz et al., "US Media Polarization and the 2020 Election," Pew Research Center, Journalism and Media, January 24, 2020. For a historical treatment of the development of public distrust of the media and its partisan implications see Jonathan Ladd, *Why Americans Hate the Media and How It Matters* (Princeton: Princeton University Press, 2011).

32. Matthew Levendusky, *How Partisan Media Polarizes America* (Chicago: University of Chicago Press, 2013), 6.

33. Ibid., 13.

34. Ibid., 21.

35. Ibid., 22–23.

36. Ibid., 23. The impact of the partisan media is uneven. The conservative media—Fox and talk radio—exercise greater influence over Republican elites and voters than do MSNBC and other liberal outlets over Democratic leaders and voters. See Kathleen Hall Jamieson and Joseph Capella, *Echo Chamber: Rush Limbaugh and the Conservative Media Establishment* (New York: Oxford University Press, 2008); and Grossmann and Hopkins, *Asymmetric Politics*, 147–179.

37. Michael D'Antonio, *Never Enough: Donald Trump and the Pursuit of Success* (New York: Thomas Dunne, 2015), 9.

38. Michael Kranish and Marc Fisher, *Trump Revealed: The Definitive Biography of the 45th President* (New York: Scribner, 2017), 184, 290.

39. Donald Trump with Dave Shiflett, *The America We Deserve* (New York: Renaissance Books, 2000), 35.

40. Joshua Green, *Devil's Bargain: Steve Bannon, Donald Trump, and the Storming of the Republican Party* (New York: Penguin, 2017), 38.

41. Trump and Shiflett, *The America We Deserve,* 31–32, 169, 208.

42. Donald Trump, *Time to Get Tough: Make America Great Again* (Washington: Regnery, 2011), 1. The slogan "make America great again" was first used in modern conservative rhetoric at the 1980 Republican Convention. It was inserted in the preamble to the party platform: "And in this Republican platform, we call out to the American people: with God's help, let us now, together make America great again." Quoted in Rick Perlstein, *Reaganland: America's Right Turn, 1976–1980* (New York: Simon & Schuster, 2020), 797. Reagan often invoked the slogan in 1980 campaign speeches.

43. Trump, *Time to Get Tough*, 106, 112.

44. Ibid.

45. Ibid.

46. Ibid., 12–14.

47. Ibid., 176.

48. Ashley Parker and Steve Elder, "Inside the Six Weeks Donald Trump Was a Birther," *New York Times,* July 2, 2016.

49. Ibid.

50. Sam Farrell, "One in Five Americans Still Think Obama Is Foreign Born," *Time,* September 14, 2015.

51. Kranish and Fisher, *Trump Revealed,* 291.

52. Green, *Devil's Bargain,* 116–117.

53. Ross Perot created the Reform Party in 1995 after his 1992 independent presidential campaign. Because of his success in getting on the ballot in multiple states and his near 20 percent of the vote, the party qualified for federal campaign financing, which made the party nomination more valuable than the typical third-party designation.

54. Stanley, *The Crusader,* 332.

55. Ibid. See also David Mark, "Trump Apologized to Pat Buchanan for Calling Him an Anti-Semite and Racist," *Washington Examiner,* July 21, 2019.

56. Ibid., 182.

57. Patrick Buchanan, *Day of Reckoning: How Hubris, Ideology, and Greed Are Tearing America Apart* (New York: St. Martin's Press, 2007), 176. The journalist Katherine Stewart in engaging, muckraking reportage contends America's White, Christian nationalists are part of a well-funded global movement that is seeking to undermine liberal democracy and replace it with a nationalist, theocratic, autocratic form of government. See *The Power Worshippers: The Dangerous Rise of Religious Nationalism* (New York: Bloomsbury, 2020).

58. According to James Davison Hunter, Buchanan derived some of his thinking for the culture war speech from his book *Culture Wars: The Struggle to Define America* (New York: Basic Books, 1991). Hunter understands the issues that shape the culture wars as inherently polarizing and nonnegotiable, writing, "But in the end, whether concerned with abortion, homosexuality, women's rights, day care or any other moral or political issue of the day, the tools of logic and evidence from science, history and theology can do nothing to alter the opinions of their opposition. Because each side interprets them differently, logic, science, history and theology can only serve to enhance and legitimate particular ideological interests. . . . [D]ialogue is irrelevant" (130–131). On Buchanan deriving some of his thinking for the culture war speech from the book, see the remarks by Hunter at a debate at Brown University between Hunter and Morris Fiorina, "Ideological Culture Wars in America," broadcast on C-SPAN, November 28, 2007.

59. Stanley, *The Crusader,* 61, 95.

60. Ibid.

61. Ibid., 136.

62. Buchanan, *Day of Reckoning,* 11. Buchanan devotes an entire book to discussing what he views as the baneful effects of immigration from non-White countries on the future of the United States as a White Christian republic. See *State of Emergency: The Third World Invasion and the Conquest of America* (New York: St. Martin's Griffin, 2007).

63. Stanley, *The Crusader,* 160.

64. Donald Trump with Tony Schwartz, *The Art of the Deal* (New York: Random House, 1987), 39.

65. "The Growth and Opportunity Project: Post-Election Progress Report" (Washington: Republican National Committee, 2015), 14.

66. Patrick Buchanan, *Suicide of a Superpower: Will America Survive to 2025?* (New York: Thomas Dunne, 2011), 34.

67. Ibid., 347.

68. Ibid., 349.

69. Green, *Devil's Bargain,* 6, 21.

70. Ibid., 21–22.

71. Buchanan, *Suicide of a Superpower,* 355.

72. Richard Schickel, *Intimate Strangers: The Culture of Celebrity* (Garden City, NJ: Doubleday, 1985), viii. See also Lauren Wright, *Star Power: American Democracy in the Age of Celebrity* (New York: Routledge, 2020).

73. C. Wright Mills, *The Power Elite* (New York: Oxford University Press, 1956), 74.

74. Green, *Devil's Bargain,* 96–97.

75. Ibid., 99.

76. Ibid. For example, his realtor firm was charged with racial discrimination, a case settled out of court in which, without admitting guilt, the firm agreed to an affirmative action rental plan.

77. David Masciotra, *I Am Somebody: Why Jesse Jackson Matters* (London: I. B. Tauris, 2020), 44.

78. Ibid.

79. Green, *Devil's Bargain*, 102.

80. Ibid., 101.

81. James Ceaser, "Demagoguery, Statesmanship, and Presidential Politics," in Joseph Bessette and Jeffrey Tulis, eds., *The Constitutional Presidency* (Baltimore: Johns Hopkins University Press, 2009), 249. For example, Andrew Jackson is viewed by many as one of the nation's greatest presidents. Although one of the most racist presidents and a White supremacist, he advanced the interests of the White working class against the aristocratic pretensions of the Washington establishment and financial elites. Eric Posner contends that Jackson, who he describes as a "white Christian nationalist" was also the only demagogue to become president prior to Trump. See *The Demagogue's Playbook: The Battle for American Democracy: From the Founders to Trump* (New York: All Points Books, 2020).

82. Ibid., 259.

83. Jennifer Mercieca, *Demagogue for President: The Rhetorical Genius of Donald Trump* (College Station: Texas A&M University Press, 2020).

84. Ann Ruth Willner, *The Spellbinders: Charismatic Political Leadership* (New Haven: Yale University Press, 1984), 6.

85. Trump made this remark at a campaign event in January 2016 shortly before the state's caucuses. Kate Reilly, "Donald Trump Says He Could Shoot Somebody and Not Lose Support," *Time,* January 23, 2016.

86. Philip Bump, "23 Things Trump Said That Would Have Doomed Another Candidate," *Washington Post,* June 17, 2016.

87. Ross Douthat, "Is Donald Trump a Fascist?" *New York Times,* December 3, 2015; Pam Grier "Is Donald Trump Really A Fascist?" *Christian Science Monitor,* November 25, 2015; Dana Milibank, "Donald Trump Is a Racist and a Bigot," *Washington Post,* December 1, 2015; David Hershey, "Donald Trump's Fascist Inclinations Do Not Bother His Fans," *Los Angeles Times,* December 14, 2015; "The New Fuehrer," *Philadelphia Daily News,* December 8, 2015; Timothy Egan, "Goose-Steppers in the GOP," *New York Times,* December 12, 2015; Robert Kagan, "This Is How Fascism Comes to America," *Washington Post,* May 19, 2016; and Nicholas Kristof, "Donald Trump Is a Racist," *New York Times,* July 24, 2016.

88. Interview with Wolf Blitzer, CNN, June 10, 2016.

89. CNN, May 3, 2016.

90. Willner, *The Spellbinders,* 6, emphasis in the original.

91. The data are reported in E. J. Dionne, Norman Ornstein, and Thomas Mann, *One Nation After Trump: A Guide to the Perplexed, the Disillusioned, the Desperate, and the Not-Yet Deported* (New York: St. Martin's, 2017), 165.

92. A 2019 poll by Public Religion Research Institute (PPRI) found that 33 percent of Trump's followers indicated "there was nothing he could do to lose their approval." See *A Fractured Nation: Widening Partisan Polarization and Key Issues in 2020 Election* (Washington: PRRI, 2019), 22. A further

illustration of Trump's charismatic hold on a segment of his followers is shown in a 2020 poll that found 49.5 percent of White weekly church attending Protestants agreed with the statement "Trump was anointed by God to be President." See Paul Djupe and Ryan Burge, "Trump the Anointed," http://religioninpublic.blog/2020/05/11/trump-the-anointed/. For a revealing series of interviews with Trump's White Christian supporters in a small Iowa town see Elizabeth Dias, "Christianity Will Have Power," *New York Times,* August 9, 2020. The respondents indicated they understood that Trump did not share their values, but they supported him because he nevertheless defended those values they view as under attack from a hostile secular society.

93. Oliver Hahl et al., "The Authentic Appeal of the Lying Demagogue: Proclaiming the Deeper Truth About Political Illegitimacy," *American Sociological Review* 83 (2018): 1–33.

94. James Campbell, "A Recap of the 2016 Election Forecasts," *PS: Political Science and Politics* 50 (2017): 331–338. These forecast models predicted Clinton's (the Democratic Party's) popular vote share quite accurately; the popular vote usually corresponds to the electoral college vote (only five exceptions in presidential election history). Finally it should be noted that it would be very difficult to model the electoral college vote.

95. Gary Jacobson, "Polarization, Gridlock, and Presidential Politics in 2016," *Annals of the American Academy of Political and Social Sciences* 667 (2017): 84. Samuel Popkin argues that Cruz "opened the door for Trump" by, among other things, waging a relentless campaign to sabotage the Republican Party's efforts, led by Marco Rubio, to fashion a bipartisan compromise on immigration. See *Crackup: The Republican Implosion and the Future of Presidential Politics* (New York: Oxford University Press, 2021), 61–86. See also Ann Marie Cox, "The Tragedy of Ted Cruz," *Harpers' Magazine,* November 11, 2018.

96. Trump was outspent in both the primaries and the general election. In the primaries Trump spent, according to Federal Election Commission data, $76 million, compared to Bush's $138 million and Rubio's $111 million. In the general election Clinton spent almost twice as much, $640 million compared to $302 million. Trump also did not employ a professionalized campaign organization of speechwriters, ad makers, opposition researchers, consultants, and others usually associated with modern campaigns. Although there were several persons who had the title "campaign manager," Trump, as Michael Genovese writes was "the campaign manager. He did what he wanted, went with his instincts, defied tradition, upended logic, rejected custom, eschewed civility. He simply could not be managed." See *How Trump Governs: An Assessment and Prognosis* (Amherst, NY: Cambria Press, 2017), 63. Trump's unorthodox, instinctual style of staffing and decisionmaking is a core part of his presidential character, which continued in his conduct of the office.

97. Michael Tesler and John Sides, "How Political Science Helps Explain the Rise of Trump: The Role of White Identity and Grievances," *Washington Post,* March 3, 2016. See also Tehama Lopez Bunyasi, "The Role of Whiteness in the 2016 Presidential Primaries," *Perspectives on Politics* 17 (2019): 679–698.

98. Tesler and Sides, "How Political Science Helps Explain the Rise of Trump."

99. Carol Swain, *The New White Nationalism in America: Its Challenge to Integration* (New York: Cambridge University Press, 2004).

100. Trump reportedly instructed his aides to listen to talk radio to get a sense of what was on the mind of conservatives, and they found immigration was a salient issue. See John Sides, Michael Tesler, and Lynn Vavreck, *Identity Crisis: The 2016 Presidential Campaign and the Battle for the Meaning of America* (Princeton: Princeton University Press, 2018), 84. Some also attribute a major influence on Trump's thinking on immigration to campaign and White House aide Stephen Miller. See Nick Miroff and Josh Dawsey, "The Advisor Who Scripts Trump's Immigration Policy," *Washington Post,* August 17, 2019. On the political salience of the issue, especially for Republicans, see Marisa Abrajano and Zoltan Hajnal, *White Backlash: Immigration, Race, and American Politics* (Princeton: Princeton University Press, 2017).

101. The question read: Some people say that because of past discrimination, blacks should be given preference in hiring and promotion. Others say such preferences in hiring and promotion discriminates against whites. What about your opinion—are you for or against preferential hiring and promotion of blacks?

102. The 2016 Republican platform included language opposing affirmative action: "We continue to encourage equality for all citizens and access to the American dream. Merit and hard work should determine advancement in our society, so we reject unfair preferences, quotas and set-asides as forms of discrimination." Quoted in Gwendoline Alphonso, "'One People, Under One God, Saluting One American Flag': Trump, the Republican Party, and the Construction of American Nationalism," in Zachary Callen and Philip Rocco, eds., *American Political Development and the Trump Presidency* (Philadelphia: University of Pennsylvania Press, 2020), 62.

103. Hillary Rodham Clinton, *What Happened* (New York: Simon & Schuster, 2017), 226.

104. Seymour Martin Lipset and Gary Marks, *It Didn't Happen Here: Why Socialism Failed in the United States* (New York: Norton, 2000).

105. Robert C. Smith, "Race, Democracy and the Socialist Project in the United States," *National Review of Black Politics* 1 (2020): 38.

106. See Justin McCarthy, "In U.S., Socialist Presidential Candidates Least Appealing," Gallup, June 22, 2015, https://news.gallup.com/poll /183713/socialist-presidential-candidates-least-appealing.aspx.

107. Thomas Patterson, *Pre-Primary News Coverage of the 2016 Presidential Race: Trump's Rise, Sanders' Emergence, and Clinton's Struggle* (Cambridge: Harvard University, Shorenstein Center, 2016).

108. Harry Enten, "Americans Distaste of Both Trump and Clinton Is Record-Breaking," FiveThirtyEight, May 5, 2016, https://fivethirtyeight.com /features/americans-distaste-for-both-trump-and-clinton-is-record-breaking.

109. American Psychological Association, "APA Survey Reveals 2016 Presidential Election Source of Significant Stress for Half of Americans," October 13, 2016, http://www.apa.org/news/press/release/2016/10/presidential -election-stress.

110. Trump's victory in the electoral college was by the narrowest of margins. He won Michigan, Pennsylvania, and Wisconsin by 0.2, 0.7, and

0.8 percentage points respectively, or by 10,704, 46,765, and 22,177 votes, which provided the 46-vote margin in the electoral college. Philip Bump, "Donald Trump Will Be President Thanks to 80,000 People," *Washington Post,* December 1, 2016.

111. Patterson, *Pre-Primary Coverage of the 2016 Election.*

112. Nicholas Confessore and Karen Yourish, "Measuring Trump's Big Advantage in Free Media," *New York Times,* March 17, 2016. During the early primaries, Fox News provided somewhat less coverage of Trump than the more liberal CNN and MSNBC, apparently because Rupert Murdoch, the owner of Fox's parent company, and Roger Ailes, the Fox News president, were opposed to Trump—favoring Bush, Rubio, or Kasich. Some Fox News commentators were often hostile, and Trump got more attention, often unfiltered, on CNN and MSNBC. See Karl, *Front Row at the Trump Show,* 23. After Trump won the nomination, Fox commentators were mainly supportive while CNN and MSNBC tended to be hostile.

113. Ronald Walters, *White Nationalism, Black Interests: Conservative Public Policy and the Black Community* (Detroit: Wayne State University Press, 2003), 21.

114. Richard Alba contends that race replaced ethnic identities among southern and eastern European immigrants to the United States as result of their integration into American society. Coming to America poor and dispossessed, they faced discrimination from the dominant Anglo-Saxon group. However, through family, church, and hard work, they made it. This pan-ethnic perspective of European immigrants creates bonds of solidarity that unites them as a distinctive White ethnic group, while at the same time excluding Blacks because they say Blacks have failed to pull themselves up as did their ancestors from Poland, Italy, and Ireland. See *Ethnic Identity: The Transformation of White America* (New Haven: Yale University Press, 1990).

115. Walters, *White Nationalism,* 29.

116. Ibid., 32

117. Ibid., 155.

118. Sheldon Danziger, "Budget Cuts as Welfare Reform," *American Economic Review* 73 (1983): 65. In White nationalist lexicon Social Security (and Medicare) are viewed as programs for Whites. Donald Kinder and Cindy Kam write, "The connection between Social Security and in-group vocabulary imply in a subtle way that Social Security is for white people while programs like food stamps or aid to dependent children are viewed as programs for blacks." See *Us Against Them: Ethnocentric Foundations of American Public Opinion* (Chicago: University of Chicago Press, 2009), 186, 188. See also Nicholas Winter, "Beyond Welfare: Framing and Racialization of White Opinion on Social Security," *American Journal of Political Science* 50 (2006): 400–420.

119. Walters, *White Nationalism, Black Interests,* 35, 53–54.

120. Corey Cook, "White Nationalism, Black Interests, and Contemporary American Politics," in Robert C. Smith, Cedric Johnson, and Robert Newby, eds., *What Has This Got to Do with the Liberation of Black People: The Impact of Ronald W. Walters on African American Thought and Leadership* (Albany: SUNY Press, 2014), 238. Cook "coded over twenty thousand bills for their content, attempting to discern those that contain the

intention of producing, whether explicitly or implicitly, 'racially disparate outcomes.'" Over the eight years of the study "white members increasingly sponsored or co-sponsored legislation implicitly or explicitly promoting white interests relative to legislation promoting black or Chicano interests" (232). Rogers Smith and Desmond King analyze a number of White interest policies pursued by the Trump administration, which they label White protectionism. See "White Protectionism in America," *Perspectives on Politics* 19 (2021): 460–478.

121. "White Racial Consciousness and White Identity in the U.S.," ANES Pilot Study, the University of Michigan, n.d.

122. Diana Mutz, "Status Threat, Not Economic Hardship, Explains 2016 Election," *Proceedings of the National Academy of Sciences* 115 (2018): 331–351; Eric Kaufman, "White Identity and Euro-Traditional Nationalism in Trump's America," *Forum* (2019); and Sean McElwee, "Fear of Diversity Made People More Likely to Vote for Trump," *The Nation,* March 14, 2017.

123. Ashley Jardina, *White Identity Politics* (New York: Cambridge University Press, 2019); Sides, Tesler, and Vavreck, *Identity Crisis;* and Alan Abramowitz, *The Great Realignment: Race, Party Transformation, and the Rise of Donald Trump* (New Haven: Yale University Press, 2018).

124. Sides, Tesler, and Vavreck, *Identity Crisis,* 175. See also Jon Green and Sean McElwee, "The Differential Effects of Economic and Racial Attitudes on the Election of Donald Trump," *Perspectives on Politics* 17 (2018): 358–369.

125. Jardina, *White Identity Politics,* 113–114. Jardina found only a "small association" between White identity and evangelism, southern residence, and living in rural areas.

126. Abramowitz, *The Great Realignment,* 124, 140. Diana Mutz agrees with this understanding of the election, writing it "was an effort by members of an already dominant group to assure their continued dominance and by those in an already powerful and wealthy country to assure its continued dominance." Mutz, "Status Threat, Not Economic Hardship, Explains 2016 Election," 350. Strikingly, race had greater impact on voter attitudes in 2016 than in the elections of the first Black president. See Michael Tesler, "Views About Race Mattered More in Electing Trump Than in Electing Obama," *Washington Post,* November 22, 2016.

127. Jardina, *White Identity Politics.* 23.

128. Brian Schaffner, Matthew MacWilliams, and Tatishe Nteta, "Understanding White Polarization in the 2016 Vote for President: The Sobering Role of Racism and Sexism," *Political Science Quarterly* 133 (2018): 9–34. It should be clear that while there may be a correlation between White racism and White nationalism, they are distinct phenomena in Walters's formulation and the subsequent research.

129. Lilliana Mason, *Uncivil Agreement: How Politics Became Our Identity* (Chicago: University of Chicago Press, 2018), 3.

3

The Importance of Presidential Personality and Character

THE GREAT POLITICAL SCIENTIST HAROLD LASSWELL was the first to introduce personality concepts to the study of political leadership. Trained in the theories of Sigmund Freud at the University of Berlin, his 1948 book *Power and Personality* was an attempt to insert Freudian ideas into the social science study of the relationship between personality and power, political leadership and the pursuit and maintenance of democratic values. Although judged by contemporary standards the book would seem rather crude and overreliant on Freudian psychiatric ideas, it is nevertheless a valiant pioneering attempt by political science to get an empirical handle on the vexing but important problem of the role of personality or character in the exercise of power.

As a general hypothesis, Lasswell asserts, "Power is expected to overcome the low estimates of self."[1]

> The attenuation of power is to be understood as the compensatory reaction against low estimates of the self (especially when coexisting with high self-estimates); and the reaction occurs when opportunities exist for both the displacement of ungratified cravings from the primary circle to public targets and for the rationalization of these displacements in the public interest; and finally skills are acquired appropriate to the effective operation of the power balancing process.[2]

Although I judge this focus on self-esteem too narrow to base a study of the problem of personality and political leadership, and shall

43

not use it in this work, it is noteworthy that James David Barber makes relatively high self-esteem a major variable in his classification of "crude clues" to presidential character types.[3] That Barber, in the most renowned and systematic work on the subject of personality and the presidency, uses Lasswell's notion is evidence of his seminal influence on the study of personality, power, and leadership.

Power, Personality, and the Presidency

It is likely useful to focus on the personality, character, or psychology of any person who exercises power over others, whatever the scope or domain of their power. In the case of the US presidency this is all the more important because Article II of the Constitution vests all of the executive power in a single person. (It is said that Lyndon Johnson used to say, "I am Article II.") There was some discussion but very little support at the Philadelphia convention for a plural executive—a council of state. Although the idea was embraced by such influential figures as Benjamin Franklin, George Mason, and Roger Sherman, James Madison's argument that plurality in the executive would encourage factionalism and regional rivalries prevailed. On the positive side, Madison and Alexander Hamilton made the case that a single, unitary executive would promote national unity, vigorous administration, and secrecy in the conduct of diplomacy and war.[4]

While there was debate at Philadelphia about sharing the executive power, there was none about whether the office would combine the symbolic, ceremonial role of head of state with the executive role of head of government, combining in one person, to use the British example, monarch and prime minister. At the time, there were no republican models for a ceremonial head of state and a political leader who would administer the government and command the military. As head of government the president is expected to occasionally be the manipulative partisan politician amassing power to advance an ideological or policy agenda, while as head of state he is expected to be above politics and serve as a role model, a moral exemplar, and the embodiment of the values and traditions of republican democratic government. These roles may sometimes be in conflict, which is why most modern states separate them. As head of state, the US president is due some of the deference accorded a king or queen, which may have the tendency to contribute to the egotism likely inherent in any personality exercising great power.

Based in part on his experience as an adviser to President Lyndon Johnson, George Reedy calls attention to the importance of assessing personality in the presidency. First, he notes the "court-like" atmosphere of the White House where the president is "treated with all the deference due to monarchs" and its structure is designed for one purpose only, "to serve the material needs and desires of a single man."[5] It is essential, he writes, "to emphasize the crucial importance of personality to the success of a president [because] in the White House, character and personality are extremely important because there are no other limitations which govern a man's conduct. Restraint must come from within the presidential soul and from within the presidential mind. The adversary forces which temper the actions of others do not come into play until it's too late to change course."[6]

Scholars of the presidency have reached the same conclusions. Edward Corwin writes, "What the presidency is at any particular moment depends in large measure on who is president."[7] Joseph Bessette and Jeffrey Tulis concur, "The presidency is by constitutional design such a highly personalized office that it will necessarily reflect the particular virtues (and vices), talents and goals of its occupant."[8]

These generalizations about character and power in the presidency apply to all forty-four persons who have held the office, but with greater force to the mercurial forty-fifth president.

Important Studies of
Personality and the Presidency

Erwin Hargrove's *Presidential Leadership: Personality and Political Style* is one of the early efforts to specifically apply Lasswell's insights to the study of the presidency. He contended political scientists could use a "biographical approach" and historical case studies to describe the role of personality in the exercise of presidential power. He notes the presidential office is "shapeless," the personality of each president "fills it out to suit himself."[9] Personality—"the amalgam of drives, values and traits" of the leader—is not necessarily the determining factor in presidential leadership behavior,[10] rather, personality interacts with culture and institutions to shape presidential leadership behavior.[11]

In *Personality and Politics: Problems of Evidence, Inference, and Conceptualization,* Fred Greenstein is specifically concerned with how to separate the effects of personality from culture and institutions in assessing leadership behavior. In gathering evidence and drawing inferences on the possible impact of personality or character, one must be careful to take account of variables such as social background, ideology, partisanship, and electoral, institutional imperatives.[12] Greenstein puts the theoretical point this way, which is useful in evaluating the impact of Trump's character on policies or events: "In each case what presumably concerns us is personal input—including again the failure to take an available course of action—that diverts the course of events from what otherwise would have been expected if the actor's personal capacities had been more typical."[13] The concept of "actor indispensability" is key here, whether the leader's personality or character was a necessary link in some decision or event.[14]

Ten variables that may foster actor dispensability or indispensability are listed. Two of these variables seem particularly relevant to the analysis of Trump. One, "the opportunities for the impact of personality increases to the degree the political actors lack socially standardized mental sets which might lead them to structure their perceptions and resolve ambiguities."[15] Two, personality factors "are likely to be exhibited in certain kinds of spontaneous behavior—notably actions that proceed from personal impulse, without effort or premeditation."[16]

Stanley Renshon's *The Psychological Assessment of Presidential Candidates* is concerned, as is Barber, with developing a psychologically grounded theory that would be helpful in predicting the "psychological suitability for office" of presidential candidates.[17] This is a daunting—valiant perhaps—but likely impossible endeavor. Renshon claims through reading memoirs, biographies, and press reports that it is possible to get some leverage on the "basic psychological building blocks" of the personality of would-be presidents and avoid "severe psychological impairment" among presidents and presidential candidates.[18] Yet, he writes:

> concern with the psychological impairments of presidential candidates are still legitimate. [But] many severe psychological disturbances do not result in obviously bizarre behavior . . . or necessarily appear continuously. . . . The problem is compounded by the fact that a person with more than moderate degrees of psychological impairment can often present a clinical picture that includes . . . personality strengths. As if this didn't make the task difficult, some personality traits such as [narcissism] may be found in persons' traits that make them more attractive as candidates.[19]

The most renowned study of personality and the American presidency is Alexander George and Juliette George's *Woodrow Wilson and Colonel House* (like Barber's work, often criticized because of its crude formulation, derived partly from Lasswell). The Georges find that for Wilson, power was a "compensatory value, a means of restoring the self-esteem damaged in his childhood."[20] In its nature, the notion that Wilson's "compulsive character," if compulsive it was, derived from childhood needs, can at best be only a limited explanation of Wilson's leadership behavior. At the outset, the Georges concede the point, "It is important to bear in mind the situational context in which the individual operates. Personality traits of leaders, in short, do not 'determine' events although they are frequently important."[21] This is a theoretical point of departure for all studies of personality, power, and leadership.

Another theoretical point of the Georges' work for which there is general agreement is the importance of "developmental biography," that is "tracing the subject's total personality throughout his formative years, and indeed sometimes into adult life . . . paying attention to his familial, cultural and social milieu. For it is in this interaction with his milieu that the individual finds himself."[22]

The Presidential Character: James David Barber and His Critics

James David Barber's 1972 work *The Presidential Character: Predicting Performance in the White House* is the most systematic attempt by political science to develop an understanding of the role of personality or character on presidential behavior.

Barber defines *character* as "what life has marked into a man's being . . . the way the *president orients himself toward life*, not for the moment, but enduringly."[23] As used by Barber, "character is the person's stance as he confronts experience. And at the core of character, a man confronts himself. The president's fundamental self-esteem is his prime personal resource; to defend and advance that, he will sacrifice much else he values. Down there in the privacy of his heart, does he find himself superb, or ordinary, or debased, or in some intermediate range?"[24]

The personality of the president is "patterned" in a "dynamic psychological package" observable in terms of his character, style, and worldview. The most visible part of the pattern is style, which is "the president's habitual way of performing his three political roles: rhetoric, personal relations and homework."[25]

> Style is how the President goes about performing what the office requires him to do—to speak directly or through media, to large audiences; to deal face to face with other politicians, individually and in small groups; and to read, write, and calculate by himself in order to manage the endless flow of details that stream onto his desk. No President can escape doing at least some of each. But there are marked differences in stylistic emphasis from President to President. The *balance* among the three style elements varies; one President may put most of himself into rhetoric, another may stress close, informal dealings, while still another may devote his energies mainly to study and cogitation. Beyond the balance, we want to see how each President's peculiar habits of style, his mode of coping with and adapting to these presidential demands.[26]

Worldview consists of the president's

> *primary, politically relevant beliefs, particularly his conceptions of social causality, human nature, and the central moral conflicts of the time.* This is how he sees the world and his lasting opinion about what he sees. Style is his way of acting; world view is his way of seeing. Like the rest of us, a President develops over a lifetime certain conception of reality—how things work in politics, what people are like, what the main purposes are. These assumptions or conceptions help him make sense of his world, give some semblance of order in the chaos of existence. Perhaps most important: a man's world view affects what he pays attention to, and a great deal of politics is about paying attention.[27]

A biographical portrait from early childhood through adulthood to what Barber calls a president's "first political success" is the best way to identify the patterns in presidential world view, character, and style. In general,

> character has its main development in childhood, world view in adolescence, and style in early adulthood. The stance I call character grows out of the child's experiments in relating to parents, brothers and sisters, and peers at play and in school, as well as his own body and the objects around it. . . . Thoughts about the way the world works and how one might work in it, about what people are like and how one might be like them or not, and about the values people share and how one might share them too—these are the typical concerns for the post-child, pre-adult mind of the adolescent. These themes come together in early adulthood, when the person moves from contemplation to responsible action and adopts a style.

In most biographical accounts this period stands out in stark clarity—
the time of emergence, the time the young man found himself. I call
it his first independent political success. It was then he moved
beyond the detailed guidance of his family; then his self-esteem was
dramatically boosted; then he came forth as a person to be reckoned
with by other people. The way he did that is profoundly important
to him. Typically he grasps that style and hangs onto it. Much later,
coming into the Presidency, something in him remembers this earlier victory and re-emphasizes the style that made it happen.[28]

This is the core of Barber's theory and method. He might have
stopped at this point. However, he goes further, and in the most controversial aspect of the theory, he develops a four-cell typology of
presidential character. Indeed, he writes, the typology is the "argument (which organizes the structure of the book) is that Presidential
character—the basic stance a man takes toward his Presidential experience—comes in four varieties. The most important thing to know
about a President or candidate is where he fits among these types,
defined according to (a) how active and (b) whether or not he gives
the impression he enjoys his political life."[29] Why, he asks, might we
expect these two simple dimensions to outline main character types?
Because, he writes, "they stand for two central features of anyone's
orientation toward life."[30] In every personality study, Barber claims
the active-positive contrast—"the tendency to act or be acted
upon"—and the affect dimension—"optimistic-pessimistic, happy-
sad"—are present.[31] Barber concludes his case, "The two baselines
are clear and they are independent of one another: all of us know
people who are very active but seem discouraged, others who are
quite passive but seem happy, and so forth. The activity baseline
refers to what one does, the affect baseline to how he feels about
what he does."[32] He concedes these are "crude clues" and "a matter
of tendencies" rather than fixed traits that one possesses or does not:
"We all have all of them but in different amounts."[33]

The four types are active-positive, active-negative, passive-
positive and passive-negative. He defines and explains each in some
detail, but in summary, "Active-positive presidents want most to
achieve results. Active-negatives aim to get and keep power. Passive-
positives are after love. Passive-negatives emphasize their civic
virtue. The relation of activity to enjoyment in a President thus tends
to outline clusters of characteristics, to set apart the adapted from the
compulsive, compliant, and withdrawn types."[34]

No other part of Barber's theory has been more criticized than
the typology.[35] It is not central to the theory, and I will not use it in

my analysis of Trump. That is, I will not attempt to classify Trump on the basis of the baselines of activity, self-esteem, or joy in political life.

Like most scholars of personality and politics, Barber is careful to specify that presidential character must be analyzed in the context of the political culture and institutions; as he puts it, "Presidential character resonates with the political situation the President faces."[36] He discusses two interrelated situational or contextual variables, the "power situation" and the "climate of expectations."[37] The power situation involves such things as the president's party balance in Congress, the relative influence of interest groups, or the thrust of Supreme Court opinions. The climate of expectations structures all presidential behavior in that presidents are expected to provide a sense of "reassurance" to the country that "things will be alright"; a sense of "action and progress"; and a "sense of legitimacy" and "moral idealism." Presidents are expected to behave with the "dignity" and "propriety" inherent in the office.[38]

Before turning to applying the theory to an assessment of Trump, it is useful to discuss some of the important reviews and critiques of it.[39] In the first chapter I referred to Michael Lyons's review of *The Presidential Character*, in which he writes that the book was "much maligned and much praised," but it remains "the most influential study of the type."[40]

The most detailed review of the book is Alexander George's "Assessing Presidential Character." He finds Barber's "tentative, uncertain theory a valuable contribution to the literature on personality and power because it enables the investigator to pull together his observations and interpretations about a president into a coherent pattern."[41] George's principal reservation concerns the typology, which he finds problematic because without a "mixed type. . . . To tag a subject with a label drawn from a typology is to place him in a pigeonhole . . . and does not provide the biographer what he needs most: Namely, a more discriminating, differentiated theory regarding the individual's more complex personality."[42] He also takes Barber to task for his neglect of ideology in his discussion of style, for his tendency to allow his (liberal) ideology to shape the analysis, the tendency to "impose theory on data simply because it seems plausible," and his wish to "popularize his theory," which rendered it "not as documented . . . to persuade professionals."[43]

Erwin Hargrove's main criticism of Barber's theory also regards its typology. He acknowledges Barber's theory of personality and presidential behavior is "the best to date" and is "useful as a sensitizing device to scan political leaders [but] the difficult methodological and conceptual problem comes with fitting individuals into boxes . . . since most talented individuals are likely to be some mix of both."[44] Like George, Hargrove also raises the problem of ideological bias: "Barber is the liberal searching for the ideal type of liberal leader. All of his active positives are liberal and presented in an idealized form."[45]

James Qualls raises several reservations about Barber's project. First, he views the focus on character as a species of "psychological reductionism," as "the sole or major explanation of political behavior rather than one among many contributing factors."[46] Second, he is also critical of the typology, not only because adequate biographical data are not likely to be available, but more importantly, because "typing a candidate is difficult, . . . even with the right kind of information; and without that information, typing a candidate in the manner Barber proposes can be expected to produce accurate conclusions no more frequently than typing at random."[47] But more concerning, Qualls concludes, "[This] assumes a true theory. If in the end, the truth of Barber's theory can only be determined empirically, then the process will be lengthy, spanning some minimum number of cases multiplied by a factor of four years. . . . Of course, in assessing personality of a presidential candidate, a student of politics may well employ the theory. But he should do so only with caution, aware of the speculative nature of the theory, and the absence of adequate information."[48]

Studying these reviews and others of Barber's work was useful in thinking about how to use Barber in the study of President Trump.[49] I was skeptical about Barber's typology and the baselines of activity and self-esteem from which he derived them when I first read the book. Reading the reviews reinforced this skepticism and my decision in this study not to use it. The reviews also reminded me as a liberal to be ever mindful of the problem of ideological bias. And I shall be careful in observations and inferences to try not to force the data to fit the theory. Overall, the reviews, however, strengthened my view that if one wishes to study the role of character in the Trump presidency, Barber's work is the best we have. As Michael Nelson concludes, "Barber's theories may be seriously flawed. For all their limitations—some of them self-confessed— they offer one of the more significant contributions a scholar can make to an unfamiliar but useful way of looking at a familiar thing—the presidency—through the lens of personality."[50]

The theory here is that Trump's presidency is shaped more by his personality or character than any other in history. Thus, character, like demagoguery and charisma, no matter how slippery the concept and ambiguous the data, is something we dare not ignore if we are to understand this extraordinary phenomenon in US politics. Other variables—ideology, the power situation here and abroad, polarization, and Barber's overall "climate of expectations"—are included, but the hypothesis here is that character will matter.

Notes

1. Harold Lasswell, *Power and Personality* (New York: Norton, 1948), 39.
2. Ibid., 53.
3. This quote and all that follow are from the paperback edition of James David Barber, *The Presidential Character: Predicting Performance in the White House* (Englewood Cliffs, NJ: Prentice Hall, 1972), 12.
4. Donald Robinson, *To the Best of My Ability: The Presidency and the Constitution* (New York: Norton, 1987), 69–76.
5. George Reedy, *The Twilight of the Presidency* (New York: New American Library, 1970), 18.
6. Ibid., 30.
7. Edward Corwin, *The Presidency: Office and Powers,* 5th ed. (New York: New York University Press, 1984), 29.
8. Joseph Bessette and Jeffrey Tulis, "The Constitution and the Presidency," in Bessette and Tulis, eds., *The Presidency in the Constitutional Order* (Baton Rouge: Louisiana State University Press, 1981), 16.
9. Erwin Hargrove, *Presidential Leadership: Personality and Style* (New York: Macmillan, 1966), 3.
10. Ibid.
11. Ibid., 142.
12. Fred Greenstein, *Personality and Politics: Problems of Evidence, Inference, and Conceptualization* (Chicago: Markham, 1969), 40.
13. Ibid., 46.
14. Ibid., 42
15. Ibid., 51.
16. Ibid., 55.
17. Stanley Renshon, *The Psychological Assessment of Presidential Candidates* (New York: New York University Press, 1996), 13.
18. Ibid., 19.
19. Ibid., 12.
20. Alexander George and Juliette George, *Woodrow Wilson and Colonel House* (New York: John Day, 1956), 320.
21. Ibid., xvi.
22. Ibid., 318–319.
23. Barber, *The Presidential Character,* 8, emphasis in original.

24. Ibid.

25. Ibid., 7.

26. Ibid.

27. Ibid., 8, emphasis in original.

28. Ibid., 10.

29. Ibid., 6.

30. Ibid., 12.

31. Ibid.

32. Ibid.

33. Ibid., 7, 12.

34. Ibid., 13.

35. For a particularly churlish critique see Garry Wills, *The Kennedy Imprisonment: A Meditation on Power* (New York: Pocket Books, 1982), 190–194.

36. Barber, *The Presidential Character,* 8.

37. Ibid., 8–9.

38. Ibid.

39. In addition to *The Presidential Character,* it is useful to read Barber's dissertation-turned book, *The Lawmakers: Recruitment and Adaptation to Legislative Life* (New Haven: Yale University Press, 1967); and his "Strategies for Understanding Politicians," *American Journal of Political Science* 18 (1974): 443–467.

40. Michael Lyons, "Presidential Character Revisited," *Political Psychology* 18 (1997): 790.

41. Alexander George, "Assessing Presidential Character," *World Politics* 26 (1974): 279.

42. Ibid., 273.

43. Ibid., 240, 246, 252, 258.

44. Erwin Hargrove, "Presidential Personality and Revisionist Views of the Presidency," *American Journal of Political Science* 17 (1973): 823, 831.

45. Ibid., 882.

46. James Qualls, "Barber's Typological Analysis of Political Leaders," *American Political Science Review* 71 (1977): 185. This is a somewhat unfair criticism of Barber's theory since he does not present character as the sole or even major determinant of presidential behavior but rather as an important contributing factor that on occasions may be decisive.

47. Ibid., 211.

48. Ibid.

49. Other reviews include Jeffrey Tulis, "On Presidential Character," in Bessette and Tulis, eds., *The Presidency in the Constitutional Order*; Betty Glad, "Evaluating Presidential Character," *Presidential Studies Quarterly* 28 (1998): 861–872; and Donald Kinder, "Presidential Character Revisited," in Richard Lau and David Sears, eds., *Political Cognition* (New York: Psychology Press, 1985).

50. Michael Nelson, "The Psychological Presidency," in Nelson, ed., *The Presidency and the Political System* (Washington: Congressional Quarterly Press, 1998), 201.

4

Trump's Character:
A Developmental Biography

USING AVAILABLE BIOGRAPHIES OF TRUMP, ACADEMIC writing, and journalists' reports, I attempt in this chapter to provide an account of the development of Trump's character focusing on worldview and style. In subsequent chapters I assess the role character played in select domestic and foreign policy issues and events. Compared to other presidents or presidential candidates, there is a larger volume of writings on Trump than typical, including many by Trump himself. Trump has been a public figure for some time, facilitating observations and inferences. Thus, the methodological concern about adequate source materials is to some extent attenuated. Some of this material is especially good on his childhood, adolescence, and his first independent business success.[1]

How did Trump's character develop? How was it constructed? He was born in 1946, the fourth of five children to Frederick Trump and Nancy Ann MacLeod. Trump's grandfather Friedrich, an immigrant from Germany, was a successful businessman, a saloon and brothel-owner, and Trump's father, Fred, was a real estate developer. Entrepreneurship and the accumulation of wealth was thus a part of young Donald's family of which all members are said to be proud.[2] Gwenda Blair summarizes the familial legacy: "Despite obvious differences in lifestyle and affect, Friedrich, Fred, and Donald were similar types. . . . All three were energetic people who would almost do anything to make a buck; all three possessed a certain ruthlessness, all three had a free and easy way about the truth; and all three had a range of solid, practical skills."[3]

Trump's mother, a Scottish immigrant, was a housewife, who occasionally did volunteer work in schools and local charities, along with assisting her husband in the business. There is very little in the biographical sources about Trump's relationships with his siblings or his mother, but he recalled that he probably got his "sense of show-manship from his mother. She always had a flair for the dramatic."[4]

Because of his father's success in business, Trump grew up in relatively affluent circumstances in Jamaica Estates in Queens, New York, a mostly homogeneous, White, middle- to upper-middle-class community. The Trumps lived in a large, twenty-three-room house with a White maid and a Black chauffeur for the two Cadillacs the family owned. His family milieu is described as a "source of warmth and security that nothing in life could ever match."[5]

Trump admired his father, and in many ways saw him as a role model. Described as strict and domineering, in *The Art of the Deal* Trump writes, "whenever pushed, he would push back harder."[6] Young Donald occasionally did yard and maintenance work with his father's employees at various developments. This was part of learning the business as well as a source of discipline. Of his father Trump writes, "Fortunately for me, I was drawn to business early, and I was never intimidated by my father, the way most people were. I stood up to him and he respected that."[7] Always meticulously dressed like his father, Donald, unlike his older brother Fred Jr., abstained from drinking and smoking because his father intensely disliked both (Fred Jr. died in 1982 from complications related to alcoholism). Yet in adolescence he was, as he put it, "a little wild,"

> always a leader in my neighborhood. Much of the way it is today, people either liked me a lot or they didn't like me at all. . . . I was mostly interested in creating mischief, because for some reason I liked to stir things up, I liked to test people . . . make a ruckus. . . . Even in elementary school, I was a very assertive kid. In the second grade I actually gave my music teacher a black eye—I punched my music teacher in the nose because I didn't think he knew anything about music and I almost got expelled. I'm not proud of that, but it is clear evidence that even early on I had a tendency to stand up and make my opinions known in a very forceful way. The difference now is I use my brains instead of fists.[8]

Interestingly, the incident with the music teacher may have never occurred. Michael Kranish and Marc Fisher suggest Trump may have made the story up to embellish his image as a tough guy, a fighter.[9] Whether true, a lie, or a Trump boast, the incident provides insight into Trump, specifically his worldview, which in adolescence seems to have taken on a Hobbesian quality.

After an incident where Trump and several friends were caught sneaking into Manhattan, his father sent him at age thirteen to a military academy to provide some discipline for his "wildness." Fred Trump visited the academy nearly every weekend to keep watch over young Donald to reinforce its discipline. Whether this was successful is unclear, but after the academy Trump enrolled at Fordham University, and subsequently the Wharton School of Business at the University of Pennsylvania. But he was really interested in following his father in business rather than pursuing a college education. Attending college, however, was a useful way to avoid the draft, and the Wharton School's prestige was alluring (he later received draft deferments for bone spurs on his feet). A lackluster student—he claimed he rarely attended classes—he recalls the one thing he learned at Wharton was not to be impressed by professors or academic credentials.[10] Michael Wolff writes, "*professor* was one of his bad words, and he was proud of never going to class, never buying a textbook, never taking a note."[11] Trump and his father, while admiring, often mocked his uncle John Trump, a distinguished professor of engineering at MIT, "He had the brains, I made the money."[12]

Worldview

After graduating from Wharton, Trump returned to Queens to join his father's business. By then the basic structure of his worldview seems to have been established, and it informed his entry into his father's real estate development enterprises at age 26. His worldview may be described as Hobbesian: a world of competitiveness, fear, and apprehension where women in the private sphere and both women and men in the public sphere are out to get you, to take advantage.[13] So, one has to get them first and get them hard. Like Thomas Hobbes's "war of everyman against everyman," every player in business, politics, or relationships is pursuing his or her own interest at the expense of everybody else. As he told an interviewer in 2015 who was writing a biography, "I think I probably expect the worst of people because I've seen so much."[14] The biographer suggests of Trump, "He approaches all life as an unending contest, which explains why he often uses the word *winner* when describing himself and calls people he dislikes *losers*."[15] Another chronicler of Trump's life writes that as a young person Trump said that "he liked to push people, to create tensions, to see how far he could assert himself to the misery of others. He was aggressive, assertive. . . . These were virtues . . . they led to power."[16] Longtime observer of Trump, David Cay Johnston, describes him as a "street fighter," who believed in "hitting back," "get[ting] even,"and quotes him as saying, "If somebody screws you, screw 'em back ten times over. At least you feel good about it. Boy, do I feel good."[17]

Tony Schwartz, who wrote *The Art of the Deal* with Trump, writes that from Trump's "perspective, he operated in a jungle full of predators who were forever out to get him, and he did what he had to do to survive."[18] In *The Art of the Deal*, Trump says, "I am very easy to get along with. I am very good to people who are good to me. But when people treat me badly or unfairly or try to take advantage of me, my general attitude has been to fight back very hard. The risk is you will make a bad situation worse, and I certainly don't recommend this approach to everyone. But my belief is that if you are fighting for something you believe in—even if it means alienating some people along the way—things usually work out for the best in the end."[19] And "I'm the first person to admit I am very competitive and I'll do anything within legal limits to win. Sometimes, part of making a deal is to denigrate your competition."[20]

Although not particularly religious, the Trump family attended Norman Vincent Peale's Marble Collegiate Church in Manhattan. When asked on a radio program in 2016 what was his favorite Bible verse or story that had influenced his thinking or character, Trump responded, "Well, I mean when we get into the Bible, I think many, so many. And some people look at an eye for an eye. That's not a particularly nice thing. But you know, if you look at what's happening to our country, I mean when you see what's going on with our country, how people are taking advantage of us . . . we have to be firm and have to be very strong. And, we can learn a lot from the Bible, that I can tell you."[21]

Trump's Manichaean outlook involves not just the public sphere, but also attitudes about women in intimate relationships where he avers, "People are really vicious, and in no place are they more vicious than in relationships with the opposite sex."[22] Trump described women as sexually voracious "killers who traded on their beauty to dominate men."[23]

Trump's Hobbesian worldview is combined with a narcissistic personality. Most if not all persons are to some degree narcissistic, and the trait is probably exaggerated among persons who seek to exercise power. Narcissism may be loosely associated with Barber's high self-esteem, which he contends is a critical trait in presidents with the preferred active-positive presidential character. Thus, some degree of narcissism is likely an inevitable and necessary part of leadership character. Trump's case is exaggerated. Examples abound: his tendency to attach his name to everything from his father's company to hotels, casinos, golf courses, airplanes, helicopters, and a university; his craving for press attention—"issuing a stream of press releases of news about his every move. He returned calls from the press, and when the calls didn't come, he made them himself."[24] For decades his daily routine included a review of everything said about him in the previous twenty-four hours; his tendency to "surround himself with sycophants who applauded his every move" rather than questioning his logic;[25] or his habit of keeping in a conference room stacks of magazines with his photo on the covers.[26] Michael D'Antonio observes, "Trump was offered as a journalist's paragon of narcissism at least as far back as 1988. The academics and psychologists got involved a few years later and would make diagnosis of Trump into a kind of professional sport."[27]

In 2009, writing in *The Narcissism Epidemic: Living in an Age of Entitlement,* Jean Twenge and Keith Campbell use Trump as a case study:

> The phenomenon is easy to see in the media. Donald Trump, who puts his name on everything he builds . . . and picks fights with talk show hosts, is a great example of someone who is both successful and appears to be narcissistic. We know about Trump's success *because* he is relentlessly self-promoting. It is hard to miss The Donald in the media, and he is rich—but there are other rich real estate tycoons you've have never heard of because they are not self-promoters and don't want to be in the lime-light.[28]

Trump has often vividly revealed this aspect of his character: "Throughout my life, my two greatest assets have been mental stability and being, like, really smart. . . . I went from successful businessman, to top TV star . . . to President of the United States on my very first try. I think that would qualify as not smart, but genius . . . and a very stable genius at that."[29]

Although as a political scientist I will not address the issue, some psychologists and psychiatrists view Trump's narcissism as malignant—a case of serious mental impairment.[30]

Style

At age twenty-six, shortly after graduating from college, Trump joined his father's company. Soon thereafter his father made him president. Immediately he changed the company name to the Trump Organization. Most of his father's real estate business was in Queens; this was too narrow a playing field for Trump. Although he and his father earlier had a multimillion-dollar project—Swifton Village—in Cincinnati, the ambitious Donald had his eye on Manhattan as the place where he could compete with the "big boys" in development and become his own man: successful and independent of his father, "against whom he would compete all his life."[31]

Fred Trump was supportive of his son's ambitions and used his connections with the New York City political establishment to provide access and "crucial legitimacy" with city politicians.[32] New York mayor Abraham Beame reportedly said after Trump's move to Manhattan, "Whatever my friend Fred and Donald want in this town, they get."[33]

Barber contends the style part of the presidential character develops in early adulthood, the time when the young man finds himself in what he calls his first political success. Narrowly defined, Trump's first political success came at age seventy when he was elected president. This of course is too limited because an individual's quest for power need not be confined to the quest for public office but can find expression in other arenas. For Trump that arena was business—real estate development in Manhattan. His first major success in that arena, "the project that launched his career," was the renovation and opening of the Grand Hyatt Hotel in 1980.[34] By this time, "he was not relying on his father's network of aging Brooklyn politicians. . . . Now [he was] ready to play with the big boys."[35]

Real estate developers tend to be private, but Trump thrived on publicity, which alienated many of his fellow developers. They particularly resented his "pattern of lying and exaggerating and boasting."[36] For example, when the Grand Hyatt in 1980 opened he falsely claimed that its ballroom was the biggest in the city, and when Trump Tower opened in 1983, he boasted the project and himself "as the best," "the greatest." His deals, he proclaimed, "would have taken an older man a lifetime to do, if he could have ever got them done."[37] One of his aides during this time said, "Donald believes in the big lie theory. If you say something again and again people will believe it."[38]

Trump justified his propensity to prevaricate and exaggerate as serving the people: "The final key to the way I promote is bravado. I play to people's fantasies. People may not always think big them-selves, but they can still get very excited by those who do. That's why a little hyperbole never hurts. People want to believe something is the biggest and the greatest and the most spectacular."[39]

Making false claims about the size of hotel ballrooms might be considered harmless "verbal inflation," but Trump also likely made false claims when his organization was sued by the Department of Justice for racial discrimination in his apartment complexes. Unlike his father, Trump initially refused to discuss a settlement, hired the McCarthy-era lawyer Roy Cohen (who became something of a mentor), then held a press conference and claimed the federal gov-ernment was trying to force him to rent to welfare recipients. Cohen then filed a $100 million defamation suit against the gov-ernment, which was summarily dismissed. The Trump firm later settled the case in an agreement that required it to seek out Black tenants aggressively and to include welfare payments in determin-ing income.[40] Years later Trump continued to defend his behavior in the case, writing, "The idea of settling the case drove me crazy. The fact is we did rent to blacks in our buildings. What we didn't want was welfare cases, black or white. I'd watched what happen when the government came after Samuel Lefrak . . . [and] he caved and started taking welfare cases. They virtually ruined his buildings."[41]

In his business career, Trump developed a distinctive style in personal relations, staffing, decisionmaking, homework, rhetoric, and media relations that, as Barber's theory predicts, carried over to his conduct of the presidency. In the Trump Organization, there was lit-tle structure in terms of staff; no one was in charge like a chief of staff. Meetings were open to all advisers with Trump as his own staff chief. Nor were there long memoranda or written reports. When asked what kind of homework he did before deciding to open a casino in Atlantic City, he pointed to his nose and said, "That's all the study I needed."[42] Long discussions were anathema, because he has "an extremely short attention span . . . and gets bored easily."[43] Describing his homework and decisionmaking process, Trump notes,

"I listened to my gut, no matter how good something sounds on paper. . . . I like to think I have that instinct. That's why I don't have a lot of number-crunchers, and don't trust fancy marketing. I do my own surveys and come to my own conclusions. . . . [I] learned more from conducting random surveys than I could from the greatest consulting firms."[44]

Trump's activity baseline apparently was extremely high, "Sleeping only a few hours a night; taking amphetamines that suppressed appetite and produced a sense of euphoria and boundless energy—precisely the sort of manic behavior that staffers often saw their boss exhibit."[45] The results showed at staff meetings when things went wrong, and Trump would "erupt like a volcano, yelling profanities, hurling accusations of laziness."[46] A result of this behavior was frequent staff turnover, and "those who lasted were those who learned never to argue back."[47]

Trump wanted not only to be a successful businessman and make a lot of money, he wanted to be famous. Thus, he likely spent as much time cultivating his rhetoric and relationships with the media as he did on his research and sound decisionmaking, which may in part account for his multiple business failures and bankruptcies. Operating on the principle that "bad publicity is sometimes better than no publicity at all,"[48] he had, an aide said, "A way of getting into print whatever he would say, even if it wouldn't be the whole and honest truth. . . . That was the thing with him that they call the big lie. You say something enough times it becomes the truth."[49]

Barber contends that the patterns of worldview that Trump developed in adolescence, and style patterns at the time of his early adulthood and in his first business success, are keys to understanding presidential behavior. The next several chapters demonstrate the intellectual acuity of Barber's theory.

Notes

1. I read the book by Trump's niece, Mary Trump, *Too Much and Never Enough: How My Family Created the World's Most Dangerous Man* (New York: Simon & Schuster, 2020); National Security Adviser John Bolton's, *The Room Where It Happened: A White House Memoir* (New York: Simon & Schuster, 2020); and Omarosa Manigault Newman's, *Unhinged: An Insider Account of the Trump White House* (New York: Simon & Schuster, 2018). I elected not to use them as sources because they were clearly bitter and biased toward President Trump.

2. Gwenda Blair, *The Trumps: Three Generations That Built an Empire* (New York: Simon & Schuster, 2000), 16. This is probably the most thorough and comprehensive of the Trump biographies.

3. Ibid., 456.

4. Donald Trump with Tony Schwartz, *The Art of the Deal* (New York: Random House, 1987), 15.

5. Blair, *The Trumps,* 229.

6. Trump, *The Art of the Deal*, 49.

7. Ibid.

8. Ibid.

9. Michael Kranish and Marc Fisher, *Trump Revealed: An American Journey of Ambition, Ego, Money, and Power* (New York: Scribner, 2016), 49. They write that in interviews none of Trump's "pals could recall the incident. Nor did the teacher recall it" (35).

10. Trump, *The Art of the Deal,* 53.

11. Michael Wolff, *Fire and Fury: Inside the Trump White House* (New York: Henry Holt, 2018), 188.

12. Blair, *The Trumps,* 226.

13. Thomas Hobbes, *Leviathan.* Introduction by John Plamenatz (New York: Meridian Books, 1966), 142. Hobbes wrote, "And therefore if any two men desire the same thing, which nevertheless they cannot enjoy, they become enemies; and in the way to their end, which is principally their own conservation, and sometimes their delectation only, endeavor to destroy one another. And hence it comes to pass, that where an invader hath no more to fear, than another man's power; if one plant, sow, build or possess a convenient seat, others may probably be expected to come prepared with forces united, to dispossess, and deprive him, not only of the fruit of his labor, but also his life or liberty" (140). Trump wrote, "Lions kill for food. People kill for sport. The same burning greed that makes people loot, kill, and steal in emergencies like fire and floods, operates daily in normal everyday people. It lurks beneath the surface, and when you least expect it, it rears its nasty head and bites you. Accept it. The world is a brutal place. People will annihilate you just for the fun of it or to show off to their friends." Donald Trump and Bill Zanker, *Think Big: Make It Happen in Business and Life* (New York: Harper Business, 2008), as quoted in Carter Wilson, *Trumpism: Race, Class, Populism, and Public Policy* (Lanham, MD: Lexington Books, forthcoming).

14. Michael D'Antonio, *Never Enough: Donald Trump and the Pursuit of Success* (New York: Thomas Dunne, 2015), 326.

15. Ibid., emphasis added.

16. Stephen Mansfield, *Choosing Donald Trump: God, Anger, Hope, and Why Christian Conservatives Supported Him* (Grand Rapids, MI: Baker Books, 2017), 48.

17. David Cay Johnston, *The Making of Donald Trump* (New York: Melville House, 2016), 351, 362–363.

18. Tony Schwartz, "I Wrote *The Art of the Deal* with Donald Trump," in Bandy Lee, ed., *A Duty to Warn: The Dangerous Case of Donald Trump* (New York: St. Martin's, 2017), 41.

19. Trump, *The Art of the Deal,* 41.

20. Ibid., 74.

21. Victor Morton, "Donald Trump's Favorite Verse Is One Jesus Specifically Repudiated," *Washington Times,* April 4, 2016.

22. D'Antonio, *Never Enough,* 226.

23. Ibid.

24. Blair, *The Trumps,* 330.

25. Ibid., 100.

26. Ibid.

27. D'Antonio, *Never Enough,* 53.

28. Jean Twenge and W. Keith Campbell, *The Narcissism Epidemic: Living in the Age of Entitlement* (New York: Free Press, 2009), 52.

29. Quoted in Victor Davis Hanson, *The Case for Trump* (New York: Basic Books, 2019), 339.

30. Bandy Lee, ed., *The Dangerous Case of Donald Trump.* For an extended critique of Lee and other psychologists who view Trump's narcissism as malignant or pathological, see Stanley Renshon, *The Real Psychology of the Trump Presidency* (New York: Palgrave Macmillan, 2020), chaps. 6–8.

31. Blair, *The Trumps,* 361.

32. Ibid., 259.

33. Ibid. On Trump's father's role in helping him in the early Manhattan years, see also Kranish and Fisher, *Trump Revealed,* 74.

34. Ibid., 85.

35. Ibid., 308.

36. Ibid., 316.

37. Ibid., 330.

38. D'Antonio, *Never Enough,* 216.

39. Trump, *The Art of the Deal,* 40.

40. Blair, *The Trumps,* 252.

41. Trump, *The Art of the Deal,* 67. The evidence, including an audit study and documents subpoenaed by the Justice Department, appears to show that race, not welfare status, was the determining factor in the case. See David Graham et al., "An Oral History of Trump's Bigotry," *The Atlantic,* June 2019.

42. Blair, *The Trumps,* 347.

43. Ibid.

44. Trump, *The Art of the Deal,* 36.

45. Blair, *The Trumps,* 386.

46. Ibid., 357.

47. Ibid.

48. Trump, *The Art of the Deal,* 118.

49. Kranish and Fisher, *Trump Revealed,* 109.

5

Presidential Character and Trumpian Rhetoric

THE POLITICAL CONTEXT WHEN TRUMP ENTERED OFFICE was a deeply polarized nation, divided by region, race, religion, party, and ideology. Winning the election while losing the popular vote, Trump was the most polarizing and unpopular president at inauguration than any president since polling began. Since he had not won a majority vote of the people, many Americans viewed his presidency as lacking legitimacy (the day after inauguration a million persons marched in protest). Yet, he had won the most stunning presidential election upset in history by mobilizing a White majority animated by economic anxiety, White nationalism, and racial resentment. This base constituency was an important part of the 35–40 percent of the conservative Republican coalition that elected him. It was loyal to Trump and undoubtedly had great expectations he would do all he could to deliver on his promise to "make America great again," by cutting taxes, repealing and replacing the Affordable Care Act (Obamacare), building a southern border wall to stop the flow of illegal Mexican and Latin American immigrants, and reviving the nation's economy by renegotiating NAFTA and other trade agreements. Trump, ideological chameleon that he was, nevertheless was likely committed to keeping as many of these promises as he could. Doing so, however, would surely deepen the polarized polity he was about to lead.

At the outset of the administration, the relative balance of power in the nation was favorable to the president. His party governed a majority of the states, had majorities in both house of Congress, and, with a Supreme Court vacancy, would shortly have a majority on the Supreme Court. Meanwhile, all economic indicators— unemployment, inflation, the stock market, consumer confidence—were positive, and the nation was not engaged in a major war, although it was involved in low-level conflicts in Iraq and Afghanistan.

The inaugural address is the first opportunity a new president has to heal the wounds of the election, by invoking the nation's traditions, reconciliation, patriotism, national unity, legitimacy, and reassurance that things will be better under his stewardship. Trump's address, reflecting to some extent his worldview as well as the insurgent nature of his campaign, was in many ways as divisive and polarizing as his campaign rhetoric. Many commentators used "American Carnage" as a label for the address. He began by attacking the political establishment seated behind him as "a small group in the nation's capital" that "has reaped the rewards of government while the people have borne the cost."[1] Then he invoked what he called "carnage" in America—"mothers trapped in poverty, rusted-out factories, students deprived of knowledge, crime, gangs and drugs."[2] Revisiting themes from campaign speeches, he spoke of "defending of other nations' borders while refusing to defend our own; the wealth of our middle class ripped from their homes and distributed all over the world; and spending overseas while our infrastructure is in disrepair and decay."[3] But, he concluded, "from this day forward, it's going to be America first . . . and together we will make America great again."[4]

Trump began his first day in office lying, saying that the size of his inaugural crowd was larger than Obama's, when this was easily demonstrated as false.[5] Angered after seeing news reports of the inauguration, Trump in his first hours in the White House called the acting director of the Park Service (which manages the National Mall) and in effect asked him to doctor photos to make his crowd appear larger than Obama's.[6] Thus, literally from his first hours in the presidential office, Trump demonstrated the character trait of lying, which he had displayed in his first business success as a young man and would characterize his presidency nearly fifty years later.

After the inaugural address, the next set of events that illuminate the climate of expectations the new administration intends to establish is the appointment of the cabinet and the first address to Congress. The Trump cabinet was the most unambiguously conservative since the Coolidge administration, with no representation of the marginalized moderate faction of the party. In the Reagan and both Bush administrations at least one cabinet position was held by an individual identi-fied as a moderate or even liberal; none were in Trump's cabinet. In the immediate aftermath of the election, there was speculation that Trump might assemble a "team of rivals" to heal the divisions of the primary by nominating persons such as New Jersey governor Chris Christie as attorney general and Mitt Romney as secretary of state. But in cabinet appointments Trump adhered to conservative orthodoxy.

The cabinet was also reportedly the wealthiest in history, con-stituted disproportionately by businessmen with little prior gov-ernment experience.[7] The cabinet was the least ethnically diverse since Reagan. It included one Black, one Hispanic, and one Asian American. Two women were appointed to the cabinet and one to the senior White House staff. Similarly, the White House staff included only one minority person, Omarosa Manigault Newman, the marginally competent former *The Apprentice* personality, who served briefly as director of communications in the Public Liaison Office, before leaving to write a scathing memoir suggesting the president was a racist.[8] After Newman's departure, Ja Ron Smith, a Black man, was appointed an assistant to the president for domestic policy.

As was the case in the Trump Organization, there was relatively rapid turnover in the White House staff and cabinet in the first years: two secretaries of state, defense, and attorneys general; three Home-land Security secretaries; four White House chiefs of staff; three press secretaries; and four national security advisers. In addition, Trump left a relatively large number of posts filled with acting heads.[9] In less than three years, Trump had twenty-eight acting cabi-net secretaries, compared to a total of twenty-seven in eight years of the Clinton administration and twenty-three in Obama's two terms.[10]

As I will discuss below, some of Trump's rapid turnover in cab-inet and White House staff was due to his character—his style of per-sonal relations and decisionmaking.

Trump's first address to Congress, compared to the inaugural, was more unifying and statesman-like. Delivered a month after taking office, Trump began the speech by noting it was the end of Black His-tory Month and condemning recent attacks on Jewish community cen-ters and burial places and calling for national unity and strength.[11] The president then articulated his legislative agenda to the Republican-controlled Congress. It included tax cuts and reforms, funds to build the southern border wall but without a specific appropriations request, a call for a merit-based immigration system, a promise to repeal and replace Obamacare, and a trillion-dollar infrastructure program. Except for the tax cuts and reform, none of these proposals were enacted. The failure to repeal and replace Obamacare and to enact infrastructure legislation I attribute at least partly to character: his failure to pay attention, to do his homework, demand staff preparation, and his poor decisionmaking process.

Finally, as is often the case with Republican presidents since Nixon, President Trump appointed a number of persons to cabinet and cabinet-level agencies hostile to their missions, such as the Environmental Protection Agency and the departments of Housing and Urban Development and Interior.[12] This phenomenon of the foxes guarding the chickens is structural in Republican administrations. The domestic policy bureaucracies in the environment, education, civil rights, and housing have a tendency to be committed, ideologically and programmatically, to their agencies' missions, while conservative Republican presidents tend to be hostile and committed to scaling-back and deregulation. This routinely results in structural "clashing beliefs within the executive branch" between presidential appointees and career civil servants.[13]

Trump came to office with a determined agenda of deregulation, especially in energy and the environment, consistent with Republican orthodoxy. Thus, from the beginning of the administration, this systemic problem was apparent.[14] Trump sometimes also had unorthodox views on foreign and defense policies, which frequently led to clashes with the diplomatic, defense, and intelligence bureaucracies, including his appointees to head them.[15]

Trump's Style and the Primacy of Rhetoric

The impact of Trump's character on the presidency is most observable in his style, which Barber, in any case, contends is the most visible part of the presidential character. In personal relations with the White House staff; interactions with congressional leaders, the media, and others in the Washington community; his homework; and his prioritization of rhetoric, the imprint of Trump's character is unmistakable.

Since the institutionalization of the White House staffing structure during the presidency of FDR, a pattern of organization and decisionmaking has evolved that operates to organize and constrain the behavior of most presidents, with the White House chief of staff coming to be seen as integral to the operation of an effective presidency. FDR, John F. Kennedy, Lyndon Johnson, Jimmy Carter for his first three years, and Gerald Ford for a brief time operated without a designated staff chief, preferring the "spoke in the wheel" structure where several key aides had access to the Oval Office and the president acted as his own chief of staff. General Eisenhower brought the hierarchical staff structure of the military to the White House; Nixon followed this model with a powerful chief of staff, and, with minor variations, this has been the model of subsequent presidents. Most students of the modern presidency see a chief of staff and some clearly delineated decisionmaking process as imperative in the conduct of modern presidencies.[16]

The Reagan pattern of staffing and decisionmaking is somewhat unique in the modern presidency, and it offers a useful comparison with the pattern of the Trump presidency. Paul Quirk refers to Reagan as a "minimalist" president, that is, as "one who requires little or no understanding of specific issues and problems and instead can rely almost entirely on subordinates to resolve them."[17] This "chairman of the board" style of staffing and decisionmaking accommodated Reagan's "disinclination to do much reading or sit through lengthy meetings." Thus, he would "personally establish the general policies and goals of his administration, select cabinet and other key personnel who shared his commitments, then delegate broad authority to them so they could work out the particulars."[18] In other words, Reagan's style was to personally do as little homework as possible, placing near complete confidence in his staff for policy development. That is, policy came from below, rather than being initiated by him. This "pattern of staff supremacy" worked reasonably well in the development of policies that corresponded broadly to the president's ideology. [19] Yet, what one observer called "the most centralized and staff-dominated presidency in history" depended on the competence and commitment of the staff to the president's agenda than would have been the case if Reagan had been a more "active" self-reliant decisionmaker.[20]

If Reagan was a minimalist president who relied on staff for policy development and routinized decisionmaking, Trump was a minimalist president who distrusted experts, and relied on his "gut" and "instincts" to make decisions and who refused to be managed by his staff.[21] Thus, both domestic and foreign policy decisions were often made in ad hoc, nonroutine ways.

The White House staff, housed in the White House and the nearby old and new executive office buildings, is itself a large and complex bureaucracy of multiple offices and responsibilities. The first task of a chief of staff is to manage and give direction to this bureaucracy. A second equally important task is to manage the flow of papers and persons into the Oval Office. And, finally, a chief of staff must establish a rational, routine decisionmaking process, assuring the inclusion of the views of all relevant departments and agencies.[22] The handful of academic studies of the early years of the Trump presidency conclude that it was not effectively organized, lacking a strong chief of staff, and a staff characterized by factionalism and an irregular, free-wheeling decisionmaking process.[23] Most attribute the staff dysfunction to Trump's character. Pfiffner writes, "After he was elected president, Donald Trump's instinct was to continue the approach to management that had been so successful in his real estate business . . . personal and informal . . . [with a] disinclination toward formal organization."[24] Michael Genovese characterizes Trump staffing as an "unstructured, open system in the extreme. . . . His personal style is to be open, accessible, unencumbered. . . . No chain of command . . . minimal attention span, tendency to say more than he knows. Intelligence officials tend to put as much as possible of his briefings in pictures," preferably on a single page with bullet points.[25]

Trump did not formally adopt the FDR/JFK/LBJ spoke-of-the-wheel structure, but nor did he embrace the Eisenhower strong chief of staff model. He designated a chief of staff, but "Trump was used to running his own one-man show and was unwilling to transfer any of his power to a chief of staff."[26] Although four persons held the title, in fact, "Trump was his own chief of staff."[27] General John Kelly (ret.), Trump's second chief of staff, tried, with some success for a time, to bring structure to staffing and decisionmaking, exercising discipline on the flow of persons and papers to the president, and ending the open door policy to the Oval Office.[28] But Trump did not like being managed, and after a year Kelly was replaced. His successor, Mick Mulvaney, the director of the pivotal Office of Management and Budget, a position he retained while serving as "acting" chief of staff, from the outset did not attempt to manage the president. As he put it, "[My] job was not to manage the president but to manage the staff. . . . [I] wouldn't try to limit the people coming into the Oval Office, and wouldn't try to push the president in any particular direction."[29] In other words, he would let Trump be Trump.

Managing the staff was difficult because from the beginning Trump created an ideologically factionalized staff of traditional conservatives, paleoconservatives, globalists, populists,[30] and his daughter, Ivanka, and son-in-law, Jared Kushner. Ivanka and Kushner were given broad portfolios over a range of domestic and foreign policy issues, although their only qualifications were kinship. This inevitably created friction with others on the staff. Trump reportedly recognized that appointing them was a mistake but was unwilling to dismiss them.[31]

Trump was an active president in the sense that he required very little sleep but he put little emphasis on homework, rather he spent a lot of time upstairs watching cable news, making phone calls, and tweeting.[32] As was his practice in business (and apparently in college), he did not read. Robert Porter, his cabinet secretary, told Bob Woodward, "He refused to read briefing books, background papers or policy memos."[33] Another aide said, "Trump didn't read. He really didn't even skim. If it was print, it might as well not exist."[34] Meetings to discuss policy frequently went off topic;[35] one aide wrote, "The president's leadership style [is] impetuous, adversarial, petty and ineffective. . . . Meetings with him veer off topic and off the rails, he engages in repetitive rants and his impulsiveness often results in half-baked, ill-informed and occasionally reckless decisions."[36]

Trump sometimes announced major policy decisions on Twitter, without advice or consultation from staff. Adjusting to this policy by Twitter, Robert O'Brien, Trump's third National Security Council (NSC) adviser, reportedly often convened meetings by distributing Trump's latest tweets on the subject. The message to the staff was that "[your] job is to find out ways of justifying Trump's policy, not advise him on what it should be. This is the reverse of what the NSC was created to do, that dynamic has been turned on its head."[37]

Barber writes, there are "marked differences in stylistic emphasis from president to president. The *balance* among the three elements varies; one president may put most of himself into rhetoric, another may stress close, informal dealing, while still another may devote his energies mainly to study and cognition."[38] In Trump's case, among the three he clearly prioritized rhetoric.

Barber gave short shrift to the rhetorical element of style in *The Presidential Character,* but since publication a robust subfield among political scientists and communications scholars has developed devoted to the study of presidential rhetoric.[39] The rhetorical presidency—where the president "goes public" to rally or shape public opinion—is historically a relatively recent development, traced to the presidencies of Theodore Roosevelt and Woodrow Wilson.[40] Prior to their presidencies, it was considered inappropriate for presidents to

address the public to mobilize public support for himself or his policies. Rather, the head of state addressed Congress in writing, which
might shape public opinion through the press or the responses of
members of Congress. In addition to being beneath the dignity of the
office, Samuel Kernell suggests appealing to the public undermines
the personal relations and bargaining of the president in the Washington community.[41]

Although the rhetorical presidency is traced to Roosevelt and
Wilson (and one should also include FDR's radio "fireside chats"),
the prominence of the phenomenon is traced to the development of
the modern media as an autonomous institution, especially television
and the Kennedy presidency.[42] The media becomes a "surrogate public," and presidents "respond to the demands by the media with rhetoric designed to manipulate public passions."[43] After Kennedy, Reagan is the next notable rhetorical president.[44] More so than Kennedy,
he was called the "Great Communicator" who went public, in an
often-cited example, to pressure Congress perhaps successfully to
enact his 1981 tax cuts, although this cannot be proven. This is the
pattern where a president attempts to use rhetoric to garner public
support and increase, contrary to Kernell, their bargaining power in
the Washington community. That is, presidential rhetoric becomes an
essential power of the office, to the extent Richard Neustadt's famous
formulation about presidential power as mainly the power to persuade is correct.[45] In addition, as Barber suggests, study of presidential rhetoric can provide insight into a president's worldview.[46]

Beginning with Reagan, presidential rhetorical displays have
become more carefully staged, less intellectual, and more conversational and anecdotal.[47] Increasingly, they are more like Oprah's talk
show couch than the bully pulpit. Finally, there is a blurring between
campaign and governing rhetoric, which is obvious in Trump's rhetoric. Of the difference, Wendt writes, "A campaign rhetoric will be one
of either/or choice, a war-like rhetoric seeking defeat of the enemy
and victory for the candidate. A governing rhetoric, at least theoretically, will be one of decorum stressing accommodation and compromise while still retaining partisan or ideological commitments."[48]

Probably no president, not even Reagan, put more emphasis on
the rhetorical element of style than Trump.[49] Certainly, if one looks at
the elements as good staffing and staff work, cultivating personal
relations in the Washington community, or presidential homework,
Trump is much more a rhetorical than a staff-dependent, bargaining,
or studious president.

Trump's presidency of rhetoric differs in several ways from his predecessors. First, he generally did not go public to build support for policies and enhance his bargaining power with Congress. Rather, his rhetoric from the weeks after the election to the reelection in 2020 was designed to promote himself and rally and maintain the support of his base constituency. Second, there is little distinction between campaign and governing rhetoric. Third, consistent with recent trends, exaggerated for sure, his rhetoric was nonintellectual, conversational, improvisational, and often emotional. Kernell offers a possible insight into why Trump gave so much primacy to rhetoric: "The outsider whose career success is founded largely upon stylized public presentation of self will derive greater gratification and even stimulation traveling around the country delivering speeches and appearing on television than in following the private, daily all-too-mysterious rituals of cultivating support from politicians."[50]

After the election, Trump resumed his campaign-style rallies in a series of what he called "Thank You" victory rallies across the country, which began the first week after the election and ended several days before his inauguration. After becoming president, Wikipedia tabulated forty-two campaign-style rallies in 2017–2018 and twenty-seven in 2019–2020 until they were interrupted by the Covid-19 lockdown.[51] Again, these rallies were not to advance policies or pressure Congress, but to promote himself and his accomplishments, and attack, often vituperatively and mendaciously, his adversaries, especially the "fake, dishonest" media.

Trump also used Twitter as a rhetorical platform. According to a detailed report of Trump's tweets by the *New York Times* between inauguration day and October 15, 2019, Trump posted 11,000 tweets.[52] Tweeting was a rhetorical innovation he used during the campaign—he believed successfully—and thus he integrated into his presidency. Tim Alberta notes, "He used Twitter during the campaign to rewrite the rules of mass communication in politics, circumventing media gatekeepers and reaching millions of people instantly. . . . He told friends without Twitter he would never have won . . . [and] without Twitter his presidency would be derailed by a hostile press."[53] Like his rallies, Trump used his Twitter rhetoric to attack his adversaries, boast about his accomplishments, but also to occasionally announce policy or appointments. While some of his aides saw his tweeting as a problem, others saw it, like his rallies, as an "essential tool to present him as someone strong, willing to stand up to political elites . . . [and] believe his unvarnished rhetoric, poor punctuation, and increasing profanity as a signal of authenticity."[54]

Authentic or not, Trump's rhetoric disturbed the norms of civic discourse in US democracy. In Chapter 1, I quoted from presidential scholar George Edwards's paper "The Bully in the Pulpit: The Impact of Donald Trump's Public Discourse," in which he claims that Trump's rhetoric was beyond the norms of the presidency. Kathleen Hall Jamieson is equally concerned about Trump's "norm-shattering rhetoric," which "flouts evidence, disdains institutions," such as the courts and the media, and "demonizes those with whom he disagrees."[55] Trump's rhetoric therefore is also implicated in personal and constitutional character, subjects I take up in Chapter 8.[56]

Radio facilitated FDR's rhetorical presidency, television John Kennedy's and Ronald Reagan's. Although Trump employed television (his rallies were always broadcast live on C-SPAN and usually also on Fox), Twitter is the technology that extended the reach of his words. But the president's rhetoric, whether on television, Twitter, or at rallies, was unusual. Rarely was it used to advance a policy or program. Rather, it usually was the war-like rhetoric of the campaign—shrill, bombastic, often inflammatory and vituperative, and occasionally profane. While it perhaps rallied the base, it did little to advance his agenda and likely undermined his capacity to govern, which are the subjects of the next two chapters.

Notes

1. For the full text, see "2017 Donald Trump Inauguration Speech Transcript," *Politico,* January 21, 2017.

2. Ibid.

3. Ibid.

4. Ibid.

5. Side-by-side photos of inaugural crowds show that Obama's crowds were clearly much larger than Trump's. See Tom Wallace, Karen Yourish, and Tray Griggs, "Trump's Inauguration vs. Obama's: Comparing the Crowds," *New York Times,* January 20, 2017.

6. Karen Tumulty and Juliet Eilperin, "Trump Pressured Park Service to Find Proof of His Claims About Inauguration," *Washington Post,* January 26, 2017.

7. Jim Tankersley and Ana Swanson, "Trump Assembling the Richest Administration in Modern American History," *Washington Post,* November 30, 2016; and Michelle Tindirera "The Definitive Net Worth of Trump's Cabinet," *Forbes,* July 25, 2017.

8. Omarosa Manigault Newman, *Unhinged: An Insider Account of the Trump White House* (New York: Gallery Books, 2018).

9. Aaron Blake, "Trump's Government Full of Temps," *Washington Post,* February 21, 2020.

10. Natasha Bach, "All the Acting Heads in Trump's Presidency," *Fortune,* November 27, 2019.

11. "Full Text of President Trump's First Address to Congress," *USA Today*, March 1, 2017.

12. James Pfiffner, "Organizing the Trump Presidency," *Presidential Studies Quarterly* 48 (2018): 153–167.

13. Joel Aberbach and Bert Rockman, "Clashing Beliefs Within the Executive Branch: The Nixon Administration and the Bureaucracy," *American Political Science Review* 70 (1976): 456–468. The senior civil service also tends to be liberal in ideology and Democratic in partisan affiliation. For example, a 2014 survey by Princeton Research Associates and Vanderbilt University's Center for the Study of Democratic Institutions found 10 percent were conservative and 16 percent Republican, compared to 21 percent liberal and 44 percent Democratic. The data are reported in Matt Grossmann and David Hopkins, *Asymmetric Politics: Ideological Republicans and Group Interest Democrats* (New York: Oxford University Press, 2016), 305.

14. Pfiffner, "Organizing the Trump Presidency."

15. Peter Bergen, *Trump and the Generals: The Cost of Chaos* (New York: Penguin Books, 2019); and Philip Rucker and Carol Leonnig, *A Very Stable Genius: Donald J. Trump and the Testing of America* (New York: Penguin Press, 2020).

16. John Burke, "The Institutional Presidency," in Michael Nelson, ed., *The Presidency and the Political System* (Washington: Congressional Quarterly Press, 1998). On the complex of offices and organizations of the more than 5,000 persons who make up the White House staff (the Executive Office of the President), see Bradley Patterson, *The White House Staff: Inside the West Wing and Beyond* (Washington: Brookings Institution, 2001). On the central role of the chief of staff since Nixon, see Chris Whipple, *The Gatekeepers: How the White House Chiefs of Staff Define Every White House* (New York: Crown, 2017).

17. Paul Quirk, "Presidential Competence," in Nelson, *The Presidency and the Political System,* 174.

18. Ibid., 175.

19. Ibid.

20. Hedrick Smith, *The Power Game: How Washington Works* (New York: Random House, 1988), 300.

21. Trump's often stated skepticism about the value of experts goes back to his days managing the Trump Organization, but as president, Philip Rocco argues, it went beyond his personal skepticism to the fostering of "an organizational culture hostile to expert knowledge production in many federal agencies and has attempted to engineer significant cuts to the federal statistical system. He has also used the ad hoc production of new information to reinforce his view of political reality." See "The Policy State and the Post-Truth Presidency," in Zachary Callen and Philip Rocco, eds., *American Political Development and the Trump Presidency* (Philadelphia: University

of Pennsylvania Press, 2020), 116. Rocco, however, notes that Trump's downplaying and degrading of the government's knowledge base is not unique, perhaps more extensive, but part of a pattern of behavior of Republican presidents that began with the "anti-analytic" presidency of Reagan. See Walter Williams, *Mismanaging America: The Rise of the Anti-Analytic Presidency* (Lawrence: University of Kansas Press, 1990).

22. Whipple, *The Gatekeepers.*

23. Pfiffner, "Organizing the Trump Presidency"; Pfiffner, "The Unusual Presidency of Donald Trump," *Political Insight,* August 9, 2017; and David Lewis, Patrick Bernard, and Emily York, "President Trump as Manager: Reflections on the First Year," *Presidential Studies Quarterly* 48 (2018): 480–501.

24. Pfiffner, "Organizing the Trump Presidency," 153.

25. Michael Genovese, *How Trump Governs: An Assessment and Prognosis* (Amherst, NY: Cambria, 2017), 121. On the failure of Trump to organize a competent staff and rational decisionmaking process see also Kenneth Mayer, "The Random Walk Presidency," *Presidential Studies Quarterly* 51 (2021): 71–95.

26. Ronald Kessler, *The Trump White House: Changing the Rules of the Game* (New York: Crown Forum, 2018), 140.

27. Ibid.

28. Rucker and Leonnig, *A Very Stable Genius,* 157–158; and Jonathan Karl, *Front Row at the Trump Show* (New York: Dutton, 2020), 209.

29. Karl, *Front Row at the Trump Show,* 278. For detailed analysis, see David Cohen and Karen Hult, "The Office of the Chief of Staff in the Trump White House," *Presidential Studies Quarterly* 50 (2020): 392–417.

30. Shirley Ann Warshaw, "The Struggle to Govern in the Trump White House: Competing Power Centers, Personalities and World Visions," *Forum* 15 (2017): 567–581. See also Martha Kumar, "Energy or Chaos: Turnover at the Top of the Trump White House," *Presidential Studies Quarterly* 49 (2019): 291–236; and Dunn Tenpas, "White House Staff Turnover," *Presidential Studies Quarterly* 49 (2019): 502–516.

31. Kessler, *The Trump White House,* 47; and Rucker and Leonnig, *A Very Stable Genius,* 20, 157.

32. Ibid.

33. Bob Woodward, *Fear: Trump in the White House* (New York: Simon & Schuster, 2018), 230–231.

34. Wolff, *Fire and Fury,* 116.

35. Ibid.

36. Anonymous, "I Am Part of the Resistance Inside the White House," *New York Times,* September 5, 2018. This person, who was generally supportive of the president's policies, subsequently wrote a book about what he saw as the president's inept style and decisionmaking process. See Anonymous, *A Warning* (New York: Twelve, 2019). Shortly before the 2020 election, he revealed his identity, Miles Taylor, former chief of staff at the Department of Homeland Security.

37. Michael Crowley and David Sanger, "Under O'Brien N.S.C. Carries Out Trump's Policy, but Does Not Develop It," *New York Times,* February 22, 2020.

38. Barber, *The Presidential Character,* 7.

39. Theodore Wendt, "Presidential Rhetoric: Definitions of a Field of Study," *Communications Studies* 35 (1984): 24–34. Martin Medhurst since 1998 has convened a series of conferences on the subject, and edited *The Prospects of Presidential Rhetoric* (College Station: Texas A & M University Press, 2018). See also Elvin Lim, "Five Trends in Presidential Rhetoric: From George Washington to Bill Clinton," *Presidential Studies Quarterly* 32 (2002): 366–386; and David Zarefsky, "Presidential Rhetoric and the Power of Definition," *Presidential Studies Quarterly* 34 (2004): 607–619. See also Terri Brimes, "Understanding the Rhetorical Presidency," in George Edwards and William Howell, eds., *Oxford Handbook of the Presidency* (New York: Oxford University Press, 2009).

40. Jeffrey Tulis, *The Rhetorical Presidency* (Princeton: Princeton University Press, 1987); Samuel Kernell, *Going Public: New Strategies of Presidential Leadership* (Washington: Congressional Quarterly Press, 1997); Martin Medhurst, "From Retrospect to Prospect: The Study of Presidential Rhetoric, 1915–2005," in James Arnt Aune and Martin Medhurst, eds., *The Prospects of Presidential Rhetoric;* and Lim, "Five Trends in Presidential Rhetoric." Tulis, in *The Rhetorical Presidency,* and James David Barber, in "Adult Identity and Presidential Style: The Rhetorical Emphasis," *Daedalus* 97 (1968): 938–968, identify Andrew Johnson as the first rhetorical president, the first to go public in an attempt to rally public opinion to pressure Congress to support his policies. Both conclude Johnson's efforts failed and served as an object lesson to future presidents. Barber writes that Johnson violated virtually all the nineteenth-century norms of presidential behavior, and "his speeches damaged his reputation [one of the articles of impeachment against Johnson alleged his 'intemperate, inflammatory and scandalous harangues' brought the office of president into ridicule and disgrace]. But he never learned that lesson. Again, and again, he repeated the same performance, illustrating how a particular strategy can become a permanent feature of presidential style. . . . Although, he 'knew' or saw the destructive effects of his speeches, he believed he had extraordinary power as a speaker. . . . In a sense, he was right: Success in terms of audience responsiveness, success in the immediate environment, was often his. He won applause and perhaps equally important to him the charge from the crowds" (949–950).

41. Kernell, *Going Public,* 11.

42. David Paletz and Robert Entman, *Media Power Politics* (New York: Free Press, 1981).

43. Ibid.

44. William Muir Jr., "Ronald Reagan: The Primacy of Rhetoric," in Fred Greenstein, ed., *Leadership in the Modern Presidency* (Cambridge: Harvard, 1988).

45. Richard Neustadt, *Presidential Power and the Politics of Leadership* (New York: Wiley, 1960). It is not clear if Neustadt's model is useful in today's era of polarization, partisan media, and a fractured public, but Trump in any event did not attempt to use it, which limited his legislative achievements. See Todd Schaefer, *Presidential Power Meets the Art of the Deal: Applying Neustadt to the Trump Presidency* (New York: Palgrave Pivot,

2021); and George Edwards, *Changing Their Minds: Donald Trump and Presidential Leadership* (Chicago: University of Chicago Press, 2021).

46. Zarefsky, "Presidential Rhetoric and the Power of Definition."

47. Lim, "Five Trends."

48. Wendt, "Presidential Rhetoric: Definition of a Field," 112.

49. In an afterword to a new edition of *The Rhetorical Presidency* (Princeton: Princeton University Press, 2017), Jeffrey Tulis describes Trump's presidency as the first almost purely rhetorical presidency.

50. Kernell, *Going Public,* 46. Mary Stuckey concludes Trump was more interested in using rhetoric "to demonstrate his personal predilections than as means of enacting policy or managing government." See "The Rhetoric of the Trump Administration," *Presidential Studies Quarterly* 51 (2021): 125–150.

51. "List of Post-Election Trump Rallies," *Wikipedia,* April 2020.

52. Michael Shear et al., "How Trump Reshaped the Presidency in Over 11,000 Tweets," *New York Times,* November 2, 2019.

53. Tim Alberta, *American Carnage: On the Front Lines of the Republican Civil War and the Rise of Donald Trump* (New York: Harper Collins, 2019), 462.

54. Ibid. In May 2020, after years of criticisms that it allowed the president to disseminate false and misleading information on its platform, Twitter designated a Trump tweet about mail-in ballots as "potentially misleading" and directed its users to articles by CNN and the *Washington Post* for more accurate information. Elizabeth Dwoskin, "Twitter Labels Trump's Tweets with a Fact Check for the First Time," *Washington Post,* May 26, 2020. Days later, when Trump, in the midst of violent protests in Minneapolis after the police murder of George Floyd, tweeted, "When the looting starts, the shooting starts," Twitter censored the president, claiming the tweet violated its policy of not inciting violence. Mark Scott, "Twitter Labels Trump Tweet as 'Glorifying Violence,'" *Politico,* May 29, 2020. And as discussed in Chapter 10, after the violent uprising at the Capitol, Twitter permanently banned the president from its platform.

55. Kathleen Hall Jamieson and Doron Taussig, "Disruption, Demonization, Deliverance, and Norm Destruction: The Rhetorical Signature of Donald Trump," *Political Science Quarterly* 132 (2017–2018): 619–650. Jennifer Mercieca presents a detailed analysis of Trump's rhetorical excesses during the 2016 campaign in *Demagogue for President: The Rhetorical Genius of Donald Trump* (College Station: Texas A & M University Press, 2020). See also the afterword to Tulis's new edition of *The Rhetorical Presidency.*

56. Susan Hennessey and Benjamin Wittes cite a passage from an 1872 address by Alexander Hamilton that they write seems "almost to be describing Trump." Hamilton, on the dangers "popular demagogues" might pose to constitutional government, wrote of "a man unprincipled in private life, desperate in his fortune, bold in his temper, possessed of considerable talents, having the advantage of military habits—despotic in his ordinary demeanor—known to have scoffed in private at the principles of liberty. . . . It may justly be suspected that his object is to throw things into confusion that he may 'ride the storm and direct the whirlwind.'" See *Unmaking the Presidency: Donald Trump's War on the World's Most Powerful Office* (New York: Farrar, Straus and Giroux, 2020), 88.

6

Presidential Character and Trump's Domestic Policy

IN THIS CHAPTER, I ANALYZE DOMESTIC POLICIES OF the Trump administration to learn how his character may have impacted decisionmaking and outcomes.[1] Trump's character—worldview and style—may have affected some of his policy decisions and outcomes while others may be a result of party, ideology, context, or the balance of power in Washington, or, in the case of foreign affairs (examined in the next chapter), the complexities of the global situation. And many policies are likely a complex interaction of multiple factors that are difficult to disentangle. I am mainly concerned here with Fred Greenstein's notion of actor indispensability, whether in any particular case Trump's character was likely indispensable in what happened. Or whether it is possible to infer that what happened would have occurred with any president or any conservative Republican president.

For domestic policy, I focus on what Richard Seltzer and I describe as the ultimate issues between the parties in this era of polarization—taxes and the budget, health insurance, and race—although in the Trump administration the principal race issue was immigration rather than the usual Black-White issue conflicts.[2] In addition, I examine Trump's campaign promises on improving infrastructure and his pledge not to cut Social Security. Finally, I examine the role of the president's character in the administration's handling of the Covid-19 pandemic and the nationwide uprisings in the aftermath of the police murder of George Floyd.

In assessing Trump's character, I am concerned with what role his worldview and style played, if any, in the advancement of a particular policy. In following James David Barber, I look at whether he did his homework, his use of staff, his decisionmaking process, his personal relations with congressional leaders, and the use of rhetoric.

Since the Reagan presidency, tax cuts that disproportionately benefit corporations and the wealthy have become conservative Republican orthodoxy.[3] With Republican majorities in both houses of Congress, and the budget reconciliation process which allows passage of tax legislation with a simple majority in the Senate and the president's support, the passage of major tax cut legislation in the first year of Trump's administration was inevitable. Its passage required little homework on the president's part, little staff work in development of a bill, and little rhetoric on Trump's part to secure support. The White House turned the drafting of the bill over to House Speaker Paul Ryan, who crafted legislation acceptable to his Republican colleagues in the House and Senate, and Trump eagerly signed it.

Like the Reagan and George W. Bush tax cuts, the Trump tax cuts predictably resulted in increases in the deficit, despite a growth economy and low unemployment. The deficits are of little concern to modern Republicans, who express concern about deficits only when Democrats are in power and seek to increase spending on domestic programs.[4] Although Trump proposed modest increases in domestic spending (the border wall, veterans' benefits), consistent with conservative Republican orthodoxy he also embraced increases in military spending, which also contributed to the deficit.

In 2020 Trump proposed a $4.8 trillion budget that projected a deficit of more than a trillion dollars. Again, not deviating from Republican ideology, the budget proposed cuts in Medicaid, housing and food assistance, foreign aid, the Centers for Disease Control (CDC), and the National Institutes of Health (NIH). It also proposed extending the tax cuts and new spending on infrastructure and the military.[5]

During the 2016 presidential campaign, Trump, consistent with his long expressed views, broke with conservative ideological orthodoxy and promised not to cut Social Security or Medicare. In order to deal with the deficit in 2020, the administration indicated it might be willing to abandon that campaign promise and propose cuts in both programs.[6] Whether he would have broken with his long-held views and campaign promise to protect Medicare and Social Security in order to accommodate party ideology, we cannot know because within weeks of the budget submission the Covid-19 crisis required the government to add more than $2 trillion to the deficit in less than three months (the Coronavirus Aid, Relief, and Economic Security Act, or the CARES Act). The crisis also made the administration's proposed cuts in the CDC and NIH budgets seem myopic.

Generally partisan and ideological commitments explain Trump's approach to taxing and spending, commitments adhered to by all Republican presidents since Reagan except George H. W. Bush, whose apostasy and subsequent defeat reenforced party ideological orthodoxy. Trump did, however, break from party ideology on another issue, consistent with his long-held views, aside from spending on the elderly; he supported a federal infrastructure program and proposed in the 2020 budget to spend more than a trillion dollars over many years to rebuild roads, bridges, ports, and air terminals.

Long before he became the Republican nominee, Trump advocated infrastructure spending. It was a major 2016 campaign promise, and he spoke of it in the inaugural address and in his first address to Congress. Yet, perhaps reflecting his failure to do the homework, that is, study the issue and have his staff develop a legislative proposal, and the absence of a routine decisionmaking process, he did not submit legislation to Congress during the two years of Republican control, nor did he consult with Republican leaders on the development of legislation. Trump may have been reluctant to consult or craft a legislative proposal because of concern it would not be supported by the Republican leaders or the rank and file. Infrastructure spending is usually an idea advanced by liberal Democrats.

In 2018 the administration did present an idea that attempted to meet Republican fiscal concerns by proposing a joint private-public partnership with a mix of private, federal, state, and local funding. Democrats, however, were not receptive because of the emphasis on private funding and the Republicans because of the federal spending.[7]

In 2019, Trump invited Senate Democratic leader Charles Schumer and House Speaker Nancy Pelosi to the White House for discussion of a $2 trillion infrastructure proposal. Prior to the meeting, the Speaker in a meeting with Democratic committee chairs declared opposition to impeaching Trump but nevertheless was quoted as saying Trump was engaging in a cover-up. Reflecting perhaps his inclination to strike back hard against his adversaries, Trump used Pelosi's comments as an excuse to walk out of the meeting three minutes after it began. Going to the White House Rose Garden to a lectern that had already been prepared, Trump declared, "I don't do cover-ups. . . . I told Schumer and Pelosi I want to do infrastructure.

I want to do it more than you want to do it. I'd be really great at it. That's what I do. But you know what? I can't do it under these circumstances. So, get these phony investigations over with."[8] This preplanned walkout of the meeting with Democratic congressional leaders may have been an excuse for not negotiating a serious infrastructure deal with the Democrats, but it also reflected his poor personal relations with Democratic congressional leaders; for example, he on more than one occasion insulted the Speaker, calling her a "third-rate politician" and a "sick woman, with mental problems."[9]

Yet, his behavior may have been partisan and ideological: unwilling in the final analysis to come to a compromise on the issue in defiance of his party's leaders, and unwilling to risk the political fallout of possibly getting a bill through the Democratic House while losing in the Republican Senate. In 2020 in the midst of massive unemployment as result of the coronavirus pandemic, Trump asked Congress for $2 trillion in infrastructure spending.[10] Democratic congressional leaders expressed support; Republican leaders were silent, and Congress once again took no action. It would have been difficult for any Republican president to get party support for a federally financed infrastructure program, but Trump's lack of attention to details, his failure to charge his staff with development of a possible bipartisan compromise, and his poor personal relations with Democratic congressional leaders doomed whatever chance there might have been to keep this campaign promise.

Before running for the Republican nomination, Trump had indicated support for a Canadian-style universal health insurance program. Yet in 2016 he joined the Republican Party consensus to repeal the Affordable Care Act, or Obamacare. However, due to the popularity of certain parts of the act (coverage for preexisting conditions, for example), Trump and Republican leaders agreed that repeal was not enough, noting that public expectations also required a replacement so the millions covered by Obamacare would not quickly become uninsured. During the campaign Trump, characteristically, had promised to repeal and replace with something "bigger and better," covering more people with lower premiums. It would have been difficult to develop legislation to provide better, broader, and less expensive coverage than Obamacare while remaining faithful to conservative Republican ideological principles of a state- and market-based insurance program. Yet, whatever possibilities there might have been were diminished by Trump's style—the absence of homework on his part, inadequate policy development by staff, and his overall inattention to the issue.

Even in his fourth year Trump had not put in place the typical White House policy development and decisionmaking process on legislation; for example, no staff were assigned to develop a legislative proposal and strategy for health insurance. And Trump himself was not interested in the substance of health policy. George Edwards writes, "The administration simply never invested in developing policies. It always had great aspirations . . . but no coherent plans for them. Thus, there was no real plan for key issues Trump emphasized during the campaign. . . . The president seems unfamiliar with the details of policy . . . willing to let others take charge of both process and substance."[11] Jon Herbert, Trevor McCrisken, and Andrew Wroe indicate that Trump was "always resistant to expertise . . . spectacularly ignorant of public policy, including his own."[12] They conclude, "By accessing expertise in relevant policy areas—health, immigration, infrastructure—Trump could have implemented his goals more effectively, but chose not to do so."[13] Pfiffner specifically observes the "lack of clear policy process or decision making process" on health insurance, and the "failure of [the] Obamacare repeal reflects this absence of process: the White House never developed a coherent alternative to sell to Congress or the public."[14] Michael Wolff notes, "Trump had little or no interest in the central goal of repealing Obamacare. . . . The details of the contested legislation were to him particularly boring."[15] And Alberta concludes on Obamacare, "The president didn't particularly care what the bill looked like. He just wanted a victory."[16]

Unlike tax cuts where there was a party consensus or infrastructure where the party was hostile, the party was divided on a replacement plan for Obamacare. Thus, Trump could not outsource the issue on health insurance to Congress or seek a bipartisan deal. Presidential leadership was required. Trump did not provide it.[17] In this case, character mattered.[18]

I discuss later in the chapter certain institutionally racist policies implemented by the bureaucracy during Trump's first two years. These policies may have been adopted without Trump's knowledge. They were consequential policies but they likely did not engage the president's attention. The race issue that did engage his attention was immigration. Indeed, in the campaign, through the paleoconservative ideological perspective, Trump racialized the issue by focusing not on immigration or even illegal immigration in general (ignoring illegal immigrants from Europe) but immigration from nonwhite places, specifically Muslim and Mexican immigrants. In his comments about "shit-hole" countries, he made clear the racial animus driving the policy. His racialization of the issue broke with the Republican orthodoxy going back to the Nixon administration. Before looking at immigration, I examine the protests at Charlottesville, Virginia, the most publicized race controversy of the Trump presidency.

In August 2017 a loose coalition of the Ku Klux Klan, neofascists, and radical White nationalists, displaying Confederate flags, swastikas, and other racist symbols, held a rally in Charlottesville ostensibly to protest the city's decision to remove a statue of Confederate general Robert E. Lee. Antiracists and antifascists organized a counterprotest. As the racists and fascists marched through the city chanting "Jews will not replace us" and similar racist and anti-Semitic slogans, one of the racist protesters drove his car into group of counterprotesters, killing a young woman and injuring twelve others.

Trump was on vacation at his New Jersey golf resort. The protests and the assault were covered extensively on the cable news channels, and Trump's first comment on the situation generated widespread criticism when he said he condemned the display of hatred, bigotry, and violence "on many sides." The "many sides" comment seemed as if the president was equating the violence of the racists with the peaceful protests of the antiracists. The next day the White House issued a statement responding to the critics: "The president said very strongly in his statement that he condemns all forms of violence, bigotry and hatred and of course that includes white supremacist, KKK, Neo-Nazi and all extremist groups."[19] It is not clear if Trump approved the statement. But when he returned to the White House several days later, he was upset. At a meeting with the attorney general, the FBI director, the homeland security adviser, and the chief of staff to discuss a federal investigation of Charlottesville, the president interrupted to make the point that the racist protesters were being treated "unfairly" because there were good reasons to protest the removal of the Lee statue. Lee, he said, was "the greatest military mind ever. . . . Next, it will be Washington and Jefferson. Does anyone think that's fair?"[20] (Trump vetoed the 2021 Defense Authorization bill in part because it required the removal of the names of Confederate generals from US military installations). The names, he asserted, are a part of the "great American heritage."[21] Nevertheless, despite these concerns Trump agreed to read on television the following statement prepared by staff: "Racism is evil. All those who cause violence in its name are criminals and thugs, including the KKK, neo-Nazi, white supremacists, and other white hate groups that are repugnant to everything we hold dear as Americans."[22]

A day later, however, Trump returned to his moral equivalency, telling reporters there was blame on both sides and "very good people on both sides."[23] Again, there were widespread criticisms, and several business executives resigned in protest from a White House advisory group. Trump was insensitive to the criticisms, apparently because he really believed there were fine people on both sides—the antiracists but also those protesting to preserve the legacy of the Confederate hero. This might also provide insight into the president's own racist or White supremacist views. Michael Nelson avers, "African Americans seemed to arouse his special ire: Obama, NBA star Stephen Curry, sportscaster host Jemele Hill, NFL players and Representatives John Lewis and Frederica Wilson."[24] Whatever the case, this is an instance of actor indispensability. Trump did not think he should have retreated from his initial statement, because it reflected his worldview. Thus, the lesson he learned from Charlottesville was not about racism and bigotry, but about fighting back and standing one's ground: "Watching the reaction he was convinced of two things: (1) he hadn't gotten any credit for saying the words everybody had said he had to say, and (2) the weakness he had displayed by giving into demands for the second statement had only emboldened his enemies to attack him harder. He would never again let anybody talk him into admitting a mistake or doing anything with even the faintest hint of an apology."[25]

Trump's racial animus was displayed in his immigration rhetoric and policies, views rooted as much in ideology as character. He has long held the view that the United States was being "invaded" by non-White people from "shit hole countries." In his speech announcing his candidacy, he described immigrants from Mexico as criminals, drug pushers, and rapists. In the course of the campaign, he called for a complete ban on immigrants from Muslim countries. And late in his second year in office, he introduced "shit hole countries" into the immigration vocabulary.

In a White House meeting with a bipartisan congressional delegation in November 2018 to discuss legislation to protect the status of immigrants from Haiti and El Salvador, Trump was quoted as saying, "Why are we having all these people from shit hole countries? Why do we need more Haitians? Take them out."[26] Instead, he proposed, "We take more immigrants from the great European countries like Norway or from Asian countries that can help us economi-cally."[27] Clearly, here Trump is wishing for a racist immigration hier-archy: Europeans, Asians, Latin Americans, Africans. This racist, White-supremacist hierarchy is implicated in Trump's attack on four non-White members of Congress: "Go back and help fix the totally broken and crime infested places from which they came."[28] These attacks on countries and peoples of color may reflect Trump's White nationalist worldview in that he, as Mary Stuckey suggests, "never conceived of nonwhite majority populations as having any value; he could not conceive of nonwhite Americans belonging to the nation in the ways whites do. Trump's United States is a white nation, and oth-ers are here merely on sufferance. Their continued welcome (such as it is) is entirely dependent on their willingness to assimilate into a narrow and particular view of nation and identity."[29]

Unlike his indifference to efforts to repeal and replace Obamacare, Trump paid attention to immigration. Immigration reform in general, and stopping the flow of immigrants at the southern border specifi-cally, including the construction of a border wall, was the signature promise of the campaign, and he endeavored to keep it. In his first week in office, he issued an executive order banning entry into coun-try of persons from thirteen predominantly Muslim countries. The hastily prepared order drafted by an inexperienced staff without con-sultation with the relevant bureaucracies was quickly overturned by the courts. Two other iterations of the order were issued, and they too were challenged in the courts. In *Trump, President of the United States vs. Hawaii* an ideologically polarized Supreme Court in a 5–4 decision upheld the third of the executive orders banning Muslim entry. The chief justice's opinion, joined by the four conservative justices, took judicial notice of the president's anti-Muslim rhetoric, but said the issue before the Court was not the president's rhetoric but his author-ity. And that statutory authority clearly sustained his right to suspend the entry of "all aliens or any class of aliens" as he deems necessary.[30]

In an unusual step for the Court, it used the case to reverse *Kore-matsu v. United States,* the 1944 case upholding the internment of Japanese Americans during World War II. In a long, passionate dis-sent, which she read from the bench, Justice Sonia Sotomayor said the Court's decision in the instant case was no better than *Korematsu,* viewing both as sanctioning racial animus, noting in her opinion Trump's frequent anti-Muslim rhetoric.[31]

Trump, as promised during the campaign, attempted to reverse the Obama administration's order allowing the children of parents who came to the country illegally to remain and to eventually become permanent residents. This action however was blocked in court. He also mused about issuing an executive order ending the Fourteenth Amendment guarantee of citizenship to all persons born in the United States. Although he did not act on this manifestly unconstitutional idea, the president did approve the "zero tolerance" policy for immigrants at the Mexican border.

Zero tolerance was a Justice Department regulation requiring the arrest and detention of persons crossing the border illegally until their request for entry could be adjudicated (previously such persons were released until their court hearing). Although a Justice Department regulation, implementation was the responsibility of the Homeland Security Department. The detention of adults with children required their separation. This required the government to find suitable care for the children, which led Homeland Security secretary Kirstjen Nielsen to delay implementation. This angered Trump, who humiliated Nielsen at a cabinet meeting and then fired her.[32] Nielsen was committed to implementing zero tolerance, but she was not aggressive enough in the face of widespread national and international criticism of the inhumane treatment of the children at the border, so Trump forced her resignation.[33]

In addition to these executive actions, Trump also presented legislation to Congress to reform immigration law to make it more merit- than family-based, and construct the border wall.[34] The Republican Congress in 2017–2018 provided modest funds for the wall, but its main focus was on tax cuts and the repeal of Obamacare. When the Democrats won control of the House, they refused to provide major funds for the construction of the wall and ignored Trump's reform proposals. In order to leverage support for the wall, Trump precipitated a month-long shutdown of parts of the government. When this failed to spur congressional action, in February 2019 he took the constitutionally dubious action of invoking the National Emergency Act and directed that the funds appropriated by Congress for military construction be used to begin building the wall. In a rare break with near unified partisan support for the president, twelve Republican senators joined the Democrats in a resolution revoking the emergency declaration, precipitating Trump's first veto.[35]

In other executive-administrative actions related to immigration, the army was dispatched to the border, enhanced border deportations were implemented, and asylum-seekers at the border were required to remain in Mexico while their cases were adjudicated. Trump's tenacity in focusing on immigration reflected his paleoconservative ideology and his commitment to keeping a major promise of his campaign. During his first years in office, there was a decrease in illegal immigration. This was only partly due to his policies since southern border crossings were declining before he became president.[36] Nevertheless, with parts of the border wall under construction, this is a policy area of achievement.

In race policy more generally, the administration adopted several institutionally racist policies. Institutional racism is understood as policies and practices of institutions, public or private, that while not overtly racist have racist effects or consequences.[37] In their cases dealing with institutional racism, courts use the term "disparate impact," wherein otherwise nonracist or neutral policies may be rendered racially discriminatory if they have a disproportionate negative impact on Black people and other minorities. In the post–civil rights era when individuals or institutions are less likely to engage in illegal, overt racism, effective enforcement of civil rights law in employment, housing, mortgage loans, and other areas requires use of the disparate impact standard. As one specialist in civil rights law said, "If you have no disparate impact enforcement, you are largely saying no discrimination enforcement at all."[38] Yet, this is precisely what the administration proposed to end.[39]

The administration also proposed to change the formula used to determine the poverty rate. The formula, established in the 1960s, determines eligibility for federal welfare programs such as food stamps and Medicaid. By changing the formula, the administration would arbitrarily reduce the number of poor people and persons eligible for assistance, persons who would be disproportionately African American.[40] In 2018 the president issued an executive order directing the social welfare bureaucracies to develop plans to get more people off welfare and into work, with the stated goal of fostering "self-sufficiency" and "economic mobility."[41] The language about self-sufficiency and economic mobility notwithstanding, the effects of these policies were to disproportionately harm poor Black people.[42]

The work requirements for Medicaid and food assistance are examples of specific institutionally racist policies. In 2017 the administration granted exemptions or waivers to states regarding the requirement for Medicaid recipients to work. In some states the work policy was implemented in an institutionally racist way. Michigan, for example, granted exemptions to the work requirement to counties with the highest unemployment. On its face it was not an unreasonable policy—except most of the counties with high unemployment were rural and White. The disparate impact: Whites who were 57 percent of the Medicaid population received 85 percent of the exemptions. Blacks who were 23 percent received only 1.2 percent.[43]

These race-related policies, implemented by Trump appointees overseeing the bureaucracy, were likely adopted without Trump's direct involvement or knowledge. They were ideologically driven, consistent with the deregulation policies and policies on race and poverty that go back to the Reagan administration. Character did not matter.

Crisis: The Pandemic and the Floyd Uprisings

What impact did character have on Trump's handling of the two crises of his presidency—the Covid-19 pandemic and the nationwide uprisings in the aftermath of the police murder of George Floyd? In the case of the virus, articles in the major newspapers suggest his approach was decisive and dangerous.[44] Trump's misleading rhetoric—"It's a Democratic hoax," "When it gets warmer, it miraculously goes away," "It's one person coming from China, we have it under control"—were reflective of his rhetorical diarrhea of the mouth and certainly were not helpful leadership behavior as the crisis emerged. Thus, Trump's character—rhetoric, staffing, homework, and decisionmaking—mattered, but so did bureaucratic arrogance and inertia, medical and scientific uncertainty, factionalism, bureaucratic infighting in the cabinet and White House staff, the novelty of the virus, and the lack of Chinese transparency and cooperation. I consider each of these variables except the last in understanding the administration's handling of the pandemic. For analysis of the virus response, I rely on detailed reports by the *New York Times* and the *Washington Post* and Bob Woodward's *Rage*. Each of these reports relied on multiple interviews with White House staff (in Woodward's case also multiple interviews with the president), science and medical experts, and officials in the various bureaucracies tasked with developing the government's response to the crisis.[45]

Robert Redfield, the CDC director, received formal notice about the virus from Chinese authorities on January 3, 2020, although China did not provide details or a sample and claimed there was no evidence of human transmission. Redfield informed Health and Human Services (HHS) secretary Alex Azar, who informed the president in a telephone conversation on January 18, 2020, as he was preparing for a trip to India. In addition, there were repeated references to the virus in the president's briefing books beginning in late January through February. It is not clear how dire or specific the warnings were about the virus, since "the preliminary intelligence on the coroanavirus was fragmentary and did not address prospects for a severe outbreak in the United States."[46] Given Trump's aversion to reading his briefing books, it is not clear he absorbed the limited information in the briefs. And at this time, the "warnings of top health officials were muddled and contradictory."[47]

The health and scientific bureaucracies—CDC and NIH—were initially unsure of the seriousness of the virus and the strategies necessary to combat it. CDC, for example, thought the outbreak would be limited and it would not need the assistance of private labs, universities, or other health organizations in combating its spread.[48] NIH's Dr. Anthony Fauci, the nation's leading authority on infectious diseases, did not have a "fixed grasp" on the problem. CDC director Redfield said he did not feel he had "his hands around the problem"; in late February he told Congress, "The immediate risk to the public remains low. It will look and feel to the American public like the flu." Fauci in late February repeatedly said the virus was low risk, while downplaying the need of people to wear masks.[49] One health official was quoted as saying "we were flying blind"; and Fauci told Trump, "We don't know what's going on. . . . It's all uncharted territory."[50] Although the Obama National Security Council in late 2016 had developed a strategy document on how to address a possible pandemic (informally called the "Pandemic Playbook"), it was not reviewed and adopted by the Trump administration.[51] The administration also abolished the White House office tasked with implementing policies to deal with a pandemic.

From the outset of learning about the virus, Trump downplayed its significance, dismissing Azar's initial briefing as "alarmist."[52] As it became clear in that the virus was a serious health threat, the administration was factionalized between those who prioritized the health dangers to the public and those (led by Treasury secretary Steven Mnuchin) concerned that mitigation for health reasons might endanger the economy. Throughout, Trump tended to side with those who prioritized the economy. Near the end of January, a task force headed by the deputy national security council adviser and the acting chief of staff was established with representatives from HHS, CDC, and the State Department. This was a kind of presidential acknowledgment of the seriousness of the problem. Shortly after its establishment, the task force recommended banning travel from China and Europe. Trump authorized the China ban, but the treasury secretary objected to the Europe ban as too disruptive to the economy. Trump agreed and delayed it for a month. There were also differences between the Office of Management and Budget and HHS over how much to ask Congress to appropriate to fight the virus, and between CDC and HHS over how fast the virus would spread and whether to enlist private entities to develop diagnostics. After the first American who had not traveled to China died of the virus on February 29, the CDC issued guidelines allowing private organizations to develop diagnostics. Yet, the president still did not appear to appreciate the gravity of the situation, telling aides it was like the flu and would go away in the spring. Although clearly uninformed, in a visit to the CDC headquarters in Atlanta in early March, Trump displayed his characteristic narcissism. Wearing a campaign "make America great again" red cap, he bragged about his brilliant medical mind: "I really get this stuff, I really get it. People here are surprised that I understand it. Everywhere these doctors say how do you know so much about this."[53]

Back in Washington the experts were increasingly worried the president did not understand. By early March the health task force was expressing increasing concern to the president about the danger of the virus, but Trump nevertheless compared it to the flu, which he said kills thousands each year and "nothing is shutdown, life and the economy goes on."[54] Still rejecting the task force recommendation of the Europe travel ban and a possible shutdown, he now worried the likely damage to the economy would undermine his chances for reelection, a view reinforced by his son-in-law who had been added to the task force.[55] In mid-March, recognizing the task force did not have a visible leader, he placed the vice president in charge. Shortly thereafter the task force again recommended the Europe travel ban and the possible imposition of a shutdown of all except essential social and economic activities. Trump, apparently reluctantly, acquiesced to the growing consensus of the health and science experts that the virus posed a greater threat to the nation than drops in the stock market or rising unemployment. On March 13, he declared a national emergency, and the country, following CDC guidelines, began to shut down on a state-by-state basis.

The nationally televised presidential address on the ban on European travel reflected aspects of Trump's character. As the *Wall Street*

Journal observed the day after the speech, the "Coronavirus has challenged Mr. Trump's unusual leadership style—blunt, improvisational and shoot-from-the-hip—like no other issue to confront his administration. . . . Inside the West Wing, Mr. Trump has decentralized power beneath him, giving as many as a half dozen White House staffers the ability to report to him and go around the chief of staff."[56] As a result, the speech was "filled with errors, some in the text and some ad-libbed by the president."[57] The sloppiness of the rhetoric of the president's first address to the nation on the crisis damaged his credibility at home and abroad.

The president may have had the statutory authority to impose uniform, nationwide guidelines—although given the nation's tradition of states' rights, it likely would have faced challenges in court—but the administration instead developed the policy of "state authority handoff." Thus, there was no national, uniform strategy but a series of state responses that often varied by which party controlled the state's government. Many states also allowed localities to establish the parameters of the shutdown, creating further incoherence and spread of the virus.

The coronavirus pandemic was the greatest national crisis since 9/11. A crisis of this magnitude requires presidential leadership that unites the country, but a combination of factors—including Trump's character, the polarized political context, the novelty of the virus, bureaucratic arrogance and hubris, the absence of an early health and science consensus—made the administration's handling of the crisis almost as polarizing as the debate on taxes and health insurance. Nevertheless, once the economy and society were on lockdown, with schools, universities, sporting events, restaurants, hotels, and all except essential economic activities closed, massive federal government intervention to ameliorate the situation was imperative, bringing factional infighting in the White House to an end. The president and congressional leaders put aside concerns about deficits and appropriated trillions of dollars to combat the virus and offer assistance to individuals and businesses. The Federal Reserve accommodated with a monetary policy that made credit available at near zero interest.

But even in this context of bipartisan consensus Trump's worldview and his poor personal relations with Democratic congressional leaders were displayed. Still angry over his impeachment, in negotiations over one of the coronavirus relief bills, he called the Speaker of the House "an inherently dumb person" who would be "over-thrown" as Speaker "either inside or out."[58] And in what seemed an arrogant display of narcissism, Trump ordered his name printed on the checks mailed to people.[59]

In its chronology of the Trump administration's handling of the crisis, the *New York Times* concluded, "The chaotic culture of the White House contributed to the crisis. A lack of planning and a failure to execute, combined with the president's focus on the news cycle and his preference for following his gut rather than data lost time, and perhaps lives."[60] Woodward puts the problem explicitly in terms of Barber's presidential character: "The failure to do his homework. To listen carefully to others. To craft a plan."[61] But the hubris of the CDC, the bureaucratic infighting, the tentative, limited knowledge of the experts, the novelty of the virus, and the lack of Chinese transparency and cooperation cast the president's behavior in a less harsh light. Trump's character mattered but so did the science, the bureaucracy, the states, and federalism. That is, it is not clear that the political system's response would have been substantively different if a person with more desirable presidential character had been in office.[62]

In addition to the style and rhetoric of the president's character, during the crisis his "fight back, hit back" worldview and narcissism raised questions of constitutional character, and the White House daily briefings on the virus, which Trump turned into a substitute for his canceled rallies, also displayed his narcissistic tendencies and "fight back" worldview.

The governors of the states, following the task force guidelines, closed their societies and economies in mid-March. Trump agreed to the state shutdowns, but remained concerned about the damage to the economy and by April was beginning to talk about reopening. As the health professionals expressed skepticism and many governors demurred, Trump displayed an extraordinary lack of understanding or appreciation for the constitutional separation of powers, federalism, and Article II. At one of the White House daily briefings on the virus, he said if the governors failed to follow his directions to reopen, he as president had the "total," "sole," "ultimate" authority to make the decision: "The President of the United States calls the shots. . . . The President of the United States has the authority to do, which is very powerful. . . . When somebody is President of the United States the authority is total. And that's the way it's got to be."[63] After extensive and predictable criticisms from constitutional scholars as well as some Republican governors and members of Congress, Trump said although he had the authority, he would leave the decisions to the governors. This episode may be no more than a case of Trump's hyperbolic rhetoric, but it also may be an indicator of the absence of constitutional character, which I discuss in a subsequent chapter.

Nevertheless, Trump continued to push the states to rapidly reopen their economies, going against the advice of the CDC and most health experts with the exception of Dr. Deborah Birk, the response coordinator for the White House task force on the virus. With an office in the White House, she told the president it was safe to begin reopening, and her advice was more influential than Dr. Fauci's and the CDC director—because it coincided with the president's inclinations. Many Republican-led states did begin to reopen in late April, and there were new surges of infections in early June and states had to return to lockdowns.

With mass rallies prohibited throughout the country, Trump turned the daily White House Coronavirus Task Force briefings into quasi-political rallies. C-Span and Fox News always covered the briefings live. CNN and MSNBC, once it became clear Trump was using them as campaign propaganda, were reluctant to provide live coverage, reflecting on how live coverage of Trump events had advantaged him during the campaign. Yet not to cover the briefings, which in addition to Trump included the top health and science experts on the virus, could be viewed as a violation of journalism ethics. For the most part, CNN and MSNBC provided live coverage, although with frequent interruptions.

Trump clearly viewed the briefings as substitutes for the rallies. An aide said after he was told about the negative polls about the briefings, he nevertheless claimed that their high ratings were a political resource against Joe Biden, the presumptive Democratic nominee, who was confined to limited video zooms from his Delaware house. "He is going to want media attention," an aide said, and "to control his message. He is the only one who thinks he can do his message best, and that's just the reality. That's how he works."[64]

The *New York Times* and the *Washington Post* did content analysis for three weeks of the briefings in April 2020.[65] The *Post* and *Times* findings were near identical. Trump monopolized the briefings at the expense of the scientists and doctors, using 60 percent of the time while the vice president, scientists, and doctors shared 40 percent.[66] Over the three weeks studied, Trump used his thirteen hours for two hours of attacks, forty-five minutes praising himself, and said something false or misleading in a quarter of his prepared comments or answers to questions.[67] The target of Trump's attacks were Obama, Biden, other Democratic leaders, China, governors and the media; three times he played videos praising himself.[68] After Trump, Vice President Pence was the second in time consumed, taking five and a half hours (Pence spent a good part of his time praising Trump), leaving eight hours to the health and science experts.

Trump frequently boasted that the late afternoon (eastern time) briefings with him in the "starring role" had higher ratings than *The Bachelor* finale and Monday Night Football. But after his especially egregiously dangerous suggestion that individuals might ingest bleach, rubbing alcohol, and other disinfectants as an antidote to the virus, Trump aides (armed with the polls showing the negative public response to his performance) persuaded him to suspend the daily briefings.[69] Some southern and western states were planning to begin reopening to limited mass gatherings, so in mid-June, the president resumed his rallies with a gathering in Tulsa, Oklahoma. Public health authorities and the city's mayor objected, citing concerns that such a mass gathering risked spreading the virus.

As indicated, after two months of the shutdown and unemployment surpassing double-digits, Trump was anxious to reopen the economy, although most medical and scientific experts warned that without adequate testing and the ability to trace the contacts of infected persons, this risked the resurgence of the virus, which began to occur in early June. Timing for reopening society and the economy mirrored the polarized state of the polity: Republican governors and voters tended to favor a quick reopening and Democratic governors, congressional leaders, and voters favored delay.[70] Another example of polarization relates to the president's ostentatious refusal to follow health authorities and wear a mask. It's not clear why he refused—vanity, skepticism about the science, worldview—but his refusal was embraced by many of his followers, resulting in further pandemic polarization. And increasingly the president and his supporters began to attack the health authorities (the head of the CDC as well as Dr. Fauci, who at one point Trump called an "idiot") that urged caution in opening schools and businesses.

Trump's attacks on the health and science bureaucracies risked undermining the confidence of the public in the CDC and the FDA. Without any evidence, Trump accused the FDA of delaying coronavirus vaccine trials for political reasons, tweeting, "The deep state, or whoever, is making it very difficult for drug companies to get people to test vaccines and therapeutics."[71] He then went on to accuse the agency of "obviously" delaying the vaccine until after the election.[72] In his press conferences and speeches, Trump repeatedly said a vaccine would be available before the election, contradicting both the CDC and the FDA and other authorities that reported a safe and effective vaccine would not likely be available until sometime in 2021.[73]

The FDA director, Stephen Hahn, repeatedly said the agency would not bow to pressure and "cut corners" to approve vaccines or therapeutics, but confidence in the agency as well as the public's willingness to use a vaccine once approved was likely undermined, as it appeared the FDA and the CDC were acceding to Trump's wishes. Shortly after the president suggested there were political motivations in the FDA's handling of a vaccine, the director announced "emergency approval" of convalescent plasma as a treatment, which Trump in a Sunday afternoon press conference boasted was a "major breakthrough." Yet, a day later the director issued a statement reporting he was mistaken in his approval of the plasma treatment, conceding the study he relied on lacked a control group that would allow scientific assessment of its benefits. The imperative of control groups to validate the effectiveness of drugs is so obvious that it is difficult to believe the head of FDA could make such a mistake. Rather, it is likely the FDA director's initial statement about the benefits of the plasma treatment was exaggerated, deliberately, almost certainly at the behest of Trump.[74]

In October, Trump contracted the virus. Although Trump and his doctors were far from transparent on how he and his wife and several close White House aides contracted the virus, it was likely a result of his refusal to wear masks and follow social distancing guidelines, which motivated his associates to follow his lead. Prior to his diagnosis, Trump held multiple rallies with no requirement or encouragement to wear masks or social distance; the last night of the Republican Convention was held on the White House lawn without masks or social distancing; Trump often mocked reporters at his press conferences for wearing masks; and days before he was diagnosed, he held a celebration for his Supreme Court nominee on the White House lawn with no masks or social distancing required. Even in the confined quarters of the West Wing of the White House, very few aides wore masks, and those who did were often told by the president,

"'Get that thing off,' an administration official said. Everyone knew Trump viewed masks as a sign of weakness."[75]

One might have thought once he contracted the virus, the president would have admitted his mistake and urged persons to follow CDC guidelines and begin to wear masks and follow social distancing rules. Instead, after he was released from the hospital (where he was apparently treated with therapeutics approved by the FDA on an emergency basis) he tweeted, "Don't be afraid of Covid, don't let it dominate your life"—touting his recovery as evidence the virus was not that dangerous or deadly.[76]

The George Floyd Uprisings

On May 25, 2020, George Floyd, a forty-six-year-old Black man, was torturously killed in Minneapolis by Derek Chauvin, a White police officer who held his knee on Floyd's neck for nearly ten minutes. The death took place in the afternoon in the presence of three other police officers who did not intervene, and multiple witnesses who repeatedly implored Chauvin not to kill Floyd, who was lying on his back, handcuffed. On May 26 videos recorded by security cameras and witnesses were repeatedly shown on television and the internet. Immediately there were mass protests around the country and across the world. The uprisings in the United States were the largest and most widespread since the riots in 1968 after the murder of Dr. Martin Luther King Jr. The protests in some cities were marked by arson, looting, and violence. In twenty states and the District of Columbia, the national guard was deployed.

Trump's response to Floyd's murder and the uprising was shaped largely by the political context of his campaign for reelection, although his worldview and rhetorical style were also likely factors. After a week of, in some places, violent protests, Trump's advisers were divided as to how he should respond. Some advised that he give a nationally televised conciliatory, unifying address about the "horror, anger and grief" of Floyd's death and discuss reforms in police practices.[77] This they suggested could reinforce the campaign's outreach to Black voters.

Throughout Trump's presidency, he was deeply unpopular among African Americans. An early 2020 poll found 83 percent viewed him as a racist; 90 percent disapproved of his job performance; 65 percent thought it was bad time to be Black in America while 77 percent thought it was a good time to be White; 75 percent viewed his policies as bad for Black people; only 20 percent gave him credit for the then good state of the economy; and 70 percent did not trust the police to be fair to Blacks.[78] Although exit polls indicated Trump received only 8 percent of the Black vote in 2016 (slightly more at 13 percent among Black men), Trump strategists thought even this small proportion of the Black vote might have made the difference in the closely contested battleground states of Wisconsin, Michigan, and Pennsylvania. They hoped to at least maintain if not expand support among Black voters in 2020. Thus, there was a well-funded and developed strategy to appeal to them.[79] In interviews, tweets, and speeches Trump frequently emphasized what he had done for Blacks, citing record low unemployment, criminal justice reform, enterprise zones, and increased aid to Black colleges and universities. In his characteristic rhetorical excess, he claimed he had done more for African Americans than any president since Lincoln and perhaps more than Lincoln.[80] Thus, some advisers (including his son-in-law) recommended he not jeopardize his campaign's outreach to Blacks with the present racial crisis.[81]

Other advisers were adamant that the violence during the uprising was a "political gold mine" that should be exploited in a tough law and order appeal to his base constituency.[82] Poll data at the time indicated a tough law and order approach would appeal only to the Republican base, since large majorities of Americans were sympathetic to the protests and favored racial conciliation.[83] While 69 percent of all Americans viewed the Floyd murder as part of a broader problem of police misconduct, only 47 percent of Republicans expressed this view; 74 percent of all respondents supported the protests but barely half of Republicans did (53 percent); 50 percent thought it was more important to heal racial divisions than "restore security," a position embraced by only 23 percent of Republicans.[84]

Trump adopted the tough law and order approach in a strategy that appealed mainly to Republicans. Deciding not to give a high-profile national address, the president gave his most detailed remarks on the Floyd murder and the protests on May 30 at Cape Canaveral in a speech mainly devoted to celebrating a space launch. The remarks at Cape Canaveral were a distillation of how he approached the crisis:

> Before going further on this exciting day for all America in space, I want to say a few words about the situation in Minnesota. The death of George Floyd on the streets of Minneapolis was a grave tragedy. It should never have happened. It has filled Americans all over the

country with horror, anger and grief. Yesterday, I spoke to George's family and expressed the sorrow of our entire nation for their loss. I stand before you as a friend and ally to every American seeking justice and peace. And I stand before you in firm opposition to anyone exploiting this tragedy to loot, rob, attack and menace. Healing, not hatred; justice, not chaos are [sic] the mission at hand. . . .

The police officers involved in this incident have been fired from their jobs. One officer has already been arrested and charged with murder. State and federal authorities are carrying out an investigation to see what further charges may be warranted, including against, sadly, the other three. In addition, my administration has opened a civil rights investigation and I have asked the Attorney General and the Justice Department to expedite it. I understand the pain that people are feeling. We support the right of peaceful protesters, and we hear their pleas. But what we are seeing on the streets has nothing to do with justice or peace. The memory of George Floyd is being dishonored by rioters, looters and anarchists. The violence and vandalism is [sic] being led by Antifa and other radical left-wing groups who are terrorizing the innocent, destroying jobs, hurting businesses, and burning down buildings. . . .

[T]here will be no anarchy. Civilization must be cherished, defended, and protected. The voices of law-abiding citizens must be heard and loudly. . . . We support the overwhelming majority of police officers who are incredible in every way and devoted public servants. They keep our cities safe, protect our communities from gangs and drugs, risk their own lives for us every day. . . .

Radical left criminals, thugs and others all throughout our country and throughout the world will not be allowed to set our communities ablaze. We won't let it happen.[85]

Trump met privately with Black families whose relatives were killed by police, issued an executive order suggesting reforms in police practices, and supported Republican Senate legislation on police reform authored by Tim Scott, the Senate's lone Black Republican. But after the address at the cape, his main response was law and order rhetoric in which he repeatedly labeled the protesters thugs, terrorists, anarchists, radical leftists, losers, and outside agitators. Invoking a comment traced back to suppression of the protests during the 1960s, Trump tweeted, "When the looting starts, the shooting starts."[86] He accused some Democratic governors of being "weak" and "looking like fools," tweeting they should "dominate" the protesters and threatening to send in the army if they did not.[87]

When the military and local police forcefully dispersed mostly peaceful protesters from a park across the street from the White House, Trump walked across to have a picture taken of him holding a Bible in front of a church. Accompanied by the attorney general, the secretary of defense, and chair of the Joint Chiefs of Staff among others, the event was clearly designed to appeal to Trump's White evangelical constituency, as the photo showed him as a "heroic defender of Christianity under siege from the secular left."[88] After the event, Trump remarked, "Religious leaders loved it. Religious leaders thought it was great. They loved it."[89]

In another example of Trump's appeal to a base constituency, in this case White nationalists, he tweeted videos of Black men attacking Whites, and asked, "Where are the protesters," suggesting equivalency between the police murder of Blacks and Blacks assaulting Whites.[90] Elements, perhaps, of Trump's worldview—the us versus them view of adversaries, and the hit back harder perspective on conflict—were displayed in his reaction to the Floyd uprising. In his rhetoric the police were the beleaguered defenders of civilization and law and order, Black Lives Matter was a "symbol of hate," and the protesters were thugs and anarchists trying to destroy America. Yet, although his rhetoric may reflect character, it also reflected what perhaps almost any contemporary conservative Republican president seeking reelection might have said and done.

Overall, Trump's handling of domestic policy, the crises of the virus, and the police murder of Floyd and the subsequent protests reflected a mix of Barber's presidential character indicators, as well as ideology, partisanship, campaign promise-keeping, the polarized political climate, reelection concerns, and perhaps other factors not known at this time. One thing is clear: Barber's theorizing that presidential character is predictable based on grasping the president's behavior at his first political success (in Trump's case his first business success) is confirmed. Trump's worldview developed apparently in adolescence, and the style he displayed in managing the Trump Organization—in terms of staffing, homework, decisionmaking, personal relations, relations with the media, rhetoric, and hyperbole—are clearly displayed in his conduct of the presidency. In the context of the international political environment, and the somewhat greater power a president has in foreign policy, the same patterns, with some variations, are observed in Trump's handling of foreign policy although his worldview appears to be somewhat more important.

Notes

1. For a detailed analysis of Trump's domestic policies in health, labor, welfare, education, taxes, and regulations, see Carter Wilson, *Trumpism:*

Race, Class, Populism, and Public Policy (Lanham, MD: Lexington Books, forthcoming).

2. Robert C. Smith and Richard Seltzer, *Polarization and the Presidency: From FDR to Barack Obama* (Boulder, CO: Lynne Rienner, 2015).

3. Iwan Morgan, *The Age of Deficits: Presidents and Unbalanced Budgets from Jimmy Carter to George W. Bush* (Lawrence: University Press of Kansas, 2009); and Bryan Jones and Walter Williams, *The Politics of Bad Ideas: The Great Tax Cut Delusion and the Decline of Good Government in America* (New York: Longman, 2008).

4. Smith and Seltzer, *Polarization and the Presidency*, 203–208, 225–227, 250–256.

5. Jim Tankersley, "Trump to Propose $4.8 Trillion Budget," *New York Times*, February 10, 2020.

6. Alan Rappeport and Maggie Haberman, "Trump Opened Door to Cuts in Medicare and Other Entitlement Programs," *New York Times*, January 22, 2020.

7. Alexander Bolton, "Lawmakers Say Trump's Infrastructure Vision Lacks Political Momentum," *The Hill*, February 16, 2018.

8. Peter Baker, Katie Rogers, and Emily Cochrane, "Trump Angered by 'Phony' Inquiries, Blows Up Meeting with Pelosi and Schumer," *New York Times*, May 21, 2019.

9. Rebecca Kheel, "Trump Calls Pelosi a 'Third-Rate Politician,' During Syria Meeting, Top Democrats Say," *The Hill*, October 16, 2019; and Morgan Chalfant, "Trump Calls Pelosi a Sick Woman," *The Hill*, May 19, 2020.

10. "President Dusts Off Infrastructure Ideas," *Bloomberg News*, April 1, 2020.

11. George Edwards, "No Deal: Donald Trump's Leadership of Congress," paper prepared for the annual meeting of the American Political Science Association, San Francisco, September 2017.

12. Jon Herbert, Trevor McCrisken, and Andrew Wroe, *The Ordinary Presidency of Donald Trump* (New York: Palgrave, 2019), 139.

13. Ibid., 150.

14. James Pfiffner, "Organizing the Trump Presidency," *Presidential Studies Quarterly* 48 (2018): 156.

15. Michael Wolff, *Fire and Fury: Inside the Trump White House* (New York: Henry Holt, 2018), 164.

16. Tim Alberta, *American Carnage: On the Frontlines of the Republican Civil War and the Rise of Donald Trump* (New York: Harper Collins, 2019), 433.

17. George Edwards, *Changing Their Minds: Donald Trump and Presidential Leadership* (Chicago: University of Chicago Press, 2021).

18. In the midst of the coronavirus health crisis, and an administration-supported case pending in the Supreme Court seeking to declare the Affordable Care Act unconstitutional, Trump issued an executive order, of dubious legality, to require health insurers to abide by the act's prohibition on using preexisting health conditions as a basis to deny coverage or increase its cost. The order also proposed to provide financial aid to older Americans for purchase of prescription drugs. Toluse Olorunnipa, "After Years of Promising

His Own Plan, Trump Settles for Rebranding Obamacare," *Washington Post,* September 25, 2020.

19. Julia Manchester, "White House Clarifies: We Condemn All Violence," *The Hill,* August 3, 2017.

20. Jonathan Karl, *Front Row at the Trump Show* (New York: Dutton, 2020), 196.

21. Congress swiftly and decisively overrode the veto, the only time his veto was not sustained during his presidency.

22. Karl, *Front Row at the Trump Show,* 199.

23. Ibid., 201.

24. Michael Nelson, *Trump's First Year* (Charlottesville: University of Virginia Press, 2018), 106.

25. Karl, *Front Row at the Trump Show,* 203.

26. Justin Beckwith, "Trump Calls El Salvador and Haiti 'Shit Hole' Countries," *Time,* January 18, 2018.

27. Ibid.

28. William Cummings, "Trump Tells Congresswomen to 'Go Back' to the Crime Infested Places from Which They Came," *USA Today,* July 14, 2019. Only one of them, Ilhan Omar, was an immigrant.

29. Mary Stuckey, "The Rhetoric of the Trump Administration," *Presidential Studies Quarterly* 51 (2021): 138.

30. *Trump, President of the United States vs. Hawaii et al.* (slip opinion), #14-965 (2020).

31. Ibid.

32. Zolan Kano-Young, "Kirstjen Nielsen Resigns as Trump Homeland Security Secretary," *New York Times,* April 17, 2019. Trump reportedly was often cruel and humiliating in his treatment of his aides. See Philip Rucker and Carol Leonnig, *A Very Stable Genius: Donald J. Trump's Testing of America* (New York: Penguin Books, 2020), 126.

33. Kano-Young, "Kirstjen Nielsen Resigns."

34. During the campaign, Trump repeatedly said Mexico would pay for construction of the wall. This was as unrealistic as his pledge to deport the millions of undocumented immigrants in the United States. In their first meeting after the election, Trump and the Mexican president agreed not to talk about Mexico funding the wall.

35. Michael Tackett, "Trump Issues Veto After Congress Rejects Border Emergency," *New York Times,* March 15, 2019. Trump's action in this instance appears to violate the provision of the Constitution (Article I, Section 9, Clause 7) stating "no money shall be drawn from the treasury but in consequence of an appropriations made by law." This would be especially compelling in this case when Congress had specifically refused to appropriate the money for the wall Trump requested. Nevertheless, the ideologically polarized Supreme Court in a 5–4 decision allowed the administration to spend the money on construction of the wall pending its resolution of the constitutional question.

36. Jynnah Radford, "Key Findings About U.S. Immigrants," Pew Research Center, July 17, 2019.

37. Robert C. Smith, *Racism in the Post–Civil Rights Era: Now You See It, Now You Don't* (Albany: SUNY Press, 1995), chap. 4.

38. Kate O'Donnell, "Trump Rolling Back Obama Efforts on Race Bias," *Politico,* May 9, 2018.

39. Renae Merle, "Trump Administration Strips Consumer Watchdog of Enforcement Powers in Lending Discrimination Cases," *Washington Post,* February 2, 2018; Linda Greenhouse, "Civil Rights Turned Topsy-Turvy," *New York Times,* August 29, 2019; and Laura Meckler and Devlin Barrett, "Trump Administration Seeks to Undo Decades-Long Rules on Discrimination," *Washington Post,* January 5, 2021.

40. Justin Sisk, "Trump May Redefine Poverty, Cutting Americans from Welfare Rolls," *Bloomberg,* May 6, 2019.

41. Loraine Woeltert, "Trump Orders Top-to-Bottom Review of Welfare Programs," *Politico,* April 11, 2018.

42. Bryce Covert, "The Not-So-Subtle Racism of Trump-Era 'Welfare Reform,'" *New York Times,* May 23, 2018; and Jonathan Chait, "The Pathological Cruelty of Trump's Medicaid Work Requirement," *New York Times,* February 12, 2018.

43. Jeff Stein and Andrew Van Dam, "Michigan's GOP Has a Plan to Shield Some People from Medicaid Work Requirements. They're Overwhelmingly White," *Washington Post,* May 11, 2018.

44. See, for instance, Dan Diamond, "Trump's Management Style Helped Fuel Coronavirus Crisis," *Politico,* March 8, 2020; Daniel Drezner, "The Unique Incompetence of Donald Trump," *Washington Post,* March 19, 2020; Lisa Friedman and Brad Plumer, "Trump's Response to Virus Reflects Long Disregard for Science," *New York Times,* April 28, 2020; and Michael Bender, "Crisis Tests President's Ad-Lib Style," *Wall Street Journal,* March 13, 2020.

45. Yasmeen Abutaleb, "The U.S. Was Beset by Denial and Dysfunction as Coronavirus Raged," *Washington Post,* April 4, 2020; Eric Lipton, "He Could Have Seen What Was Coming: Behind Trump's Failure on the Virus," *New York Times,* April 11, 2020; and Bob Woodward, *Rage* (New York: Simon & Schuster, 2020). See also David Leonhardt, "The Unique US Failure to Control the Virus," *New York Times,* August 9, 2020; and Michael Shears et al., "Inside Trump's Leadership Failure," *New York Times,* July 19, 2020.

46. Greg Miller and Ellen Nakashima, "President's Intelligence Briefing Book Repeatedly Cited Virus Threat," *Washington Post,* April 27, 2020.

47. Ibid.

48. Abutaleb, "The U.S. Was Beset by Denial." See also Eric Lipton et al., "The CDC Waited 'Its Entire Existence for This Moment': What Went Wrong?" *New York Times,* June 3, 2020.

49. Abutaleb, "The U.S. Was Beset by Denial." Redfield and Fauci are quoted in Woodward, *Rage,* 244, 254.

50. Abutaleb, "The U.S. Was Beset by Denial." Fauci is quoted in Woodward, *Rage,* 235.

51. Trump repeatedly claimed Obama had left no plan to deal with a possible pandemic. *Politico* published the sixty-nine-page Obama document "Playbook for Early Response to High-Consequence Infectious Disease and Biological Incidents." See Dan Diamond and Nahal Toosi, "Trump Team Failed to Follow NSC's Pandemic Playbook," March 25, 2020.

52. Abutaleb, "The U.S. Was Beset by Denial."

53. Lipton, "He Could Have Seen What Was Coming."

54. Ibid.

55. Ibid.

56. Michael Bender, "Crisis Tests President's Ad-Lib Style."

57. Ibid.

58. Sheryl Gay Stolberg, "Deal Near on Small Business," *New York Times,* April 20, 2020.

59. Lisa Rein, "In Unprecedented Move, Treasury Orders Trump's Name on Stimulus Checks," *Washington Post,* April 14, 2020.

60. Lipton, "He Could Have Seen What Was Coming."

61. Woodward, *Rage,* 386. For a similar assessment see Jeffrey Mayer, "Two Presidents, Two Crises: Bush Wrestles with 9/11, Trump Fumbles Covid 19," *Presidential Studies Quarterly* 50 (2020): 629–649. Mayer suggests "Trump's handling of Covid 19 will quickly and perhaps permanently become known as the worst-handled crisis in history, surpassing even the malignant passivity of James Buchanan in the face of Southern secession" (646).

62. One measure of the system's failure compared to other nations: the United States has 4 percent of the world's population but as of August 2020 it had 22 percent of the world's cases, more than all the cases in Europe, Canada, South Korea, Japan, and Australia combined. Leonhardt, "The Unique U.S. Failure to Control the Virus."

63. Jason Lemon, "Trump Insists Constitution's Article II 'Allows Me to Do Whatever I Want,'" *Newsweek,* June 16, 2020.

64. Gabby Orr and Nancy Cook, "Trump Grapples with a Surprise Threat: Too Much Trump," *Politico,* April 25, 2020.

65. Phillip Bump and Ashley Parker, "Thirteen Hours of Trump: The President Fills Briefings with Attacks and Boasts," *Washington Post,* April 26, 2020; and Jeremy Peters, Elaine Platt, and Maggie Haberman, "260,000 Words Full of Self-Praise for Trump," *New York Times,* April 26, 2020.

66. Bump and Parker, "Thirteen Hours of Trump."

67. Ibid.

68. Ibid.

69. Suggesting that people take disinfectants was not the only dangerous medical notion Trump advanced during the crisis. He suggested and later claimed he was taking the medically unproven drug hydroxychloroquine, alarming doctors who said taking the drug may cause serious heart problems and other complications.

70. Rachel Roubein, "Stark Partisan Divide on Reopening America," *Politico*, May 2, 2020.

71. "Trump Without Evidence Accuses FDA of Delaying Trials," *East Bay Times,* August 23, 2020.

72. Ibid.

73. Several weeks after the election, the FDA approved coronavirus vaccines on an emergency basis, and inoculations of health workers began in early December 2020.

74. Katie Thomas and Sheri Fink, "F.D.A. Grossly Misrepresented Blood Plasma Data, Scientists Say," *New York Times,* August 25, 2020.

75. Annie Karni and Maggie Haberman, "A White House Long in Denial Confronts Reality," *New York Times*, October 3, 2020. Throughout the fall, in deliberate contrast with his opponent, Trump held rallies where the wearing

of masks and social distancing was neither required or encouraged. A study by Stanford's Institute for Economic Policy Research concluded, "The communities in which Trump rallies took place paid a high price in terms of disease and death." The institute estimated the rallies resulted in more than 30,000 confirmed cases of the virus and likely caused more than 700 deaths among attendees and their contacts. Lisa Krieger, "Trump Rallies Linked to 30,000 Cases, 700 Deaths," *Bay Area News Group,* November 1, 2020.

76. Katie Thomas and Denise Grady, "Trump Makes Return to the White House," *New York Times,* October 6, 2020.

77. Gabby Orr, Nancy Cook, and Daniel Lippman, "How Trump's Scattered Team Scrambled to Respond to Historic Protests," *Politico,* June 1, 2020.

78. Olive Woodson, "Black Americans Deeply Pessimistic About Country Under Trump," *Washington Post,* January 17, 2020.

79. Gabby Orr and Alex Isenstadt, "Trump's Campaign to Woo Black Voters: Retail Stores," *Politico,* February 28, 2020; and Theodore Johnson, "Trump's Black Outreach Could Actually Work," *Washington Post,* February 6, 2020.

80. Glenn Kessler, "Trump Claims He Has Done More for Black Americans Than Lincoln," *Washington Post,* June 5, 2020.

81. Orr, Cook, and Lippman, "How Trump's Scattered Team."

82. Ibid.

83. Scott Clement and Dan Balz, "Big Majorities Support Protest Over Floyd Killing, Say Police Need to Change, Poll Finds," *Washington Post,* June 9, 2020. A year later a Minnesota jury found Chauvin guilty of second-degree murder, third-degree murder, and manslaughter. Opinion on the verdict was polarized. A CBS poll found 90 percent of Democrats approved of the verdict, but only 54 percent of Republicans did. Jemina McEvoy, "Nearly Half of Republicans Think Derek Chauvin Verdict Was Wrong," *Forbes,* April 25, 2021.

84. Ibid.

85. "Text of President Donald Trump's Speech at Kennedy Space Center," May 30, 2020 (Washington: The White House).

86. Michael Wines, "Looting Comment from Trump Dates Back to Racial Unrest of the 1960s," *New York Times*, May 20, 2020.

87. Robert Costa, Seung Min Kim, and Josh Dawsey, "Trump Slams Governors as 'Weak': Urges Crackdown on Protesters," *Washington Post,* May 31, 2020.

88. Sarah Posner, "White Evangelicals Think Trump Is Divinely Ordained, He'll Do Almost Anything to Keep It That Way," *Los Angeles Times,* June 14, 2020. General Mark Milley, the Joint Chiefs chair, and Mike Esper, the defense secretary, both later apologized for their participation in what looked like an obvious political event.

89. Ibid.

90. Tim Elfrink, "Trump Tweets Videos of Black Men Attacking White People, Asks Where Are the Protesters," *Washington Post,* June 23, 2020.

7

Presidential Character and Foreign Policy

TRUMP'S FOREIGN POLICY, TO SOME EXTENT MORE than domestic policy, seems to have been shaped by his worldview and ideology more than his character in terms of homework, decisionmaking processes, and rhetoric, although character is not unimportant.

Trump did not like memorandums or reports, was skeptical of expertise, and tended to want briefings to be short and preferably visual. His first national security adviser, H. R. MacMaster, told his staff after he had spent some time on the job, that they were going to have to "adapt to the style of the commander-in chief. He was not going to read seventy-page briefing papers. He might read one-pagers, but even so staff should aim to fit everything on an index card . . . compress complex issues into an elevator pitch. And when a 'decision package' is sent to the President, nice to include a couple of suggested tweets."[1] Intelligence officials in charge of briefing Trump said he "rarely absorbs information he disagrees with or that runs counter to his world view. Briefing him has been so great a challenge compared to his predecessors that the intelligence agencies hired outside consultants to study how to better present information to him."[2]

Trump's third national security adviser, Robert O'Brien, reduced the size of the NSC staff because he understood Trump's distrust of experts and his wish to make decisions on his own initiative without a lot of staffing or paperwork.[3] When he hired O'Brien, Trump quipped that the job would be "easy. You want to know why it's easy because I make all the decisions. They don't have to work."[4] An example of Trump's idea of doing the work was his decision to receive the President's Daily Brief, which covers events around the world that may affect US interests, weekly rather than daily.[5] The failure of the president to read and study left him without expert information on complex issues such as Korean nuclear weapons or trade. On trade, for example, most economists disagreed with his decision to impose across-the-board tariffs on China, Canada, and European countries. His principal trade adviser prepared a thoroughly researched paper on the subject, but said "he knew [Trump] had not read it and probably never would. He hated homework."[6]

Trump's foreign policy, however, was not based primarily on style. Unlike with domestic policies, his foreign policies often derived from his worldview, specifically his view of the role of the United States in the post–World War II era and from an ideology he has held and articulated for decades. He viewed international politics as Hobbesian struggles, with winners and losers, and for years in books, interviews, and tweets he has argued the United States has been a loser, and allies and adversaries have been winners. The United States has been losing, he contended, because the nation's leaders have been fools. These views are not merely Trumpian whims or impulses but deeply rooted in the isolationist, "America first" history, expressed currently in paleoconservatism. Paleoconservatives view the bipartisan American foreign policy establishment as "globalist" and "internationalist" and as having abandoned the country's national interests.

Again, unlike his domestic policy views on taxes, health insurance, or abortion, Trump's foreign policy views are deeply held, based not on the political context or climate but on a worldview not easily altered by experts, whether professors or generals. As Charlie Laderman and Brendan Simms argue, "It would be a mistake to see Trump's foreign policy positions as establishment Republican ones. For in almost every area of international policy Trump's pre-presidential stance represents a fundamental departure not only from his Democratic predecessors and recent Republican incumbents, but from the entire bipartisan consensus that has existed in US foreign policy since World War II."[7] Although perhaps crudely expressed, the core of Trump's view is that the United States is being "ripped-off" and "taken advantage of" internationally by its supposed friends, Japan, Germany, South Korea, and Saudi Arabia. He viewed his election as a mandate to change this and "put America first."

Trump articulated his foreign policy ideology in his first meeting as president with his national security team held in the Pentagon's secret tank. In what has been described as "Trump's tirade in the tank,"[8] Bob Woodward reports the president proceeded to lecture and insult the entire group of the nation's top military and diplomatic officials, telling them they didn't know anything about defense or national security.[9] Peter Bergen in his account of the meeting writes, "The tank meeting was one of the most important moments of Trump's presidency. [He] for the first time laid down a marker in front of pretty much his entire cabinet that an isolationist, protectionist America first policy was the Trump doctrine."[10] It is after this meeting that Secretary of State Rex Tillerson reportedly said the president was a "moron." Within a year, Trump—on Twitter—fired him.

Trump's character mattered in his conduct of foreign policy, although more so in domestic policy; his foreign policy is best understood in terms of ideology, campaign promise-keeping, and what I call personalism—his personal relations with certain countries and their leaders.

For decades Trump has argued that NATO, particularly its major powers, has taken advantage of the United States, with America bearing the financial and military burden of Europe's defense while it prospered through unfair trade practices. Why, he asked, should the United Kingdom and Germany not pay for the US troops stationed in their countries? Why indeed should US troops be stationed in those countries? After the collapse of the Soviet Union and the end of the Cold War, skepticism about the value of NATO to US interests became a core tenet of paleoconservative thought.

During the 2016 campaign, Trump often inveighed against NATO because of its members' failure to pay a proportionate share of the budget. This was not a new complaint. Since the 1960s US presidents and congressional leaders have complained, but none had done it so crudely, personally attacking leaders of the countries. Trump in a break with past presidents also openly questioned the continued relevance of NATO, and refused to unambiguously affirm that he would uphold Article 5 of the NATO charter, which commits each member state to consider an attack on one an attack on all. Trump also kept an implied promise and withdrew a substantial number of US troops stationed in Germany, a move opposed by most congressional Republicans. Confronting this opposition, he defended the decision as resulting from

Germany's long-standing failure to meet its NATO financial obligations and its unfair trade practices.[11]

All of Trump's national security cabinet—the secretary of state, the secretary of defense, the chair of the Joint Chiefs, the national security adviser—were committed to NATO as, in their view, the most successful alliance in history, and as integral to global security. They urged the president, without success, to be less confrontational in his public rhetoric and private discussions with NATO leaders. Nevertheless, partly due to his forceful attacks, most NATO members did agree to increase their contributions. Yet, his attacks alienated the leaders of France, Germany, and Canada, undermined alliance solidarity, and led some European leaders to muse about the need to think about charting a course independent of the United States.[12]

For decades and during the election campaign, Trump also objected ideologically to the liberal, globalist trade regime established on a bipartisan basis after World War II. He argued that most of the agreements were unfair and had contributed to the decline of the manufacturing base of the economy. Against the counsel of most of his advisers and Republican Party orthodoxy, he imposed unilateral tariffs on China, Canada, and European trading partners. Trump also withdrew from the Trans Pacific Partnership trade agreement and negotiated modest improvements in a new NAFTA agreement. Although he did not label China a currency manipulator as he had promised during the campaign, the relatively high tariffs he unilaterally imposed precipitated a reciprocal Chinese response and a trade war. This eventually resulted in a tentative agreement with somewhat more favorable US access to Chinese markets and protection of intellectual property rights.[13] But the retaliatory Chinese tariffs resulted in rising US trade deficits and significant harm to US farmers.[14] Overall, Trump was able to "revolutionize" US trade relations with China and other nations, but observers worried that his use of trade as a "coercive weapon" in foreign policy may have negative long-term consequences for the global economy.[15]

The origin of Covid-19 in China and China's lack of transparency and refusal to allow US scientists to visit in order to gain firsthand knowledge resulted in further deterioration in US-China relations. Trump frequently labeled the disease the "China virus" and sometimes implied China may have deliberately fostered its global spread.

Trump also withdrew from the Paris climate agreement and the Iran nuclear accord. During the campaign he promised to withdraw from both agreements and in doing so he was acting in line with the

Republican Party consensus as well as keeping campaign promises. That these withdrawals were contrary to the wishes of US allies and the consensus of the international community did not bother Trump. Defiance of the global community in pursuit of perceived US interests is integral to his ideology.

Trump also defied allies and the global consensus in dealing with the Palestine-Israel conflict. He moved the US embassy in Israel to Jerusalem, recognized Israel's authority over the Golan Heights, sanctioned continued settlements in the occupied territory, withdrew recognition and economic assistance to the Palestine Authority, and in a "peace" agreement brokered by his son-in-law, he gave Israel everything it wanted while completely ignoring the interests of Palestine. During the campaign Trump promised to take an even-handed approach to the conflict and negotiate the "deal of the century." Instead, of "the art of the deal," as Bergen quipped, Trump negotiated "the art of the giveaway."[16]

Trump's policy on the conflict was not ideologically driven, it was not party orthodoxy, it was not based on character, not based on his gut, nor was it keeping a campaign promise. So, what happened? Why did Trump the dealmaker give away everything to Israel, and possibly damage the long-term prospects of a two-state solution and a viable, lasting peace. I suggest personalism—his personal relations with the key actors in the decisionmaking processes. The first of these personal relationships is with his son-in-law, Kushner, a Zionist, with no expertise in diplomacy or the Middle East, who was given a near complete portfolio to arrange a deal. The second personal relation was David Friedman, Trump's appointee as ambassador to Israel. A personal friend, Friedman was Trump's longtime bankruptcy attorney, campaign contributor, and cochair of the campaign's advisory committee on Israel. A radical Zionist, Friedman supported unrestricted Jewish settlement in the occupied territories, and was skeptical about a two-state solution. His appointment was opposed by liberal Jewish organizations and approved in the Senate on a narrow party-line vote. The final personal relation was Benjamin Netanyahu, Israel's prime minister, who was a personal friend of the Kushners.

In 1995 Congress enacted the Jerusalem Embassy Act, directing the president to move the US embassy to Jerusalem. During the campaign Trump promised to do so, as had Presidents Clinton and George W. Bush during their campaigns. However, once elected Clinton and Bush used the act's national security waiver clause and declined to move the embassy. The basic reason for the waiver is that the international community considers East Jerusalem illegally occupied territory and the final status of the city is to be determined in a final peace agreement. Initially Trump, probably on the recommendation of his national security advisers, followed the Clinton-Bush precedent, but in December 2017 probably on the advice of Friedman and Kushner he moved the embassy. The Palestine Authority viewed this unilateral action by the United States as inconsistent with its role as an honest broker in the US-sponsored "peace process" and terminated its participation. The widespread protests predicted in the Arab world as a result of the embassy relocation did not happen, which likely encouraged Kushner and the president to continue down the path of capitulation to the demands of Israel. In the fall of 2019, the administration announced its Israel-Palestine "peace agreement" negotiated solely with Israel, which ceded to Israel virtually everything Netanyahu wished including all of the territory it illegally occupied. Endorsed by no other nation and near universally condemned as a violation of international law, the agreement was widely described as a sham and a hoax.[17] It did result in three Arab states agreeing to normalize relations with Israel in exchange for its promise not to annex the occupied West Bank territories along with some other US transactional concessions.[18]

In the broader Middle East, Trump's main objective—also ideologically driven—was to end what he called the "endless wars" in Iraq and Afghanistan and avoid starting another. At the beginning of the administration, the United States was involved to some degree in four wars in the Middle East, in Iraq, Afghanistan, Syria, and against ISIS (the Islamic State in Iraq and Syria), the terrorist group that emerged in the region after Obama's withdrawal of most US troops from Iraq. The top priority of the president's national security cabinet was to destroy the ISIS "caliphate." The Obama administration had made considerable progress in destroying ISIS, without committing a large number of troops. Trump accelerated this low-intensity war, and by the end of the year ISIS had been defeated insofar as its control of any substantial territory in Syria or Iraq.[19]

The defeat of ISIS, however, came with a cautionary note for Trump in terms of his wish to withdraw forces from Iraq and Afghanistan. His national security cabinet was unanimous in urging him not to repeat Obama's "mistake" by precipitously withdrawing troops from Iraq or Afghanistan and risking the reemergence of ISIS or a kindred group. Convinced that the wars in Iraq and Afghanistan were "futile" endeavors, and the generals' plans to stay the course were "bullshit,"[20] Trump nevertheless did not wish to take responsibility for the consequences of a substantial withdrawal. He, however, ordered the start of direct talks with the Taliban, which resulted in a tenuous, tentative agreement that would allow for withdrawal of most US troops (as the 2020 election approached, modest troop withdrawals from Iraq and Afghanistan were announced). In pursuit of this agreement, Trump outraged Republican conservatives and neoconservatives by extending an invitation to Taliban leaders to confer at Camp David. Trump further outraged congressional Republicans and Democrats when he agreed to the Turkish president's demand to withdraw US troops from northern Syria to facilitate Turkey's attack on Kurdish rebels. The Kurds had assisted the United States in defeating ISIS, but they were viewed by Turkey as terrorists. Trump's decision was viewed as a betrayal of a US ally and was opposed by his entire national security cabinet and congressional leaders of both parties. Later, when he proposed withdrawing all US troops from Syria, the secretary of defense resigned in protest. Trump, however, was undeterred, believing the presence of US troops ran the risk of involvement in another endless war. After the 2020 election, the administration announced further withdrawals of troops from Iraq and Afghanistan, and the complete withdrawal of the small force of 700 US troops in Somalia.

When Syria used biological weapons that resulted in the death of civilians in an attack on the rebels seeking to overthrow the government, Trump ordered a limited air strike in response, resisting the advice of some in the security cabinet to use the occasion to destroy Syrian air capabilities. Similar reluctance on his part to start a war was displayed when Iran brought down a US drone. He ordered a retaliatory bombing response but while the planes were en route to their targets, he canceled the attack concluding the likely Iranian deaths were a disproportionate response. Some congressional Republicans also criticized the president when he failed to respond militarily to a suspected Iranian-sponsored attack on Saudi Arabian oil facilities.

Trump's policy toward Iran was unrelentingly hostile. During the campaign he joined with all the Republican candidates in opposing the nuclear agreement with Iran, and he promised to withdraw from it if elected. Some in the national security cabinet urged him not to withdraw since the agreement seemed to be working to restrain Iran's nuclear capabilities, but Trump kept the promise and in addition imposed economic sanctions on Iran. Trump's decision alienated the other signatories to the agreement (Russia, China, the

UK, France, and Germany), who pledged to continue to abide by its provisions, as did Iran. Iran responded, however, by increasing its production of nuclear material, by harassing Western shipping in the Persian Gulf, shooting down a US drone, and proxy attacks on Saudi oil facilities. As tensions between the countries increased, Trump, against the advice of his advisers, offered to meet the Iranian leadership to discuss a new nuclear agreement, but Iran insisted that no meeting could take place until the sanctions were lifted.[21] And then in a surprise move, Trump approved the assassination of Iran's top military officer, General Qassem Soleimani, bringing the two countries to the brink of war. (Earlier he had approved the killing of Abu al-Baghdadi, the ISIS leader.) Iran's retaliation for the assassination was deliberately restrained (injuring only a few American soldiers) and thus war was avoided. Trump apparently was prepared to start another Middle East war if Iran had responded more aggressively, vetoing a bipartisan congressional resolution requiring him to seek authorization before engaging in further military action against Iran.[22]

If war with Iran had occurred, in perhaps a reflection of his worldview, Trump in a tweet indicated he was prepared to flagrantly violate international law by attacking Iranian cultural sites (protected from attack by a 1954 Hague Convention, to which the United States is a signatory): "They're allowed to kill our people. They're allowed to torture and maim our people. And we're not allowed to touch their cultural sites. It doesn't work that way."[23] Both the secretary of state and secretary of defense publicly rebuked the president by declaring the United States would follow international law, and the Senate Republican leader condemned the president's threat.

Trump's policy toward Iran was contradictory. He withdrew from the nuclear agreement that his intelligence chief said was working reasonably well in order to keep a campaign promise and perhaps also because of his abiding animus toward Obama, who signed the agreement. In the process, he alienated key European allies and risked yet another endless Middle East war. Yet, at the same time he defied his advisers and sought meetings with Iranian leaders to make a deal. In the end, however, the UN Security Council, despite vociferous protests by the United States, allowed its thirteen-year arms embargo on Iran to expire in 2020. The Security Council majority, including the UK and France, concluded the United States forfeited its right to retain the embargo when it withdrew from the nuclear agreement.

Trump cultivated good relations with the authoritarian leaders of Saudi Arabia, even after its principal leader was implicated in the brutal, sadistic murder of Jamal Khashoggi, US resident and *Washington Post* contributing writer. The relationship was Trumpian art-of-the-deal business transactionalism. Saudi Arabia was the main adversary of Iran in the region; it purchased huge amounts of US arms and other goods; it has huge oil reserves; it is strategically located; and its conservative regime is friendly to the United States and not overtly hostile to Israel. Thus, as he said, after the Khashoggi murder, it was important to maintain good relations with the regime no matter how murderous its leaders: "I only say they spend $400 to 450 billion over a period of time, all money, all jobs, buying equipment. I am not a fool that says we don't want to do business."[24]

In his most audacious act of diplomacy, Trump once again defied his advisers and the precedents of his predecessors and agreed to meet with Kim Jong-un, the leader of North Korea. This followed a series of provocative missile launches by North Korea and bellicose, bombastic rhetoric by Trump on Twitter and in a UN address. For a time, the two countries appeared headed for war. And then Trump abruptly agreed to a summit with Kim, arranged by South Korea. The idea of the president of the United States meeting the leader of North Korea was anathema to the foreign policy establishment, but Trump thought he could make a deal to get Kim to abandon his nuclear program (Barack Obama was sharply criticized during the 2008 Democratic primaries by his opponents and many Washington pundits for saying he would meet with the leaders of North Korea, Iran, and Cuba). An unlikely prospect but perhaps a worthy endeavor to avoid war. Overall, "Trump engineered an unprecedented opening with North Korea and significantly reduced tensions. . . . [But] his efforts to dismantle its nuclear program ultimately led nowhere, as others had in the past. The lovefest between Trump and Kim continued but so did Kim's nuclear program."[25]

At the heart of US-China relations was the trade war. Otherwise, relations were reasonably calm. However, the Chinese government's effort to restrict Hong Kong's autonomy and its repression of the resulting protests strained relations. And China's lack of transparency and cooperation on the coronavirus further strained relations. Trump and his reelection strategists also apparently decided that attacking "communist" China would be a useful 2020 campaign issue. As China's repression of Hong Kong dissent continued, Trump ended Hong Kong's special trade relationships with the United States. After the uprisings in the United States following the police murder of George Floyd, Chinese media accused the US government of hypocrisy for condemning Chinese repression in Hong Kong, while it was killing and repressing African Americans.

Trump maintained relatively good relations with Russian president Vladimir Putin, in spite of or perhaps because of Russian interference in the 2016 election to facilitate his election.[26] After one of their meetings, at a press conference Trump joked about the interference and appeared to suggest that he believed Putin rather than US intelligence about the alleged Russian interference.[27] During the campaign, he promised to pursue as policy good relations with the Russian Federation. Although there were no major deals, Putin and Trump had a couple of friendly meetings in Europe, and Trump sought unsuccessfully to have Russia readmitted to the G7, following its suspension after its annexation of Crimea. But, unlike Obama, Trump approved the sale of lethal weapons to Ukraine to fight Russian-backed insurgents. The administration also imposed multiple sanctions on Russian entities and individuals, and it withdrew from the 1987 Intermediate Range Nuclear Forces Treaty and from the 1992 Open Skies Treaty (permitting overflights by each side of the other's territory), accusing Russia of cheating. The administration also engaged in a buildup of US nuclear weapons, and hinted it might withdraw from the 2010 Strategic Arms Reduction Treaty (START) and resume nuclear testing. Administration officials suggested the purpose was to bring China into the agreement—an unlikely possibility since it has far fewer nuclear weapons than Russia or the United States.[28] Although the reporting is not clear, it is likely Trump embraced these policies on the advice of his national security cabinet. And these policies are consistent with views of the so-called conservative defense hawks. Overall, while there may have been a Trump-Putin bromance, US policy seems to have been dictated by ideology.[29]

Trump's foreign policy was characterized by no stunning successes or failures, and his style and rhetoric made for an unorthodox decisionmaking process. He attempted to keep his promises of prioritizing US interests as dictated by his worldview; he was prudent in the use of military power and only reluctantly failed to keep his promise to withdraw all US forces from the wars in Iraq, Syria, and Afghanistan; and he avoided war with Iran. Although his rhetoric was often bellicose, his policies were restrained. Here presidential character mattered less than worldview and ideology.[30]

Presidential character as Barber theorizes it deals mainly with how the president does the work of the office, and it is little concerned with the individual's personal or even democratic or constitutional character. Barber by omission seems to suggest that personal character has relatively little to do with presidential character. That is, one can be an effective president, even perhaps a great president, in spite of deficits in personal and democratic character. Whether this is the case is perhaps a normative rather than an empirical question. President Trump's personal and democratic or constitutional character are addressed in the following chapter. Although it may be debatable, it is my perspective in Chapter 8 that the personal and democratic character of the leader are important in a healthy democratic polity.

Notes

1. Peter Bergen, *Trump and His Generals: The Cost of Chaos* (New York: Penguin Press, 2019), 91.
2. John Baines and Adam Goldman, "For Spy Agencies, Briefing Trump Is a Test of Holding Attention," *New York Times,* March 21, 2020.
3. Noah Bierman, "White House Quietly Trims Dozens of NSC Experts," *Los Angeles Times,* February 13, 2020.
4. Ibid.
5. Charlie Laderman and Brendan Simms, *Donald Trump: The Making of a World View* (London: I. B. Tauris, 2017), 105.
6. Bob Woodward, *Fear: Trump in the White House* (New York: Simon & Schuster, 2018), 47.
7. Laderman and Simms, *Donald Trump,* 107.
8. Bergen, *Trump and His Generals,* 11–13.
9. Woodward, *Fear,* 226.
10. Bergen, *Trump and His Generals,* 15. Philip Rucker and Carol Leonnig report that in the meeting Trump mocked the generals, calling them "losers" and "dopes and babes," and saying "I wouldn't go to war with you people." See *A Very Stable Genius: Donald J. Trump's Testing of America* (New York: Penguin, 2020), 138–139.
11. The bipartisan 2021 Defense Authorization Act included a provision prohibiting the reduction of US troops in Germany until Congress was given the opportunity to review the decision. This provision was one of the reasons Trump vetoed the bill.
12. Anne Gearan and John Hudson, "Trump's Strong-Arm Foreign Policy Tactics Create Tensions with US Friends and Foes," *Washington Post,* January 19, 2020; and Michael Birnbaum and John Hudson, "At Munich Security Conference, an Atlantic Divide: US Boasting and European Unease," *Washington Post,* February 16, 2020.
13. Keith Bradsher et al., "U.S. and China Reach Initial Trade Agreement," *New York Times,* December 13, 2019.

14. Patricia Cohen, "Tariffs Test Farmers Loyalty to Trump: How Long Is Short-Term," *New York Times,* May 24, 2018.

15. Michael Mastanduno, "Trump's Trade Revolution," *Forum,* 17 (2020): 523–548.

16. Bergen, *Trump and the Generals,* 195.

17. Peter Waldman, "The Administration's Peace Plan Is Absurd," *Washington Post,* November 1, 2019; Robert Malley and Aaron David Miller, "The Real Goal of Trump's Middle East Peace Plan: It's Not Peace, It's Power," *Politico,* November 28, 2019; and Max Boot, "What Trump and Netanyahu Unveiled Was a PR Campaign, Not a Peace Plan," *Washington Post,* November 28, 2019. The *New York Times* reported the Trump proposal "would give Israel most of what it has sought over decades of conflict while offering the Palestinians the possibility of a state with limited sovereignty." See Michael Crowley and David Halbfinger, "Trump Issues Mideast Plan That Strongly Favors Israel," *New York Times,* February 4, 2020.

18. Bahrain based its recognition on its understanding Israel would not annex additional West Bank territory. Morocco granted recognition in exchange for US recognition of its sovereignty over the disputed Western Sahara, and the administration agreed to allow the United Arab Emirates to purchase advanced US fighter jets.

19. Dion Nissenbaum and Maria Abi-Habib, "Trump Gives Generals More Freedom on ISIS Fight," *Washington Post,* April 14, 2017.

20. Bergen, *Trump and His Generals,* 136.

21. Laura King, "Trump Says He's Open to Iran Talks Without Preconditions," *Los Angeles Times,* June 23, 2019.

22. In a meeting two weeks after the 2020 election, the president reportedly asked his advisers for options for military action against Iranian nuclear sites, after reports from the International Atomic Energy Agency that Iran had substantially increased its stockpile of nuclear material. Fearing an attack on Iran's nuclear facilities could easily escalate to major war in the last months of the administration, the vice president, the secretaries of state and defense, and the chair of the Joint Chiefs reportedly persuaded Trump that military action was too risky. Eric Schmitt et al., "Trump Sought Options for Attacking Iran to Stop Its Growing Nuclear Program," *New York Times,* November 16, 2020.

23. Maggie Haberman, "Trump Threatens Iranian Cultural Sites and Warns of Sanctions," *New York Times,* January 7, 2020.

24. Michael Shear, "Trump Shrugs Off Khashoggi Killing by Ally Saudi Arabia, *New York Times,* April 23, 2019.

25. Bergen, *Trump and His Generals,* 222.

26. There was much speculation about the source of the Trump-Putin "bromance." Was it because of Trump's affinity for Putin's strongman, authoritarian leadership or was it because perhaps Putin had derogatory information about Trump's personal or financial improprieties while in Russia? Or was it, as Trump said, simply a wish to maintain good relations with Russia?

27. Julie Hirschfeld Davis, "Trump, at Putin's Side, Questions U.S. Intelligence on 2016 Election," *New York Times,* July 16, 2018.

28. Rebecca Kheel, "Open Skies Withdrawal Throws Nuclear Treaty into Question," *The Hill,* May 25, 2020.

29. An aspect of US-Russian relations that lacked clarity at the end of Trump's term is the reporting by multiple news agencies in June 2020 that Russia offered Taliban fighters bounties to kill US soldiers in Afghanistan. The *New York Times* reported that intelligence about the bounties was included in the president's daily brief in February. However, the national security adviser insisted the president was never briefed, orally or in writing, because the intelligence was "unverified." Trump described the reports of the Russian bounties as fake news and a hoax orchestrated by the media and the Democrats. While White House aides were aware of the intelligence, it was suggested they may have not informed the president because of his aversion to bad news about Russia. Trump indicated he never raised the issue with Putin, while Secretary of State Mike Pompeo said he told his Russian counterpart that there "would be an enormous price to pay if Russia were paying bounties to kill US soldiers." Yet, he declined to say whether he thought the intelligence was credible or if he thought Trump should have been briefed about it. See Charlie Savage et al., "Trump Got Written Briefing in February on Possible Russian Bounties, Officials Say," *New York Times,* June 29, 2020; Natasha Bertrand and Kyle Cheney, "Russia Bounty Flap Highlights Intel Breakdown Under Trump," *Politico,* July 7, 2020; and Reuters, "Pompeo Warned Russia's Lavrov Not to Offer Bounties," *East Bay Times,* August 13, 2020. Shortly after it assumed power, the Biden administration indicated "low to moderate confidence" in the intelligence. See Nick Niedzwiadek, "White House Dials Down Likelihood Russia Offered Bounties," *Politico,* April 15, 2021.

30. The American foreign policy establishment in general was aghast at Trump's attacks on and disruption of the postwar world order created by the United States in alliances and trade, differing only on whether Trump was an aberration or whether the damage was permanent. See Richard Haass, "Present at the Disruption: How Trump Unmade U.S. Foreign Policy," *Foreign Affairs,* September/October 2020, http://www.foreignaffairs.com/articles/united-states/2020-08-11/present-disruption; and Daniel Drezner, "This Time Is Different: Why U.S. Foreign Policy Will Never Recover," *Foreign Affairs,* May/June 2019, http://www.foreignaffairs.com/articles/2019-04-16/time-different.

8

Does Personal
Character Matter?

JAMES DAVID BARBER IGNORED PERSONAL OR MORAL
character, presumably seeing no relationship between personal
morality and presidential character. Perhaps there is not. The case of
John F. Kennedy—Barber's ideal presidential character, the model
active-positive president—suggests there is not. Barber concludes—
and I agree—that Kennedy displayed exemplary presidential character, yet no president with the possible exception of Trump was more
misogynistic than Kennedy, who had what Nigel Hamilton described
as a "deliberately degrading, exploitative attitude toward women."[1]
However, I also agree with Pfiffner that in the presidency, personal,
moral character matters, perhaps not as much as presidential character, but it should not be ignored in a full assessment of the presidency
and character. As Pfiffner writes, "Americans agree that presidential
character is important—just as important as intellect, organizational
ability, television presence, and effectiveness in public speaking. The
values, principles, and habits of behavior that mark an individual will
strongly influence his or her behavior, and the stakes are very high in
the U.S. presidency."[2]

Americans agree, but as Scott Clifford shows, what matters as
character or morality differs on the basis of ideology. While I, following Pfiffner, will analyze the personal and moral character of Trump in
terms of honesty, sexual probity, and promise-keeping, many Americans view morality and character in broader societal terms, such as
equity and fairness or patriotism and adherence to authority. On these

broader conceptions of morality, there are sharp differences. Liberals tend to see morality in presidential character in terms of fairness and concern for those who are economically disadvantaged, while conservatives emphasize religiosity, self-restraint, law and order, and defense of US national interests.[3] Character in presidents and presidential candidates in this sense has relatively little to do with personality, as the individual's morality is determined by her adherence to party ideology. Even an ideological chameleon like Trump, once he decided to seek the nomination of the conservative Republican Party, was compelled to adhere to its moral foundations, even if his personality or character inclined him otherwise. In some cases, if a president's personal morality clashes with the moral foundations of his party's ideology, then there might be oscillations in policies and rhetoric, as appeared to be the case with George H. W. Bush.[4]

By contrast, the personal character of the individual is determined by his psychological foundations rather than by the ideological foundations of his party. Moral character in this sense may be reflective of the individual's worldview, but has little to do with one's style. That is, a person could be an effective president in homework, personal relations, decisionmaking, and rhetoric but lack moral character as measured by honesty and marital fidelity. This appears to be the inference drawn from Barber's classification of Kennedy as of the highest presidential character. Pfiffner notes that Barber's "framework can provide insights into presidents and how they approach office, but it does not try to evaluate them morally in the traditional meaning of good character."[5]

Pfiffner's framework for defining and assessing presidential moral character derives from popular understandings of morality— "the ordinary and common sense way of talking about a person's character."[6] All persons should try to behave ethically or morally, but, Pfiffner contends, persons in leadership have an *additional* duty to act ethically because of their public office. This is especially the case, he avers, for US presidents because they have "exemplary moral duties that relate to the public nature of their behavior: That is, presidents, whether they like it or not, are often seen as role models, especially for children."[7] The presidential duties of moral exemplar relevant to the dimension of presidential moral character are lies, extramarital sex, and promise-keeping.

Telling the truth is a necessary premise in human societies, but for Pfiffner it is especially important in democracies because it is essential to democratic accountability. Thus, "lies of policy deception are the worst kind of presidential lie."[8] While some presidential lies are justified, such as those told to protect diplomatic initiatives or military operations, in general telling the truth is the rule for presidential behavior. Keeping the promises or at least attempting to keep the promises a president makes in the campaign or in public declarations, unless they become clearly imprudent, is also central to democratic governance. Marital fidelity is an important character indicator because "presidents have the same obligations as private individuals not to cause pain in their families,"[9] but in addition as moral exemplars they are bound to respect societal norms. In addition, "the flouting of conventional morality regardless of its personal morality (e.g., permission of spouse) likely will result in public scandal that will undermine the ability of an administration to pursue policies it was elected to pursue."[10]

Regarding lies, Trump is the biggest, most audacious liar ever to serve as president.[11] A *Washington Post* analysis shows that in his first 649 days in office, Trump told more than 6,000 lies, an average of 30 a day.[12] The *Post* study counted only "distinct falsehoods"— excluding misleading statements, mild exaggerations, or statements that could be plausibly defended. Comparing Trump's lies to Obama's (the only other president where a comparable data set is available) is revealing. In his first ten months in office, Trump told 103 separate lies, many of them repeatedly. Obama told 18 lies over his entire eight-year tenure, for an average of about 2 a year for Obama and about 124 for Trump.[13] When Obama was made aware of his untruths, he stopped repeating them. But "Trump is different. When he is caught lying, he will often try to discredit the people telling the truth, be they scientists, FBI, CIA officials or members of Congress. It is extremely dangerous to democracy, and it's not an accident. It's the core of his political strategy."[14]

This pattern of lying by Trump goes back to his first business success when he lied about the number of floors in his hotel and the size of its ballroom. It started when he was in his early thirties and has continued into his mid-seventies. It is a core part of his character.

Trump is an admitted serial adulterer. Indeed, he has sometimes bragged about his infidelities. There are no reports he was unfaithful to his wife while president, but shortly after he was inaugurated, two women—a pornographic movie star and a former *Playboy* model—came forward with allegations they were paid by Trump to remain silent during the 2016 campaign about sexual relations with him. Unlike Pfiffner's concern, however, these and earlier revelations about the president's sexual conduct do not appear to have affected his capacity to govern or his standing with his core constituency. It may be that the conventional norms about marital infidelity Pfiffner refers to have eroded, and Americans draw a sharper line between private and public morality. This distinction would seem to be indicated by the level of support for Bill Clinton after revelations of his sexual misconduct, and retrospectively about Kennedy because in spite of the widespread dissemination of information about Kennedy's behavior, he is still held in high regard by the American public.[15]

Most presidents try to keep their campaign promises most of the time.[16] President Trump made an effort on health insurance, trade, taxes, the border wall, infrastructure, and immigration, although he was fully successful only on the tax cut promise. An analysis of Trump's promise-keeping by the *Washington Post* concluded that Trump had failed to keep 43 percent of "key" promises, kept 35 percent, and compromised on 12 percent.[17] The *Post* does not clearly distinguish efforts from success. Often presidential candidates make promises they cannot keep. This was the case with Trump; a glaring example is the promise Mexico would pay for the border wall.

Finally, I turn to an assessment of Trump's democratic character, or what Dennis Thompson calls constitutional character.[18] Of the three dimensions of character—presidential, personal, and constitutional—the last is the least developed theoretically, and the indicators are least specified. Thompson defines constitutional character as the disposition to act according to the principles of the democratic process.[19] Among the indicators of this disposition are respect for basic civil liberties, tolerance of opposition, willingness to accept responsibility, respect for the integrity of constitutional institutions—the separation of powers, independence of judiciary, the free press, and racial and religious tolerance.[20]

Although the framework and the data for constitutional character are not as systematic as is the case for presidential and personal character, there are bits and pieces of evidence that suggest Trump's constitutional character is not as robust as other modern presidents with the possible exception of Richard Nixon.[21]

Before the 2016 election, Trump showed a cavalier attitude toward perhaps the most important democratic-constitutional value when he repeatedly refused to say he would accept the outcome of the election if he did not win. One might engage in a thought experiment: what would have been Trump's response if the outcome of the election had been reversed and he won the popular vote and lost the electoral college? As discussed in Chapter 10, Trump did not accept the outcome of the 2020 election when he lost; instead, he engaged in months of distortions, obfuscations, and lies.

During the campaign and accelerating during the presidency, Trump repeatedly attacked, denigrated, and mocked the media, popularizing the moniker "fake news." Trump's attacks on the media were not random or ad hoc; they were strategic and systematic. Invoking a phrase associated with Stalin and the German Fascists, Trump labeled the press "enemy of the people," and at one of his rallies he mused about killing reporters, "I would never kill them. But I hate them. And some of them are lying, disgusting people. It's true. But I would never kill them and anybody who does would be despicable."[22] Trump's taunts and threats of the press at his rallies led some news organizations to employ security to protect their workers.

Again, the nature of the attacks was strategic. When asked by CBS *60 Minutes* correspondent Lesley Stahl why he continued to attack the media, in an off-camera response he said, "You know why I do it. I do it to discredit you all and demean you all, so when you write negative stories about me, no one will believe you."[23]

During the campaign and the presidency, Trump attacked judges who rendered decisions adverse to him; attacked his attorneys general because they refused to pursue investigations of his political adversaries; attacked the head of the independent Federal Reserve; insulted and mocked Democratic congressional leaders; abused the plenary pardon power to reward friends, family, and political associates; and, as discussed below, fired five inspectors general (IGs) because of their investigations and reporting to Congress on misconduct in the administration. And, as discussed in Chapter 6, on more than one occasion he declared the Constitution gave him "total power."

The House of Representatives in 2019 impeached the president for abuse of power, charging he withheld appropriated and legally obligated foreign aid to Ukraine in order to coerce its president to announce an investigation of former vice president Joseph Biden, at that point the likely 2020 Democratic opponent. Although the Senate acquitted the president, the transcript of the phone conversation indicated clearly the president asked the Ukraine leader for the "favor" of announcing a Biden investigation, and the aid was released only after the phone conversation became known. The day after acquittal, Trump expressed no regret for his behavior, attacked the legitimacy of the impeachment, and engaged in a vindictive and vulgar attack on the Speaker of the House.[24]

Whether Trump's solicitation of an investigation of his political opponent by Ukraine's president constituted a high crime meriting impeachment is perhaps debatable. It is also debatable whether it was prudent to impeach the president, knowing he would be acquitted in the Senate on a partisan vote. What is not debatable is that the president did direct the Office of Management and Budget and the Department of Defense to withhold the aid to Ukraine, and that he saw nothing wrong with his actions. Indeed, he described the July 25, 2019, phone conversation in which he asked for the favor as a "perfect" call. This transactional view of relationships with a foreign power is consistent with the president's worldview, the art of the deal he celebrated in his book, and with the way he conducted his business. It is also consistent with his view that Article II gives him "the right to do whatever I want as President."

In addition, the president showed contempt for the House's impeachment authority by summarily refusing to turn over documents or allow his aides to testify in response to subpoenas. The House made this defiance the second article of impeachment. Throughout the process he never expressed regret for even the appearance of impropriety in his behavior. Instead, his response was to hit back and hit back hard at those conducting the impeachment inquiry, those administration officials—mainly career diplomats and military officers—who defied his wishes and testified against him. After the acquittal, he dismissed those officials from the White House or their diplomatic posts.

The president also engaged in an unprecedented assault on the independence of the offices of the inspectors general. Congress in the aftermath of Watergate created IGs in each of the agencies and departments of government to investigate and report to it on misconduct. When Reagan was elected, he fired all of the IGs appointed by Carter. After bipartisan disapproval he rehired most of them and an informal understanding developed that IGs would not be replaced when a new president took office.[25] In his eight years Obama removed one IG and in his two terms George W. Bush removed two (there are seventy-five). Trump dismissed five during his tenure, beginning with the National Intelligence IG that first alerted Congress to the Ukraine phone call.[26] Subsequently, he dismissed IGs in Health and Human Services, and the State and Defense Departments. Each at the time of their firing had investigated or were investigating misconduct in the administration.[27]

In dismissing the IGs, Trump not only ignored the tradition of independence but specific requirements in the law requiring an explanation and a thirty-day waiting period. The intent of the dismissals was punitive, and the likely effect was to send a message to the dozens of IGs that the administration would not tolerate efforts within the bureaucracy to hold it accountable. The specific attacks on the IGs were part of a larger pattern of attacking the bureaucracy and career civil servants in the foreign policy, intelligence, health, science, and law enforcement agencies in an attempt to undermine their responsibilities to provide expert, nonpartisan decisions and information to the administration and Congress. Occasionally the president invoked the right-wing canard about the "deep state" deliberately attempting to sabotage his administration. As discussed earlier, there is a tendency for Republican presidents to clash with the bureaucracy, especially on the environment and civil rights, but in its scope Trump's clashes were unprecedented.

On several occasions the president displayed racial intolerance, most notably in the Charlottesville incident. Overall, President Trump failed to conform his conduct to the dignity, propriety, and sense of legitimacy the Constitution and democratic values require of a president who serves as head of state and role model, especially for children. There are reports that his bullying, inflammatory, often racially tinged language seeped into American classrooms, changing the way children are bullied.[28]

In the American Political Science Association's 2018 study ranking the presidents, all respondents including conservative and Republican political scientists gave President Trump the grade of F for adherence to "institutional norms."[29] Trump's routine violation of institutional norms in his rhetoric and behavior has impacted public attitudes; not surprisingly, however, those attitudes are polarized. The 2019 Public Religion Research Institute (PRRI) poll found 73 percent of Americans said they wished Trump's "speech and behavior" were more consistent with past presidents. But less than half (46 percent) of Republicans agreed compared to 88 percent of Democrats and 74 percent of independents.[30] Similarly, 65 percent of Americans said Trump had damaged the dignity of the presidency; 92 percent of Democrats, 72 percent of independents, but only 24 percent of Republicans agreed.[31]

In early summer 2020, Trump tweeted that the election scheduled for November 3 should be postponed, because he said there was a high likelihood of fraud in states using mail-in ballots. The Republican leadership in both houses of Congress swiftly rejected the idea, saying the election could be conducted fairly as scheduled.[32]

Article I, Section 4, and Article II, Section I, confer on Congress the authority to determine the day of election of members of Congress and presidential electors. Never in the history of the republic has a scheduled presidential election been delayed. During the Civil War President Lincoln, although he thought he might lose the 1864 election, did not broach the idea of delaying the election. President Trump's call for an election delay was an unprecedented and extraordinary breach of American democratic and constitutional norms.

At the time of the tweet, Trump was behind in the polls, and after his idea of an election delay was almost universally dismissed, he began to attempt to systematically undermine the results of the election by claiming that mail balloting would inevitably result in fraud. There was no evidence that mail balloting could not be done honestly. When Christopher Wray, the FBI director, told Congress his agency had no evidence "historically" of any coordinated election fraud whether by mail or otherwise, the White House chief of staff mocked the director: "With all due respect to Director Wray, he has a hard time finding emails in his own FBI."[33]

Beginning in late September until election day, Trump attacked the integrity of the election, and in another extraordinary display of deficits in democratic and constitutional character he refused to commit to a peaceful transfer of power if he lost, saying at a debate with Biden and at press conferences, "we're going to have to see what happens. You know that I have been complaining very strongly about the ballots and the ballots are a disaster."[34]

At the beginning of October, Trump begin to publicly pressure the attorney general to give his campaign an "October Surprise" by indicting Vice President Biden and President Obama for "spying" on his 2016 campaign, contending that the FBI's investigation of his campaign's possible collusion with the Russians was a ruse by Biden and Obama to spy on his campaign. The contention was without merit, as demonstrated by the special counsel's investigation,[35] but nevertheless Trump publicly pressured the attorney general to indict his political rivals, saying "unless Bill Barr indicts these people for their crimes, the greatest crimes in the history of our country, then, we are going to get little political satisfaction unless I win, and he'll just have to go, because I won't forget it."[36] Trump did not win, and as promised he refused to accept defeat, precipitating, as discussed in Chapter 10, the most disorderly transfer of power in the republic's history.

Trump violated multiple norms of the modern democratic, constitutional order. Although the data are not as systematic or robust as one might wish, it is sufficient enough that in terms of constitutional character, like presidential character, he is a most unusual president.

Trump's composite character—presidential, personal, and constitutional—is unique, a product of his personality, background, and business experience. Hopefully, we will not see another character like him for a long time, if ever. However, his ideology—a somewhat opportunistic mix of traditional and paleoconservatism—coupled with demagoguery may be replicable. Are Trump's White nationalist and paleoconservative politics the wave of the Republican future? Or are they aberrations that pass as he passes? If Trump becomes Trumpism and the dominant or even a major faction in the Republican Party, how long can it remain competitive? What will be the impact on the party system? On polarization? On American democracy? These are questions I take up in the concluding chapter. But, first, I return to the question of how Trump became president.

Notes

1. Nigel Hamilton, *JFK: Reckless Youth* (New York: Random House, 1993), 28. Kennedy was a serial adulterer, but one of the more egregious examples of his abuse of women is his coercing a young White House intern into performing oral sex for one of his aides at the White House swimming pool. Kennedy's sexual misconduct, among other ethical lapses, are discussed in multiple books on Kennedy, but the most comprehensive is Thomas Reeves, *A Question of Character: A Life of John F. Kennedy* (New York: Free Press, 1991).

2. James Pfiffner, "Judging Presidential Character," *Public Integrity* 5 (2002): 7. See also his *The Character Factor: How We Judge American Presidents* (College Station: Texas A & M University Press, 2004).

3. Scott Clifford, "Reassessing the Structure of Presidential Character," *Electoral Studies* 54 (2018): 240–247. See also Jesse Graham et al., "Liberals and Conservatives Rely on Different Sets of Moral Foundations," *Journal of Personality and Psychology* 16 (2009): 1029–1046; and Steven Green, "The Role of Character Assessments in Presidential Approval," *American Politics* 29 (2001): 196–210.

4. Throughout his political career Bush struggled with his personal moderate, preppy, patrician, Connecticut Yankee personality and background and his need to try to accommodate the Republican Party's conservative

moral foundations. See Herbert Parmet, *George Bush: The Life of a Lone Star Yankee* (New York: Lisa Drew/Scribner, 1997).

5. Pfiffner, "Judging Presidential Character," 9.

6. Ibid., 10.

7. Ibid., 12.

8. Ibid.

9. Ibid., 14.

10. Ibid.

11. Glenn Kessler, Salvador Rizzo, and Meg Kelly, "President Trump Has Made 6,420 False or Misleading Claims Over 649 Days," *Washington Post,* November 2, 2018; Bess Levin, "Report: Trump Has Told More Than 10,000 Lies, Since Being Inaugurated," *Vanity Fair,* April 29, 2019; Kessler, Rizzo, and Kelly, *Donald Trump and His Assault on Truth* (New York: Scribner, 2020); and Kessler, "Trump Made 30,573 False or Misleading Claims as President, Nearly Half in His Final Year," *Washington Post,* January 23, 2021. James David Barber writing in 1982 suggested that Ronald Reagan often said things that were not true, but he was not a liar, rather he "literally did not know what he was talking about." Barber concluded this too was a danger to democratic deliberation and governance, and argues the problem was that Reagan was "the first modern president where contempt for facts was treated as a charming idiosyncrasy." See "The Oval Office Aesop," *New York Times,* November 11, 1982.

12. Kessler, Rizzo, and Kelly, "President Trump Has Made More Than 6,420 False."

13. Ibid.

14. Ibid. Just as many of Trump's base supporters became less concerned about the personal morality of political leaders after Trump's emergence, they also became less concerned about presidential dishonesty. Kessler and his colleagues report that in a 2007 poll 71 percent of Republicans and 70 percent of Democrats considered it "extremely important" for presidential candidates to be honest. In 2018 the figure for Democrats had not changed but for Republicans declined to 47 percent. See Kessler, Rizza, and Kelly, *Donald Trump and His Assault on Truth,* 179.

15. George Edwards, *Presidential Approval: A Sourcebook* (Baltimore, MD: Johns Hopkins University Press, 1991), 161.

16. Jeff Fishel, *Presidents and Promises* (Washington, DC: Congressional Quarterly Press, 1985).

17. Glenn Kessler, "Trump Has Broken More Promises Than He Has Kept," *Washington Post,* November 17, 2020.

18. Dennis Thompson, "Constitutional Character: Virtues and Vices in Presidential Leadership," *Presidential Studies Quarterly* 40 (2010): 23–37.

19. Ibid., 23.

20. Ibid., 24–26.

21. Historian Melvin Smalls writes, "Watergate did not begin when CREEP operatives broke into Democratic headquarters in 1971. It began when Nixon took office armed with his private slush fund, prepared to do battle by means fair and foul against his enemies. No President before or after ordered or participated in so many serious illegal and extralegal acts that violated constitutional principles." *The Presidency of Richard Nixon* (Lawrence: Univer-

sity Press of Kansas, 1999), 309. Useful for details of those acts are Bob Woodward and Carl Bernstein, *All the President's Men* (New York: Simon & Schuster, 1974) and *The Final Days* (New York: Simon & Schuster, 1976).

22. Jonathan Karl, *Front Row at the Trump Show* (New York: Dutton, 2020), 39–40.

23. Lesley Stahl, "Trump Admitted Mission to Discredit Press," May 23, 2018, http://www.cbsnews.com/news/lesley-stahl-donald-trump-said-attack ing-press-to-discredit-negative-stories/. It should be noted that attacks on the media have been a staple of the conservative movement since the Goldwater campaign and was employed in the Nixon administration in a series of speeches (many written by Patrick Buchanan) by Vice President Spiro Agnew. See Jonathan Ladd, *Why Americans Hate the Media and How It Matters* (Princeton: Princeton University Press, 2011), 74, 78. Trump's attacks, however, were more routine, systematic, and incendiary and were an integral part of his strategy of campaigning and governing.

24. Eli Stokols, "From Vindictive to Vulgar: Trump Lets Loose After Impeachment Acquittal," *Los Angeles Times,* February 6, 2020.

25. David Sanger and Charlie Savage, "Flouting Norms, Trump Seeks to Bring Independent Watchdogs to Heel," *New York Times,* May 23, 2020.

26. Ibid.

27. Joe Davidson, "Trump Allergic to Independent Oversight," *Washington Post,* May 23, 2020.

28. Hannah Natanson, John Woodrow Cox, and Perry Stein, "Trump's Words, Bullied Kids, Scared Schools," *Washington Post,* February 13, 2020.

29. Brandon Rottingham and Justin Vaughn, "Official Results of the 2018 Presidential Greatness Survey" (Washington: American Political Science Association, 2018). See also James Pfiffner, "Donald Trump and the Norms of the Presidency," *Presidential Studies Quarterly* 51 (2021): 96–124.

30. PRRI, *Fractured Nation: Widening Party Polarization and Key Issues in 2020 Election* (Washington, DC: Public Religion Research Institute, 2020), 23.

31. Ibid.

32. Steve Peoples, "Trump Faces Rare Rebuke from GOP for Floating Election Delay," *Washington Post,* July 30, 2020; and David Sanger, "Debate Made Clear the Greatest Threat to the Election: The President Himself," *New York Times,* October 1, 2020. At a debate with Biden, Trump repeated his claims about fraud in mail balloting, and under repeated questioning said he could not guarantee a peaceful transfer of power if he lost.

33. Sanger, "Debate Made Clear." Reportedly, the president wanted to fire Wray and his deputy and replace them with persons he viewed as more loyal to him, but demurred when Attorney General William Barr threatened to resign. See Daniel Lippman, "Inside Trump's Push to Oust His Own FBI Chief," *Politico,* May 20, 2021.

34. Associated Press, "Trump Won't Commit to Peaceful Transfer of Power If He Loses," *East Bay Times,* October 24, 2020.

35. Rosalind Helderman and Matt Zapotosky, *The Mueller Report* (New York: Scribner, 2019).

36. Peter Baker and Maggie Haberman, "Trump Lashes Out at His Cabinet with Calls to Indict Political Rivals," *New York Times.* October 10, 2020.

9

How Did Trump
Become President?

SO, WHAT HAPPENED? HOW AND WHY DID THE OLDEST
and most powerful democracy in the world elect to its highest office
a man with multiple character deficits, manifest deficits that clearly
rendered him unfit intellectually, morally, and temperamentally for
the world's most powerful office? A man his Republican opponents
in 2016 labeled a "kook," a "fraud," a "con man," and "utterly
immoral and a pathological liar." The first answer is that the people
of the United States did not do it. The electoral college did it. More
Americans in 2016, despite Trump's fraudulent claims to the contrary, voted for Hillary Clinton than Donald Trump.

Article II and Amendment 12 of the Constitution in pertinent
parts dictate that each state in such a manner as its legislature may
determine shall appoint a number of electors equal to its representation in Congress, and those electors shall choose the president and
vice president. The citizens of the United States do not have the constitutional right to vote for president or the electors. It is a privilege
granted by the fifty state legislatures to vote for the electors, revoca-
ble at any time by any or all of them.

The origins of this undemocratic procedure are partly rooted in
race. To understand this, one starts with the most infamous of the
racist provisions of the Constitution, Article I, Section 2, Clause 3,
which designates the enslaved Africans as three-fifths of a person for
purposes of per capita taxation and allocation of seats in the US
House of Representatives. Without this provision, it is possible the

framers of the Constitution would have required direct election of the president by the citizens.

At the convention to write the Constitution, the drafters initially considered election by the Congress or the people. Election by the Congress was rejected because it violated the principles of the separation of powers and an autonomous executive. Election by the people was rejected not because of any pervasive antidemocratic sentiments but because, given the communications and transportation systems of the time, it was thought the people might not have the information necessary to make an informed choice. Nevertheless, election by the people might have prevailed if it was not recognized that it would disadvantage the slaveholding states. Wishing to accommodate the slave interests and maintain the support of the southern states for the new constitution, the electoral college became another of the convention's great compromises. Basing the choice in the electoral college gave southern slaveholders a bonus in "representation for their human property."[1] Although the historical record is ambiguous, Donald Robinson concludes, "The disenfranchisement of slaves was, in fact, the decisive consideration against the direct popular election of the president."[2]

It is this flawed, racist compromise of 1787, not the citizens of the United States in 2016, that begins to explain how and why Trump was elected. Trump's undemocratic election in 2016 was not unprecedented. Four times before—in the elections of 1828, 1877, 1888, and 2000—the choice of the people did not become president. The last two instances of a loser becoming the winner occurred in less than twenty years and both involved Republican candidates, suggesting that the electoral college may be becoming a structural advantage for the Republican Party. (A change of less than 100,000 votes in Wisconsin, Arizona, and Georgia in 2020 and Trump would have won an electoral college majority, despite Biden's near 7 million popular majority.) Estimates of the demographic and generational shifts in the electorate project Democratic popular victories through 2036. But, given the demography of different groups across the states, there are quite a few scenarios of Democratic popular victories but Republican wins in the electoral college.[3]

Yet, the electoral college is only part of the answer to how and why Trump won. While Clinton won the plurality of the popular vote in 2016, Trump won a majority of the White electorate. So, the question becomes why did a majority of Whites of virtually all demographic categories—men and women, young and old, middle class and working class, North and South, rural and suburban—vote for a man of Trump's character? The answer to this question in a word is race, which is not to suggest that Trump's voters did not support him for other reasons, such as his anti-establishment rhetoric, his championing of their religious values, his business background, or simply because of his personality. Rather, it is proposed, as much of the research suggests, that race was the focal point or pivot of his election.

In Chapter 2, discussing ideology in the mass public, I noted that since Phillip Converse's seminal work in the 1960s, studies have shown that opinions about African Americans have been the central organizing constraint in the White public's thinking about politics in America. When President Johnson signed the Civil Rights Act of 1964, he told his aide Bill Moyers, "I think we just delivered the South to the Republican Party for a long time."[4] The president was only partly correct; he should have said we have just delivered the majority of White voters to the Republicans for a long time. Not since Johnson's landslide election in 1964 has a majority of Whites voted for the Democratic candidate for president. This is mainly because since 1964 every Democratic nominee has embraced racial liberalism, more or less, and every Republican nominee, more or less, has embraced racial conservatism, racial resentment, or White nationalism.[5] A majority of Whites embraced FDR's economic liberalism and the welfare state from the 1930s until the 1960s. Then in the 1960s when the Democrats embraced racial liberalism, a majority of Whites abandoned the Democratic Party and the liberal label, and they have never returned.[6]

The conclusions have different implications, depending on whether Trump was reelected or defeated in 2020 and by what margin. If he had been defeated in a landslide, there would have been cause for optimism about democracy in America; the minority of voters who supported him in 2016 recognized their mistake and corrected it at the first opportunity. If he had won in a landslide, of course, the opposite would have been the case. If he had won narrowly as he did before with victory only in the electoral college, the despair would have been more toward the antiquated electoral system, rather than democracy itself.

Trump was narrowly defeated. Biden won approximately 81 million votes (51.3 percent), twenty-five states and the District of Columbia, and 306 electoral votes; Trump won about 74 million votes, twenty-five states, and 232 electoral votes. Meanwhile the Republicans gained seats in both houses of Congress and in state legislatures across the country. In this light, Trump's defeat might be viewed as a repudiation of him rather than his party or his version of conservatism, and rather than ratification of Biden and his version of liberalism. Conversely, Trump substantially increased his voter support in 2020, 74 million compared to 63 million in 2016. He also, according to the exit polls, modestly expanded his support among Blacks (from 8 to 12 percent), among Latinos (28 to 32 percent), and among Asian Americans (27 to 31 percent), while losing a bit of support from White evangelicals, down from 80 percent in 2016 to 76 in 2020.[7] Nevertheless, in 2020 as in 2016 Trump's coalition was constituted by the nation's White Christian majority of all demographic categories. Exit polls in 2020 indicate Biden received majority support from two categories of Whites—those in union households and those with a postgraduate education.

A majority of White Christian Americans have voted for the Republican presidential candidate since 1968, and this did not cause alarm or despair among students of democracy in America as is the case with Trump. This is so because those candidates— Nixon, Ford, Reagan, Dole, the Bushes, McCain, Romney—did not display the multiple character deficits of Trump. But this democratic despair should not, perhaps, be directed at the voting behavior of the White majority. First, many in that majority likely had reservations about Trump's character but saw him as an effective tribune, more so than his opponents, advancing their values and interests as an aggrieved declining majority. Second, in the 1960s and 1970s political science contended that democratic values were secured from the threat of a Trump-like character not by the voting behavior of the public but by the commitment to democratic norms of the elites, which came to be known as the elitist theory of democracy. The fallacy of this theory is another explanation of what happened.

The theory contended that democratic norms and values were safeguarded by party elites rather than the people, because many citizens were not supportive of those norms and values while the elites were. In this theory the elites of the Republican Party would have blocked the nomination of a candidate with Trump's character. This *may* have occurred in 2016 if elites had controlled the nomination process. They did not. Republican voters decided on Trump against the will of the party establishment. The theory then predicts that a significant number of Republican elites—senators, representatives, governors—would have joined in a bipartisan coalition to oppose Trump, as was the case with the nomination of Goldwater in 1964. The ideologically cohesive nature of the two parties, and the high degree of partisan polarization, however, made this unlikely in 2016.

But while party solidarity and polarization may partly account for the events of 2016, we now recognize the elitist theory was flawed from the start.[8] The theory is based empirically on large samples of elites and the public.[9] Both samples were asked to respond to statements about democratic norms and values, such as: I don't mind a politician's methods if he manages to get things done; to bring about great changes for the benefit of mankind often requires cruelty and ruthlessness; regardless of what some people say, there are certain races in the world that just won't mix with Americans. On the basis of their responses, it was concluded, "The evidence suggests that it is the articulate classes rather than the public who serve as the major repositories of the public conscience and carries the [democratic] creed. Responsibility for keeping the system going, falls heavily upon them."[10] And on perhaps a too optimistic note, Herbert McClosky suggested increased education, urbanization, the growth of the middle class, and the incorporation of immigrant and minority groups would "likely to beget a more articulate population and a more numerous class of political influentials committed to liberal democracy and aware of the rights and obligations attendant to this commitment."[11]

There were a number of flaws in this notion of elite commitment to democratic values. The most glaring—the elephant in the room these political scientists could not see—was these supposed democratic elitists were presiding over or acquiescing to one of the most illiberal regimes in the world—the southern racial caste system of the 1950s in which African Americans were denied the most basic democratic right, the vote.[12] As the historian Arthur Schlesinger Jr. would write of this phenomenon, "Historians of the twenty-first century will no doubt struggle to explain how nine tenths of the American people, priding themselves every day on their kindness, their generosity, their historic consideration of the rights of man, could so long have connived in the systematic dehumanization of the remaining tenth—and could have done so without just a second thought but hardly a first thought. The answer to this mystery lay in the belief, welling up from the depths of the white unconscious, in the inherent and necessary inferiority of those of darker color."[13]

Another basic flaw in the theory, identified decades later by Paul Sniderman and his colleagues in their replication of the studies, is the theory compared elites with the public rather than elites with elites. Once liberal and conservative elites are compared, it is clear "conservative elites—notwithstanding their greater involvement in politics—are consistently and markedly less committed to basic rights than other citizens whose political outlook happens to be liberal."[14]

But even if the theory of democratic elitism was not flawed methodologically, it still may not be helpful in explaining the failure of conservatives to return to democratic norms when they were assaulted by Trump during the 2016 campaign and during his presidency. In a prescient observation that is worth quoting in full, McClosky wrote:

> While disagreements among Americans on fundamental values have tended to be passive, and owing to apathy and the relative placidity of our politics, easily tolerated, while they do not follow party lines and are rarely insinuated into political struggle; and while no extremist movement has yet grown enough to challenge effectively the governing principles of the American Constitution, this happy state of affairs is not permanently guaranteed. Fundamental differences could become activated by political and economic crises, party differences could develop around fundamental constitutional questions . . . and powerful extremist movements are too familiar phenomenon of political life to take for granted their eternal absence from American politics.[15]

The relative placidity of 1950s US politics has been replaced by rancorous, polarized politics, and extremist leaders and movements that challenge constitutional and democratic norms have emerged. This in part explains why conservative elites were so obsequious in relation to Trump.

There were substantial, robust criticisms of Trump during the 2016 Republican primaries by his opponents and Mitt Romney, the 2012 nominee, as well as the conservative media. Once he was elected, the criticism virtually disappeared among conservative elites. Alas, his harshest critics during the primaries—Senators Ted Cruz and Lindsey Graham—became his most ardent defenders. Even as he departed from conservative orthodoxy, Republican legislators and activists remained silent. It seemed his trampling on the norms of presidential behavior provoked no more than passing, muted criticisms. From the beginning of his presidency until its end, Trump maintained the overwhelming support and loyalty of Republican base voters, many of whom told pollsters they believed there was nothing the president could do wrong. This base support gave Trump near total control over the party and elicited fear of his rhetorical wrath, which Republican officeholders worried could jeopardize their careers.

Dave Trott, a two-term congressman from Michigan, experienced Trump's scorn after he criticized the president's erratic approach to health insurance reform in a private meeting with colleagues. Believing it was untenable to seek reelection as an anti-Trump Republican, he decided not to run.[16] Tennessee senator Bob Corker and Arizona senator Jeff Flake, occasional critics of Trump, made similar decisions. After his decision, in an interview Trott said, "Trump is emotionally and intellectually unfit for office, and I'm sure a lot of Republicans feel the same way. But if they say that, the social media barrage will be overwhelming."[17] Anonymous interviews with some of Trott's colleagues confirmed his feelings about their concerns about Trump and their fear of retaliation if they were made public.[18]

In addition to fear of Trump's wrath if they rebuked him, many Republican officeholders likely were not bothered by Trump's norm-shattering behavior, while others, perhaps concerned, came to believe their destiny and the destiny of the party were linked to Trump. Thus, to criticize Trump would damage the party and the conservative cause.

Whatever the explanations for Republican elites bowing to Trump, it is clear that the assumptions of the classic elitist theory of democracy, that conservative elites would uphold democratic values in opposition to a popular demagogue, are fallacious. In a highly polarized, evenly divided polity, perhaps no elites, liberal or conservative, would restore democratic values.[19] Yet, it is striking that even after Trump refused to accept the outcome of the 2020 election and engaged in patterns of behavior that resulted in the most violent transfer of power in the nation's history, Republican leaders refused to uphold this most basic of constitutional and democratic values. Trump's, the Republican Party's, and the political system's response to the 2020 election are the subjects of the next chapter.

Notes

1. Donald Robinson, "The Constitutional Legacy of Slavery," *National Political Science Review* 4 (1994): 11. See also his book-length study, *Slavery in the Structure of American Politics, 1765–1820* (New York: Harcourt Brace Jovanovich, 1970).

2. Donald Robinson, *To the Best of My Ability: The President and the Constitution*(New York: Norton, 1987), 82. The electoral college provides a modest bonus to the smaller population states, based on their two senators. But this is insignificant when compared to the three-fifths clause. The percentage of additional votes going to the slave states as a result of that clause ranged from a low of 8 percent in 1872 to a high of 19 in most elections between 1788 and 1860, with a mean for the period of 17 percent. See Hanes Walton Jr., Robert C. Smith, and Sherri Wallace, *American Politics and the African American Quest for Universal Freedom,* 8th ed. (New York: Routledge, 2021), 15.

3. Rob Griffin, William Frey, and Ruy Teixeira, "America's Electoral Future: Demographic Shifts and the Future of the Trump Coalition" (Washington: Center for American Progress, 2020). There is little likelihood the Constitution will be amended abolishing the electoral college in favor of popular election of the president. In 1969 the House passed by the necessary two-thirds vote (369–70) an amendment establishing popular elections, but it failed in the Senate. Given the polarized state of American politics and the structural advantage of the college to Republicans, it is not likely the amendment could pass even the House any time soon. For an overview of the thoroughly undemocratic character of the electoral college and a systematic rebuttal of the arguments of those who would retain it, see George Edwards, *Why the Electoral College Is Bad for America* (New Haven: Yale University Press, 2004).

4. Randall Wood, *LBJ: Architect of American Ambition* (New York: Free Press, 2006), 480.

5. Edward Carmines and James Stimson, *Issue Evolution: Race and the Transformation of American Politics* (Princeton: Princeton University Press, 1989); Tali Mendelberg, *The Race Card: Campaign Strategy, Implicit Messages, and the Norm of Equality* (Princeton: Princeton University Press, 2001); Robert C. Smith, *Conservatism and Racism and Why in America They Are the Same* (Albany: SUNY Press, 2010); and Nathan Angelo, *One America? Presidential Appeals to Racial Resentment from LBJ to Trump* (Albany: SUNY Press, 2020).

6. K. Elisabeth Coggins and James Stimson, "Understanding the Decline of Liberal Self-Identification in America," manuscript, Department of Political Science, University of North Carolina, Chapel Hill, 2008. See also Eric Schickler, *Racial Realignment: The Transformation of American Liberalism, 1932–1965* (Princeton: Princeton University Press, 2016).

7. CNN Exit Polls, 2016, www.cnn.com/election/results/exit-polls /national/president. CNN Exit Polls, 2020, https://www.cnn.com/election /2020/exit-polls/president/national-results. The exit poll information should be read and interpreted with caution (especially the 2020 election when so

many ballots were cast by mail), understood as rough estimates rather than entirely valid and reliable statistical data.

8. The seminal studies are James Prothro and Charles Grigg, "Fundamental Principles of Democracy: Bases of Agreement and Disagreement," *Journal of Politics* 22 (1960): 276–294; and Herbert McClosky, "Consensus and Ideology in American Politics," *American Political Science Review* 58 (1964): 361–382. See also V. O. Key, "Public Opinion and the Decay of Democracy," *Virginia Quarterly* 22 (1960): 276–294.

9. McClosky's elite sample was constituted by "political actives"—delegates who attended the major party conventions in 1956—and a national sample of 1,500 persons.

10. Ibid., 374.

11. Ibid., 379.

12. Robert Mickey, *Paths out of Dixie: The Democratization of Authoritarian Enclaves in America's Deep South, 1944–1972* (Princeton: Princeton University Press, 2015).

13. Arthur M. Schlesinger Jr., *A Thousand Days: John F. Kennedy in the White House* (Boston: Houghton Mifflin, 1965), 929.

14. Paul Sniderman et al., "The Fallacy of Democratic Elitism: Elite Competition and Commitment to Civil Liberties," *British Journal of Political Science* 21 (1991): 365.

15. McClosky, "Consensus and Ideology in American Politics," 379.

16. Jonathan Martin and Maggie Haberman, "Fear and Fealty: Trump Has Taken Control of the Republican Party with an Iron Grip and Threat of Retaliation," *New York Times,* December 21, 2019.

17. Ibid.

18. Ibid. See also Associated Press, "GOP Sends Message, Trump's Behavior Is OK," *East Bay Times*, February 2, 2020.

19. Some conservative writers and commentators did challenge Trump's assault on democratic norms, most notably the political-scientist-turned-columnist George Will. But many did not, for example Rich Lowery, editor of *National Review.* During the 2016 campaign, Lowery was an early "Never Trump" intellectual, assembling in *National Review* twenty conservative intellectuals to make the case against Trump's nomination. But in the 2019 book *The Case for Nationalism: How It Made Us Powerful, United and Rich* (New York: Broadside Books, 2019), he urges the Republican Party to incorporate nationalist policies on trade and immigration into its ideology. The Lincoln Project, the small group of former Republican operatives opposed to Trump, gained some media attention but exerted little influence within the Republican establishment or on the party base. For a kind of manifesto of the Lincoln Project, see Charlie Sykes, *How the Right Lost Its Mind* (New York: St. Martin's Press, 2017).

10

Democratic Character and the 2020 Election

THIS INQUIRY INTO THE CHARACTER OF PRESIDENT DON-
ald Trump confirms the consensus view of political science scholars of the presidency, and likely the discipline as a whole, that
Trump's presidency is a unique and disturbing development in the
history of democracy in America.[1] What I have done in this book
is document theoretically and empirically what is obvious not just
to the community of presidency scholars and political scientists but
in all likelihood to a majority of the American people. In this chapter, an overview and summary of the findings are presented, and
then an analysis of how Trump's deficits in personal and democratic character determined or shaped his response to his defeat in
2020 election.

In carefully pursuing objectivity in this study, I adopted Barber's theory of presidential character because I thought it would be
useful theoretically and empirically in disciplining the collection of
data, analysis, and interpretation. The theory draws attention to how
Trump's first business success predicts his performance as president
in terms of style, and how his worldview, apparently developed in
adolescence, shaped his decisionmaking as president. The remarkable
consistency in Trump's style, particularly decisionmaking and rhetoric, from when he was a young thirty-something businessman and
forty years later as president are indicative both of the usefulness of
Barber's theory, and something fundamental about Trump's personality and character.

Presidential Character

Presidential character, as Barber theorizes it, has to do with the capacity of the individual to do the work of the office. In a nutshell, it involves the organizing of a competent White House staff, and a disciplined decisionmaking process in which information from all pertinent sources is considered. This requires effective, discerning use of the knowledge lodged in the bureaucracy and sometimes even from persons outside the government. However, the president cannot rely wholly on his staff and others for advice to do the job effectively; he must also do his homework, taking time, as Barber writes, "to read, write and calculate by himself,"[2] recognizing that the ultimate decision is often his alone.[3]

In addition, the modern president must "go public"—use rhetoric from time to time to advance his policies, shape public opinion, and persuade the media, Congress, and other parts of the Washington community, understanding the difference in the White House between the rhetoric of campaigning and governing. Effective presidential rhetoric requires he be disciplined and careful in his language; emotions are sometimes necessary in presidential rhetoric, but in general it should be rational and civil in order to inform and elevate the public discourse.

Furthermore, presidential character requires understanding and accommodating the climate of expectations in the Washington community, and appreciating the constraints on the exercise of power in the system of separated powers. This means that the president must maintain reasonably good personal relations even with adversaries in the Washington community, especially the bipartisan leadership of Congress. Finally, presidential character requires the individual to be cognizant that the president is head of state as well as government and must behave with the dignity and decorum that role requires. As Barber puts it, "The President is expected to personify our betterness in an inspiring way, to express in what he does and is (not just what he says) a moral idealism which in much of the public mind, is the very opposite of politics."[4]

In all of these dimensions of the presidential character, President Trump was a failure. And the absence of presidential character affected his capacity to get things done. It is *possible* that if he had possessed more of the essentials of presidential character, in his first two years, with Republican majorities in both houses of Congress, he might have negotiated a repeal and replacement of Obamacare, funding for the border wall, and perhaps some kind of infrastructure program. In these cases, character counted; Trump was the indispensable actor. And all of this was predictable, Barber teaches, on the basis of Trump's past—of his first business success where his worldview, decisionmaking, and rhetorical styles were on full display in his leadership of the Trump Organization with its multiple failures and bankruptcies.

Trump's absence of presidential character affected his capacity to govern. His absence of personal and constitutional, or democratic, character degraded the American democracy.

Personal Character

Of the first element of personal character—lying—Trump's behavior is unprecedented in the history of the office. This pattern of lying may also be traced to Trump's first business success, when he lied about the height of a building, recurred on the first day of his presidency when he lied about the size of the inaugural crowd, and continued through his last days in office. His lying was compulsive, perhaps pathological. Jonathan Karl, the ABC White House correspondent, writes, "Donald Trump lies for comic effect, he lies to make himself feel good, he lies because he likes to, because he can. . . . Trump has no problem lying if the lies sound better."[5] Susan Hennessey and Benjamin Wittes observe that "Trump lies about policy, about ethics matters, about his enemies and opponents and about his personal behavior. He lies routinely about his prior lies. Trump's lies are so pervasive, so inherent in his presidency, that it is impossible to imagine his presidency without them. He is the first president in American history whose public statements cannot be granted any kind of presumption of factual accuracy."[6]

Trump's long pattern of lying suggests a deep character deficit, a moral deficit. As the great Howard University theologian Howard Thurman argues, "The penalty of deception is to become deception, with all sense of moral discrimination vitiated. A man who lies habitually becomes a lie, and it is increasingly impossible for him to know when he is lying and when he is not."[7] If honesty between political leaders and citizens is an important currency in democracies, then Trump has done more to damage it than any of his predecessors.[8] If the hypothesis is that Trump's lying is part of his psychological makeup, then one might assume it is not likely to be easily replicated in subsequent presidents. Yet, lying on the scale of Trump and its tolerance by near half the people could be precedential.

The president's well-publicized cases of marital infidelity, his frequent misogynistic comments, and the allegations of sexual harassment by multiple women (including rape) raise concerns about this aspect of personal character. Yet, these allegations seem not to have affected his capacity to govern, were accepted by his core constituency of White evangelicals, and apparently tolerated by most of the public. Even in the era of the MeToo movement when many prominent men in media, politics, and entertainment were held accountable, the president seemed to escape sanctions. Perhaps this reflects the blasé attitudes toward Trump or perhaps a change in culture. Pfiffner contended that presidents are "bound to respect conventional sexual morality. The premise of this argument is that the conventions on sexual morality are so strongly held in the United States (in contrast to other countries) that the consequences of flouting them can have serious consequences for the President's ability to fulfill the duties of the office."[9]

Perhaps this premise is no longer operative in the United States. The Bill Clinton case may have been precedent setting. His sexual relationship with a young White House intern was, given the power and age differentials, tantamount to sexual harassment. In addition, there were allegations by multiple women of sexual harassment by Clinton, including one case of rape. Yet, his base, partly constituted by feminists, stood by him, as did a majority of the public. Trump's absence of personal character as it relates to sex is therefore not unique in this time, is the equivalent of Clinton's, and pales into insignificance when compared with the well-known sexual immorality and recklessness of the still venerated John Kennedy while he was in the White House.

The third element of personal character identified by Pfiffner is unique to officeholding. An elected official—preeminently the president—should endeavor to keep his campaign promises because promise keeping is integral to democratic accountability. Like most successful presidential candidates, Trump endeavored to keep his campaign promises. To the degree he was unsuccessful, for example on the promise of a major infrastructure program and health insurance reform, was to some extent due to the absence of presidential character—his failure to devote time and attention to the issues; his failure to organize a competent staff and direct it to come up with proposals he could send to Congress; and his failure to cultivate good personal, working relationships with key members of Congress.

On the signature promise of the campaign—working to stop the flow of immigrants across the southern border—Trump did pay attention and directed his staff and the bureaucracies to develop policies to fulfill his commitments. He, of course, could not keep his outlandish promise to deport the millions of undocumented immigrants or to get Mexico to pay for construction of the border wall, and he prudently abandoned both promises once assuming office. Otherwise from the first days as president he worked diligently to implement policies, some of which were widely disparaged as inhumane, to stop the flow of immigrants across the Mexican border. He also vigorously pushed Congress to provide funds for construction of the wall, going so far as to precipitate a partial shutdown of the government. When Congress nevertheless refused to appropriate the money, he issued an executive order directing funds for military construction to be diverted to fund construction of the wall. By the time he completed his term, several hundred miles of the wall had been built, and there had been a decline in immigration.[10]

Breaking with conservative orthodoxy, Trump during the campaign repeatedly promised not to cut Social Security or Medicare, but in preliminary discussions on the 2021 fiscal year budget the White House signaled willingness to cut those programs in order to deal with rapidly increasing deficits and debt. The onset of the Covid-19 pandemic, which required massive and rapid increases in spending, made concerns about deficits and debt seem quaint as the economy experienced a deep recession.

In foreign policy, where presidential power is more expansive, the president acted unilaterally to keep his promises to withdraw the United States from the Paris Climate Accords and the Iranian nuclear agreement. He also unilaterally imposed tariffs on China and Europe, renegotiated NAFTA, and more so than any previous president pressured the NATO allies (especially Germany) to meet their financial obligations to the alliance. All of these actions he had promised during the campaign. And, unlike Bill Clinton and George W. Bush, he kept his promise to relocate the US embassy in Israel to Jerusalem. He also wished to terminate US engagement in what he called the "endless" wars in the Middle East by withdrawing US forces from Syria, Iraq, and Afghanistan. This was a long-held Trump position, which he stated throughout the campaign. In the end, however, he listened to the near unanimous advice of his national security cabinet and Republican congressional leaders who warned that total withdrawal would likely result in the collapse of the Iraq and Afghan governments and a resurgence of terrorism.

Constitutional-Democratic Character

Overall, on the promise-keeping part of personal character, President Trump's behavior was consistent with most presidents. A disturbing aspect of his promise-keeping bears on his constitutional/democratic character. In 2016 and 2020 Trump repeatedly would not promise to accept the outcome of the election if he lost, saying if he did not win it would be because of a "rigged" election. In 2020, he also would not promise a peaceful and orderly transfer of power. In 2020 he did not win, and true to his promise, he did not accept the outcome of the election and precipitated the most violent transfer of power in the history of democracy in America.

But, beginning during the campaign and throughout his presidency Trump set about discrediting the media so that persons would not believe reporting about him and the administration. Although previous presidents, notably Jefferson and Nixon, had vigorously attacked the press, in his deliberately systematic efforts Trump was unique. Using the language of authoritarians, he repeatedly called the press "enemies of the people" and made the moniker "fake news" a part of the vocabulary. Trump admitted his attacks were a calculated strategy to demean the press so that when it published negative stories about him, they would not be believed. A free, critical press is indispensable to democratic governance—Jefferson said as important as free elections—and Trump throughout his presidency denigrated this institution.

Beginning in the 2016 campaign Trump questioned the legitimacy of the US election process, claiming, without credible evidence, that he had won the popular vote, and Clinton's popular vote victory was based on 3 to 5 million illegal votes. Behind in the polls, in early 2020, until he was quickly and forcefully rebuked by Republican congressional leaders, Trump mused about postponing the election. When he lost the election, he refused to concede, claiming, again without credible evidence, there was widespread fraud and corruption. The mainstream press was scathing in its denunciation of the president's perfidy, even Fox News—its journalists, not its commentators—questioned the president's claims of fraud, and declared Joe Biden the president-elect.[11] Yet, the president refused to concede, and for months did virtually everything in the powers of the administration to prevent an orderly transfer of power, including denial of funds, office space, and staff for a transition office; denying access to the President's Daily Brief and other national security material and secure means of communication; and denying access to government departments and agencies. Three weeks after the election, while still claiming he had won, Trump finally permitted the General Services Administration to "ascertain" that Biden had been elected, and to make available the resources necessary to begin an orderly transition. However, as late as January the president-elect indicated his office was still not getting all the resources necessary in key national security areas.

Trump fired the Department of Homeland Security's official in charge of election security after he issued statements refuting Trump's charges of massive voter fraud, and attacked the attorney general when he said that the FBI and Justice Department concluded there was no evidence of voter fraud that could alter the outcome of the election. His attorneys and supporters filed dozens of frivolous lawsuits in state and federal courts charging corruption and fraud in several states won by Biden; one of his attorneys said at a press conference that "communist" Venezuela, Cuba, and likely China had corrupted the election in order to defeat Trump.[12] The courts, Democratic and Republican judges ranging across the ideological spectrum, quickly dismissed the lawsuits as without merit. The Third Circuit Court of Appeals's curt dismissal of the Pennsylvania case was typical of how the courts treated Trump's various legal challenges: "Charges of unfairness are serious. But calling an election unfair does not make it so. Charges require specific allegations and their proof. We have neither here."[13]

Trump's ultimate strategy was to persuade Republican local and state officials not to certify the results of the election, and then have Republican-controlled legislatures appoint alternative electors to replace those selected by the voters. He personally called Republican members of the Wayne County, Michigan, board of canvassers asking them not to certify the results and invited the Republican leaders of the Michigan Legislature to the White House to lobby them on appointing alternative electors.[14] This transparent attempt to subvert the will of the voters was quickly rejected by Michigan Republican leaders, as well as Republican legislative leaders in Georgia and Pennsylvania. However, for the most part Republican national and state leaders, with the exception of Senator Mitt Romney, remained silent or acquiesced in Trump's attempts to undermine the election's integrity and legitimacy.[15]

After his initial statement on the election, which was widely disparaged as filled with exaggerations and fabrications, Trump did not meet the press again until Thanksgiving. Instead, in the three weeks after the election he posted more than 500 tweets targeted at undermining the election, repeatedly posting it was the "most corrupt" in US history.[16] On Thanksgiving, he met briefly with the press and said he would definitely "depart the White House" if Biden was selected by the electoral college. Yet, he insisted, he had won, and "Massive fraud has been found. We're like a Third World country."[17] When the electoral college confirmed Biden's election, the Senate's Republican leader—Mitch McConnell of Kentucky—acknowledged Biden's victory. Trump tweeted it was "too soon to give up."

After the electoral college meeting, Trump continued to meet with attorneys and advisers seeking ways to overturn the election. Amid concerns that he might try to use the military to remain in power, all ten former secretaries of defense (including two appointed by Trump) in early January 2021 published an op-ed in the *Washington Post* declaring the results of the election were clear, and Department of Defense officials, civilian and military, are "bound by oath, law and precedent to facilitate the entry into office of the new administration and do so wholeheartedly. They must also refrain from any political action that undermines the results of the election or hinder the success of the new team."[18]

The final constitutional procedure in electing the president is the certification and counting of each state's electoral votes in a joint meeting of the House and Senate, presided over by the vice president. In an effort endorsed by the president, twelve Republican senators led by Ted Cruz and a majority of House Republicans proposed that Congress refuse to certify the results from six states won by Biden (Georgia, Michigan, Arizona, Nevada, Pennsylvania, and Wisconsin) and instead appoint a commission to conduct an "emergency" ten-day audit of the elections in those states; on the basis of the commission's findings (presumably assuming it would find fraud) those states could convene their legislatures to appoint new electors to vote for Trump.[19]

Three days before the congressional certification meeting, Trump called Georgia's Republican secretary of state and berated, threatened, and attempted to pressure him to change Georgia's determination that Biden had won the state. After being repeatedly told during the call that the votes had been recounted and Biden had won, Trump nevertheless asked the secretary to "find 11,780 votes"—the exact amount he needed to win the state.[20] Three days after the call, he held a raucous rally in Georgia where he berated and threatened to campaign against the secretary of state and the state's Republican governor. He also laid out in detail, on a state-by-state basis, his case that the election was stolen, and called on Vice President Pence and Republicans in Congress to prevent the certification of Biden's electors from several states.

On the morning of the congressional meeting to count and certify the electoral vote, Trump supporters held a "Stop the Steal" rally to protest the expected decision to designate Biden president-elect. In an angry and vituperative speech, Trump again claimed he won the election by "a lot"; boasted he would never concede; attacked his appointees to the Supreme Court, because of their refusal to vote to hear his challenges to the election; called Republican officials who refused to support him "weak" and "stupid"; pledged to support primary challenges to Republicans who did not support his efforts to overturn the election; and called on Vice President Pence to send the votes of the contested states back for recertification—a power the vice president does not possess.[21] He concluded by urging those in attendance to go to the Capitol to protest "the steal."

A group of rally attendees did march to the Capitol, and some violently assaulted the building, breaching the chambers of both houses, resulting in five deaths. The assault on the Capitol caused a lockdown of the building and several hours of delay in the joint meeting. Trump had urged persons at the rally to go to the Capitol to protest the certification of the vote, and he may have considered that his angry words might have created a "clear and present danger" of incitement to violence. Much of the media and virtually all the Democrats labeled the protests at the Capitol an "insurrection" and accused Trump of inciting the violence. Trump in a video posted on Twitter late in the day equivocally condemned the violence, saying, "We have to have peace, and law and order, please go home." But he also said, "I know your pain. I know you are hurt. We had an election that was stolen from us. . . . There's never been a time where such a thing happened where they could take it away from us."[22] The next day Democratic Senate leader Charles Schumer called for the president's impeachment, and Speaker Pelosi called for impeachment or invoking the Twenty-Fifth Amendment to remove the president.

After the violent disorders at the Capitol, many Republican senators and members of Congress were chastened and withdrew their objections to the certification of the votes of Nevada, Georgia, Michigan, and Wisconsin. The House and Senate by large bipartisan margins rejected the challenges to the votes of Arizona and Pennsylvania. Only eight of fifty-two Republican senators voted affirmatively on one or both of the rejections, while one or both were supported by 139 of 211 Republican House members. The next day Trump, having exhausted all legal and constitutional possibilities, accepted the inevitable and said in a statement, "Even though I totally disagree with the outcome of the election, and the facts bear me out, there will be an orderly transition to January 20. . . . While this represents the end of the greatest first term in presidential history, it's only the beginning of our fight to Make America Great Again!"[23] Two days later, Trump announced he would not attend Biden's inauguration.[24]

On January 13, a week before his term expired, the House—without hearings or even the semblance of due process and on a near party-line vote—impeached the president for "incitement of insurrection." The single article of impeachment alleged at the "Stop the Steal" rally, Trump incited violence against the United States by "willfully making statements that in context encouraged—and foreseeably resulted—in imminent lawlessness in the Capitol, such as 'if you don't fight like hell, you're are not going to have a country anymore.'"[25] The article also alleged Trump's conduct on the day of the rally was consistent with prior efforts to "subvert and obstruct" the results of the 2020 election.

While Trump's rhetoric at the rally—as was the case with most of his speeches—was inflammatory, it did not likely meet the legal standard of incitement or foreseeability of "imminent lawless action," that is, that his words would create a foreseeable danger of the violence that ensued at the Capitol. Impeachment does not require violation of law. Congressional Democrats impeached Trump not so much for his legal culpability for the remarks at the rally but, as the article implied, for his weeks of subversion and obstruction of the results of the 2020 election, which was part of a long pattern of violation of constitutional and democratic norms.

The president accepted no responsibility for the violence at the Capitol, noting that he had called on his supporters to "peacefully and patriotically" protest, and he said his speech at the rally was "totally appropriate."[26]

The second impeachment of Trump resulted in a modest breach in the monolithic support of congressional Republicans. In the first impeachment, no House Republicans voted in favor. In the second, ten Republicans (5 percent) joined all the Democrats voting in favor including Wyoming congresswoman Liz Cheney, the daughter of the former vice president and chair of the House Republican Conference, the third ranking position in the party's House leadership. (Unlike in the first impeachment, the Republican leadership did not lobby members to vote against the second.) Immediately after her vote, there were calls by Republican members to remove Cheney from the leadership post.[27] The public narrowly approved of impeachment (48 to 44 percent), but opinion was polarized—81 percent of Democrats approved, 84 percent of Republicans were opposed.[28] Within weeks of the House vote, all ten Republicans who voted for impeachment had drawn primary challenges from Trump-aligned candidates.[29]

Even before the trial began in the Senate, forty-five of the fifty Republicans supported a procedural motion to effectively dismiss the case, declaring the Senate lacked the constitutional authority to try a former president. The president's attorneys in their response to the House's impeachment article also argued the Senate lacked jurisdiction to try a former president. On the specifics of the impeachment article, their brief denied that the president "incited the crowd to engage in destructive behavior." Rather, it claimed at the rally he had simply "exercised his First Amendment right under the Constitution to express his belief that the election results were suspect." The brief concluded the election results were suspect because local authorities and courts had changed laws and procedures without the "necessary approvals from state legislatures."[30] After six days of trial, the Senate voted 57 to 43 to acquit the president. In the first impeachment, Senator Romney was the only Republican voting to convict. In the second, he was joined by six others (14 percent).

Whatever Trump's culpability in the violence at the Capitol, it showed that the transition he repeatedly refused to promise would be peaceful is another promise in a sense he kept. The 2021 transition was the most violent in history. After the January 6 assault on the Capitol, more than 20,000 troops from the National Guard were deployed in Washington, on inauguration day the city was in virtual lockdown, and across the country law enforcement and militias were on heightened alert, with more than a dozen states activating the National Guard to protect their capitol buildings. Meanwhile, on his last full day in office Trump released a video farewell address wishing the new president "luck" and reviewing his domestic and foreign policy accomplishments. On January 20 he issued more than a hundred pardons, and departed Washington for Florida several hours before Biden was sworn in.

Trump's attack on the integrity and legitimacy of the election is unprecedented. Ten incumbent presidents were defeated prior to Trump. None of them questioned the outcome of the elections or even remotely tried to use the powers of the office to delegitimize his successor. Even in the closest and most bitterly contested elections of 1824, 1876, and 2000, the losers—Andrew Jackson, Samuel Tilden, and Albert Gore—after the completion of the constitutional processes accepted the outcome of the elections as legitimate.[31]

Although Andrew Jackson might be included, Richard Nixon is the only president about whom serious questions are raised regarding constitutional or democratic character—he is the only modern president, at least.[32] The 1960 contest between Nixon and Kennedy, one of the closest in history, is the only election in modern history in which there is credible evidence it might have been stolen.[33] Nixon was presented evidence of the likely fraud, and urged by the Republican National Committee chair and the Republican leader of the Senate Everett Dirksen of Illinois, among others, not to concede and seek a recount. Nixon declined. In his memoir, Nixon said he concluded "a presidential recount would require up to half year, during which time the legitimacy of Kennedy's election would be in doubt. The effect would be devastating to America's foreign relations. I would not subject the country to such situation. And what if I demanded a recount and it turned out despite the vote fraud Kennedy still would have won? Charges of 'sore loser' would follow me through history and remove any possibility of a further political career."[34] Tom Wicker in an essay considering Nixon's character observes that he did not challenge the 1960 "results in court nor in any way cloud the legitimacy of J. F. K.'s presidency. In devastating defeat, his better instincts prevailed."[35]

How does one interpret Trump's behavior? How does one understand a participant in a contest, whether a tennis match, a prize fight, or an election, who says at the outset I am going to win, and if I do not it's because the game is rigged, the referees are corrupt? Hubris? Extreme narcissism? Self-deception? Lying? As a political scientist, this is a difficult task, one perhaps best left to the psychologists and psychiatrists, although their capacities to address the question are problematic.[36] Clearly, however, character matters. Trump's behavior deeply implicates his Hobbesian worldview, wherein there are winners and losers, and he is a winner and his adversaries are losers. The very word *loser* runs counter to the image he began constructing of himself since his early days in business. He wrote in *The of Art the Deal,* "I'm the very first person to admit I am very competitive and I'll do anything within legal limits to win. Sometimes a part of making a deal is to denigrate your competition . . . and to fight back hard."[37] In 2020, he used every legal means, fought back hard to try to win, but in the process he denigrated the American democracy.

Notes

1. Perhaps the most notable exception to this consensus among political science scholars of the presidency is Stanley Renshon, who writes, "Trump is a man of extraordinary strong convictions and courage in seeing them through. He is a man of remarkable determination and resilience in the face of adversity. In his presidency, the last large act of his life, he is absolutely serious about putting into place the *Politics of American Restoration.* And, win or loose [*sic*], he never gives up. . . . The risks are high, the chances of success low, but it would be unwise to place a large bet against President Trump." See *The Real Psychology of the Trump Presidency* (New York: Palgrave Macmillan, 2020), 458–459, emphasis in the original.

2. James David Barber, *The Presidential Character: Predicting Performance in the White House* (Englewood Cliffs, NJ: Prentice Hall, 1972), 7.

3. Stephen Walker, "The Psychology of Presidential Decision Making," in George Edwards and William Howell, eds., *Oxford Handbook of the Presidency* (New York: Oxford University Press, 2009).

4. Barber, *The Presidential Character,* 9.

5. Jonathan Karl, *Front Row at the Trump Show* (New York: Dutton, 2020), 7.

6. Susan Hennessey and Benjamin Wittes, *Unmaking the Presidency: Donald Trump's War on the World's Most Powerful Office* (New York: Farrar, Straus and Giroux, 2020), 110.

7. Luther Smith, *Howard Thurman: Essential Writings* (Maryknoll, NY: Orbis Books, 2006), 137.

8. Eric Alterman, *Lying in State: Why Presidents Lie and Why Trump Is Worse* (New York: Basic Books, 2020).

9. James Pfiffner, "Judging Presidential Character," *Public Integrity* 5 (2002): 14.

10. William Frey, "The Past Decade's Foreign-Born Population Gains Will Be the Smallest in Decades" (Washington: Brookings Institutions, 2020); and Miriam Jordan, "Even as Trump Cut Immigration, Immigrants Changed America," *New York Times,* November 11, 2020.

11. Philip Bump, "In a Speech of Historic Dishonesty, Trump Tried to Reinforce His Long-Planned Effort to Stay in Power," *Washington Post,* November 6, 2020; Glenn Kessler, "Trump's White House Statement: Falsehood After Falsehood," *Washington Post,* November 6, 2020; Peter Baker and Maggie Haberman, "In Torrent of Falsehoods, Trump Claims Election Is Being Stolen," *New York Times,* November 6, 2020; and the Associated

Press, "Trump's Wild Claims Test Limits of GOP Loyalty," *East Bay Times,* November 7, 2020.

12. Aaron Blake, "Trump's Legal Team Lights Fuse Beneath Its Remaining Credibility," *Washington Post,* November 19, 2020. Trump's team focused its claims of voter fraud on cities—Atlanta, Detroit, Philadelphia and Milwaukee—with large African American populations.

13. *Donald J. Trump for President et al. v. Secretary of the Commonwealth of Pennsylvania et al.,* United States Court of Appeals for the Third Circuit, #20-3371, November 27, 2020.

14. Maggie Haberman et al., "Trump Targets Michigan in His Ploy to Subvert the Election," *New York Times,* November 19, 2020. Trump also reportedly called Georgia's Republican governor to urge him to call a special session of the legislature to override the popular vote and appoint electors that would vote for him. Amy Gardner and Colby Itkowitz, "Trump Calls Georgia Governor to Pressure Him for Help Overturning Biden's Victory," *Washington Post,* December 6, 2020. In a suit by the Texas Republican attorney general, joined by the president, seventeen other Republican attorneys general, and a majority of House Republicans in amicus briefs, the state claimed Pennsylvania and three other states won by Biden had changed their election procedures without legislative authorization, which violated Texas's rights under the Equal Protection Clause of the Fourteenth Amendment. The suit asked the Supreme Court to direct the legislatures of the states (all controlled by Republicans) to appoint new electors, who presumably would have voted for Trump. In a 7–2 unsigned opinion the Court summarily dismissed the case: "Texas has not demonstrated a judicially cognizable interest in the manner in which another state conducts its elections." *Texas v. Pennsylvania, et al.* (Order List: 592 U. S.), December 11, 2020. Justices Clarence Thomas and Samuel Alito wrote they would have heard the case but "would not grant other relief."

15. *National Review,* perhaps the leading journal of conservative opinion, assailed the Republican Party for "desperately trying to find something, anything" to support "the petulant refusal of one man to accept the verdict of the American people." See its editorial, "Trump's Disgraceful Endgame," November 30, 2020, http://www.nationalreview.com/2020/trump-election-fraud-disgraceful-endgame/. A month after the election, only 25 of the 222 Republican members of the House and Senate were willing to acknowledge Biden's victory. See Paul Kane and Scott Clement, "Just 25 Congressional Republicans Acknowledge Biden's Win, Washington Post Survey Finds," *Washington Post,* December 5, 2020.

16. Karen Yourish and Larry Buchanan, "Since Election Day, a Lot of Tweeting and Not Much Else," *New York Times,* November 24, 2020.

17. Jeff Mason and Simon Lewis, "Trump Takes Another Step Closer to Conceding," *Bay Area News Group,* November 27, 2020.

18. "All Ten Living Former Defense Secretaries: Involving the Military in Election Disputes Would Cross into Dangerous Territory," *Washington Post,* January 3, 2021. On January 12, in a memorandum to all members of the armed forces signed by all members of the Joint Chiefs of Staff, the nation's eight senior military commanders wrote the "violent riot" at the Capitol was a "direct assault on the U.S. Congress, the Capitol building, and

our constitutional processes. . . . We support the Constitution. Any act to disrupt the constitutional processes is not only against our traditions, values and oath; it is against the law." Paul Sonne, "Joint Chiefs Call Riot a Direct Assault on the Constitutional Order, Affirm Biden as Next Commander-in Chief," *Washington Post,* January 12, 2021.

19. Senate Majority Leader McConnell opposed this effort, saying it was a threat to the integrity of the electoral college and the constitutional order; the people, the states, and the courts had spoken; and Biden was the legitimately elected president. Mike DeBonis, "McConnell Warns Overturning Biden's Election Would Push Democracy into Dangerous Territory," *Washington Post,* January 6, 2020.

20. Amy Gardner, "In Extraordinary Long Call, Trump Pressures Georgia Secretary of State to Recalculate Vote in His Favor," *Washington Post,* January 3, 2021. The *Post* obtained a recording of the conversation.

21. The Electoral Count Act of 1887, establishing the procedures for counting the electoral votes in Congress, specifies the limited, largely ministerial role of the vice president. The rejection of a state's electoral votes requires the concurrence of both houses, and both houses may overrule any decision of the vice president. In a letter to Congress on the date of the meeting, Pence wrote, "My oath to support and defend the Constitution constrains me from claiming unilateral authority to determine which electoral votes should be accepted and which should not. My role as presiding officer in Congress is ceremonial." Josh Wagner, "Pence Says He Will Not Intervene to Change Outcome of the Election, Rejecting Trump's Pleas," *Washington Post,* January 6, 2021.

22. Felicia Sonmez and Josh Dawsey, "Trump Tells Those Who Stormed Capitol to Go Home," *Washington Post,* January 6, 2021. The following day Trump released a video with a more forthright condemnation: "The demonstrators who infiltrated the Capitol have defiled the seat of democracy. To those who engaged in the acts of violence and destruction. You do not represent our country. And to those who broke the law. You will pay." Amy Wang, "Trump Acknowledges a New Administration Will Be Inaugurated on January 20," *Washington Post,* January 7, 2021.

23. Antonia Noori Farzan, "Trump Promises Orderly Transition to Biden, One Day After Inciting Mob to Storm Capitol," *Washington Post,* January 7, 2021.

24. Three defeated incumbent presidents did not attend the inaugurations of their successors: John Adams in 1801, John Quincy Adams in 1829, and Andrew Johnson in 1869. The most acrimonious transfer of power prior to Trump-Biden was in 1869 between Johnson and Ulysses Grant. While Johnson did not contest the election results, he lambasted Grant as a "dissembler" and a "desperate deceiver" and said he would not "debase" himself by attending the inauguration—"a fitting end," Ron Chernow writes, "to a sad, somewhat shabby presidency." See *Grant* (New York: Penguin Books, 2017), 629.

25. H. RES. 24, Impeaching Donald John Trump, January 11, 2021, https://www.congress.gov/117/bills/hres24/BILLS-117hres24ih.pdf.

26. David Jackson, "Donald Trump Defends Speech as Totally Appropriate, Won't Accept Responsibility for Deadly Capitol Riot," *USA Today,* January 13, 2021. Trump's characterization as "totally appropriate" recalls

his description of his phone conversation with the Ukrainian president that led to his first impeachment, which he described as "perfect."

27. Several weeks after the impeachment vote, the House Republican Conference voted 145 to 61 not to oust Cheney as chair. The vote was by secret ballot, allowing members to back her without fear of retaliation by Trump loyalists. Mike DeBonis and Colby Itkowitz, "House Votes to Keep Cheney in Leadership Role," *Washington Post,* February 3, 2021. Several days after the House vote, the Wyoming Republican Party voted overwhelmingly to censure Cheney and called on her to resign, indicating it would not support her in the 2022 election. Several months later as Cheney continued her criticisms of Trump, the Republican Conference reversed itself and by a voice vote removed Cheney. Marianna Sotomayor and Jacqueline Alemany, "House Republicans Oust Cheney for Calling Out Trump's False Election Claims," *Washington Post,* May 12, 2021. A Quinnipiac poll conducted shortly after Cheney's ouster found only 12 percent of Republicans had a favorable opinion of her (https://poll.qu.edu/poll-results/).

28. Nick Niedzwiadek, "Poll: Americans Narrowly Back Trump's Impeachment," *Politico,* January 11, 2021.

29. Alex Isenstadt, "Republicans Who Impeached Trump Already on the Chopping Block," *Politico,* January 21, 2021.

30. U.S. Senate, Answer of President Donald John Trump, 45th President of the United States to Article 1: Incitement of Insurrection, February 2, 2021. See also "Trump Defense Memo," *New York Times,* February 8, 2021. The argument of Trump, his lawyers, and some conservative commentators and Republican politicians during the election controversy was that the election was suspect because in some states election officials and courts changed election procedures (allowing mail-in ballots and extending election hours or the time for receipt of ballots) in violation of the Article II provision, which states, "Each state shall appoint, in such manner, as the Legislature thereof may direct . . . the Electors." However, once the legislatures decide the appointment will be through an election, local and state election officials and the courts are authorized to change the procedures for presidential elections in the same manner as for any other state or federal election. But in 2021, consistent with the ideas advanced by Trump and his lawyers, Republican-controlled legislatures in several states considered or passed laws to increase their control over state and local election officials. See Amy Gardner, "After Trump Tried to Intervene in 2020 Vote, State Republicans Moving to Take More Control of Elections," *Washington Post,* March 27, 2021.

31. The one possible exception is Andrew Jackson, Trump's favorite president. In the 1824 election Jackson won a plurality of the popular and electoral votes. Since he did not have a majority, the election was decided in the House, which voted for John Quincy Adams, who finished in second place. Jackson charged Adams's victory was the result of corruption, specifically Adams's promise to appoint Henry Clay the secretary of state in exchange for his delivery of votes from several states. Jackson used the "corrupt bargain" argument to indict the Adams presidency and the entire political system as elitist and corrupt, which became a rallying point for his defeat of Adams in 1828. Most historians have accepted Jackson's argument that Adams's election was the result of corruption and vote buying, but one

rigorous analysis of the vote patterns in the House does not support the corrupt bargain hypothesis. Rather, it concludes, "House balloting was driven by ideological considerations that were generally consistent with preferences of members' constituencies." See Jeffrey Jenkins and Brian Sala, "The Spatial Theory of Voting and the Presidential Election of 1824," *American Journal of Political Science* 42 (1998): 1178.

32. Melvin Small, *The Presidency of Richard Nixon* (Lawrence: University Press of Kansas, 1999). See chap. 8, note 21.

33. On the evidence of voter fraud in Texas and Illinois sufficient to change the results in those states to Nixon and thus the election, see Victor Lasky, *J. F. K.: The Man and the Myth* (New York: Macmillan, 1963), 495–496; Seymour Hersh, *The Dark Side of Camelot* (Boston: Little, Brown, 1997), 187–190; W. J. Rorabaugh, *The Real Making of the President: Kennedy, Nixon, and the 1960 Election* (Lawrence: University Press of Kansas, 2009), 19–20; and James Giglio, *The Presidency of John F. Kennedy* (Lawrence: University Press of Kansas, 2006), 21–23.

34. Richard Nixon, *RN: The Memoirs of Richard Nixon* (New York: Grosset and Dunlap, 1978), 224.

35. Tom Wicker, "Richard M. Nixon," in Robert Wilson, ed., *Character Above All: Ten Presidents from FDR to George W. Bush* (New York: Simon & Schuster, 1995), 145.

36. See Bandy Lee, ed., *A Duty to Warn: The Dangerous Case of Donald Trump* (New York: St. Martin's, 2017). See also Dan McAdams, *The Strange Case of Donald Trump: A Psychological Reckoning* (New York: Oxford University Press, 2020). Some psychological impairments may be simply eccentric behavior or, like narcissism, even helpful in leadership. Furthermore, complicated, often esoteric psychological analyses of a leader's mental incompetency are not likely to be accepted by people not otherwise disposed against that person. And as George Reedy writes of psychological assessments of presidents, "Anyone who has ever listened to conflicting testimony in criminal proceedings will never be willing to accept a technical verdict as to whether a man's psychic health is sufficient for him to exercise the instruments of power." *The Twilight of the Presidency* (New York: New American Library, 1970), 170. On this point with specific reference to Trump see Renshon, *The Real Psychology of the Trump Presidency,* chaps. 6–9.

37. Donald Trump with Tony Schwartz, *The Art of the Deal* (New York: Random House, 1987), 41, 74.

11

The Trump Legacy:
Speculating on the Future

THE ELECTION OF DONALD TRUMP. DOES IT REPRESENT a phenomenon of personality? Or does it represent an "ism," a set of beliefs—Trumpism? Or, to put the question in terms of Stephen Skowronek's theoretical studies of the presidency, is Trump an "affiliated" president, a "disjunctive" president, or a "reconstructive" president?[1] It is difficult at this point to answer these questions, but it is useful to raise them in an attempt to understand Trump's legacy beyond character. Trump's character is sui generis.[2] But what are the likely legacies of his paleoconservative, White nationalist politics on the Republican Party and conservatism in America?

While Trump's character (and his character deficits) is new in the presidency, his politics have roots in the Reagan reconstruction and its progeny. While I have identified Patrick Buchanan as a Trump precursor, his rhetoric and style of politics have also been traced to Spiro Agnew's politics in the 1970s and Newt Gingrich's in the 1990s.[3] Agnew and Gingrich injected a right-wing populism into the conservative movement, focused on the heightened mobilization of White working- and middle-class resentment of the social changes of the 1960s. They also brought a style of hyperbolic, no-holds barred, mean-spirited rhetorical attacks on the media and the Democratic Party, portraying them as radical, elitist, corrupt, and vaguely anti-American—all in what Gingrich described as a "nasty fight for power."[4]

Finally, the Tea Party is a Trump precursor. The Tea Party, Theda Skocpol and Vanessa Williamson contend, was the product of "three interrelated forces: grassroots anger and activism at the conservative base; financial support from 'ultra–free market advocacy groups' such as the Club for Growth; and propaganda from the conservative media including Fox News and right-wing talk radio."[5] Overwhelmingly White, well-educated, middle-class, married, older than forty-five, disproportionately southern and evangelical, the 18 percent of Americans who identified with the Tea Party were especially concerned about being taxed to pay benefits to "undeserving categories of people," which for them included "young people, minorities and illegal immigrants."[6] In essence, Skocpol and Williamson conclude, the Tea Party was a political reaction by very conservative Republicans alarmed by the presidency of Barack Obama. Abramowitz also concludes that "racial resentment and dislike of Obama had significant effects on support for the Tea Party."[7] But, he writes, "the Tea Party did not suddenly emerge in 2009 in response to the progressive agenda set forth by President Obama and the Democratic Congress. Rather, it was the natural outgrowth of the growing size and conservatism of the activist base of the Republican Party during preceding decades."[8]

Thus, Trump is an extraordinary character in the presidency, but his political style, his rhetorical bombast, and his appeal to White nationalist sentiments are not new in conservative Republican politics, although they are more explicit. His appeal may in part be due to his character but also in part to the growth in White racial consciousness and identity in the last decade.[9] The sentiments are familiar, but Trump gave them a sharper emphasis, and it is possible his presidency may represent the consolidation of a more empowered White nationalist faction that could sustain as well as transform the Republican Party and conservatism. Has Trump built a White nationalist, paleoconservative coalition that has more appeal than the more traditional conservatism represented by the Republican establishment—Trumpism?

It is unlikely, as I indicated before, that Trump's deficits in presidential and personal character will soon be replicated. But his constitutional character and demagogic, norm-shattering flouting of democratic values could become a new normal, easily replicated following paths traveled by Agnew, Buchanan, and Gingrich. There are a number of young, dynamic Republican personalities willing to embrace Trumpism: his son Donald, Senators Tom Cotton and Josh Hawley, television commentators Sean Hannity and Tucker Carlson, Secretary of State Mike Pompeo, and 2016 presidential contenders Ted Cruz and Lindsey Graham.

The only way Trump might not have become an ism is if he and Republicans in Congress had lost the 2020 election in a landslide. Losing narrowly in the electoral college, while claiming he did not lose, allows Trump, elements of the Republican Party, and conservative media to manufacture a "lost cause," portraying him as a victim of the liberal establishment—the media, high tech, the academy, and the "deep state."[10] Narrowly defeated, continuing the canard that the 2020 election was stolen, Trumpism could become a major if not dominant faction in the party.[11] Trump, with his fervent base, his likely command of the conservative media, rhetorical prowess, and probable fundraising abilities, could be major force in the party as long as he is willing and able to be active.[12]

Theoretically in terms of Skowronek's classifications, it is not clear where Trump should be located in "political time," that is, in relationship to the established governing regime. First, since the Reagan reconstruction there has been no established, governing regime. Rather, both parties have been engaged in a decades long struggle to establish partisan and ideological hegemony. In this context, Trump could be an affiliated presidency, faithfully carrying forward the legacy of the Reagan regime in ways that accommodate the rise of more explicit White nationalist politics since the 1980s.[13] Or his presidency could be disjunctive, representing the beginnings of the unraveling of the Reagan reconstruction. Or finally, it could be a reconstructive presidency, not in terms of establishing a new governing regime but in the sense of remaking the Republican Party into a more thoroughly White nationalist paleoconservative formation, as the Reagan reconstruction did in the 1980s with respect to traditional conservatism.[14]

At this time, it is difficult to locate Trump or Trumpism, if that's what it is, in political time, because of the "waning" or "scrambling" of time.[15] But, if his is a reconstructive presidency that remakes the Republican Party and conservatism along more explicit White nationalist lines, its likely legacy is disjunctive because the White nationalist base of the party is, even as Patrick Buchanan acknowledges, *"the emerging white minority,"*[16] and the multiethnic Democratic Party is the emerging majority. Estimates of the effects of demographic and generational changes in the electorate yield future Democratic popular vote and electoral college victories (although the latter is more problematic) based on the projected rise of Democratic leaning groups—Blacks, Asians, Latinos—and the decline of the Republican leaning White share of the electorate.[17] These projections, however, assume stability in the voting behavior of the various ethnic groups, which may not be the case, especially for Latinos and Asians.

First, although it is common for social scientists and journalists to refer to Latinos and Asian Americans as if they are single, discrete ethnic groups, they are obviously not. Rather, each constitutes multiple ethnicities with distinctive histories, cultures, and political attitudes. Second, most Latinos identify as White (more than two-thirds); as a result of this identification, the White population rather than declining grew by 6 percent between 2000 and 2010.[18] Thus, demographic changes may sustain the White majority and its nationalist sentiments. Latinos and Asians tend to share the same negative stereotypes about Blacks as Whites,[19] and as Latinos and Asians become incorporated these stereotypes may become more pronounced. These tendencies may incline some Asians and Latinos to accept what Guinier and Torres call the "racial bribe": "The racial bribe is a strategy that invites specific racial or ethnic groups to advance within the existing black-white hierarchy by becoming 'white.' The strategy expands the range of physical characteristics that can fall within the definition of white in order to pursue four goals: to defuse the previously marginalized group's oppositional agenda; to offer incentives that discourage the group from affiliating with blacks; to secure high status for individual members within existing hierarchies; and to make the social position of 'whiteness' appear more racially or ethnically inclusive."[20]

Even if a majority of Latinos and Asians reject the "bribe" and align with the liberal Democratic coalition, a minority of the groups (exit polls indicate about a third of each group voted for Trump in 2016 and 2020) aligning with the Republicans coupled with Buchanan's strategy of maximizing the vote of the shrinking White majority could result in extended victories by a more diverse White nationalist coalition.[21]

Cautious Thoughts About the Future

To the extent Trump embraced an ideology or a coherent set of beliefs, it is best labeled *paleoconservative*, which is contrasted with the traditional Goldwater-Reagan conservatism that displaced the more moderate conservatism of Eisenhower and Nixon. I expect aspects of this ideology—immigration, trade, and neoisolationism— to endure as a powerful faction, if not the dominant faction, of the

Republican Party. White Christian nationalism was also embraced by Trump, which may be understood as a subset of paleoconservatism. White nationalism was dormant during the Goldwater-Reagan era, although Reagan mobilized the Christian right and skillfully exploited White racial grievances.[22] By 2016, fueled by increased non-White immigration and by the election of a Black president, among a segment of White conservatives a distinct White consciousness matured—a consciousness organized around a perceived loss of status and power, a wish to maintain their race privileges, and a desire for the United States to remain a White Christian nation. This consciousness is likely to endure after Trump, but this ideology of the past has no future. The civil rights reforms of the 1960s (including liberal immigration reform) set in motion changes that inevitably resulted in the loss of White power and status. These changes are continuing and are not reversible. Relatedly, the loss of Christian dominance in a more multicultural and secular society is irreversible.[23] For example, on two issues important to devout evangelicals—abortion and LGBTQ status—public opinion tends to be hostile to their values and is likely to become more so.[24]

As discussed above, demography is not necessarily destiny politically, but demographic trends are irreversible in that Whites, as denoted by European ancestry, are going to become a minority in the United States (according to the 2020 census, the White share of the population fell from 63.7 percent in 2010 to 57.8 percent, the lowest decline on record). And while one should always be cautious in projecting ideological trends, given the notorious ideological innocence of the public, at this time an emerging liberal majority, especially on social issues, appears to be the future. As Richard Seltzer and I maintain, polarization in the US two-party system historically ends when one party utterly defeats the other and establishes a new governing coalition and policy regime, as was the case with the laissez-faire conservatives in the 1890s or the New Deal liberals in the 1930s.[25] Again, projecting is hazardous, but a multicultural, multiethnic liberal majority seems more likely than a paleoconservative White nationalist majority. Many in the Republican Party accepted this projection and urged outreach to racial minorities and the LGBTQ community. Alas, then came Trump.

Trump represents those, most notably Patrick Buchanan, who foresee the coming demographic and ideological changes but cling to the past on the assumption that militant mobilization of the declining White Christian majority will allow them to hang on to power for perhaps another generation or more,[26] given the structural advantages of the GOP in the malapportioned Senate,[27] electoral college, gerrymandering, and voter suppression.[28]

And then there is the ominous possibility of a violent reaction to the ascendancy of the new majority. That is, some elements of the White nationalist minority, unwilling to accept the inevitable, may resort to violence or other undemocratic means of political conflict. We know from the elitist theory of democracy data collected in the 1950s that antidemocratic sentiments exist among the elites and the public of both parties, but especially among conservatives. We also know those sentiments are more pronounced in the early twenty-first century among Republicans than Democrats. We also know that adherence to democratic values is not strongly correlated with political engagement or higher education. As Larry Bartels writes, based on 2020 survey data, "The typical antidemocrat was not some rural, low education, uninvolved citizen, but suburbanites with some college and a healthy interest in politics."[29]

Given that "antidemocratic tendencies loom larger in the Republican Party—especially in the rhetoric of President Trump—than among Democrats,"[30] Bartels in January 2020 conducted a large survey of Republicans (1,151 persons identifying as Republican or leaning Republican) in an attempt to identify the sources or correlates of antidemocratic sentiments among the Republican rank-and-file. Several possible variables were identified—attitudes toward Trump, economic conservatism, political cynicism, Republican effect, and ethnic antagonism. Allegiance to democratic values was determined by responses to this fundamental statement: The traditional American way of life is disappearing so fast that we may have to use force to save it. The statement was agreed to by 50.7 percent of respondents, 27.7 percent were unsure, and 21.7 percent disagreed. Of the several predictor variables, Bartels writes, "the strongest predictor by far, for the Republican rank-and-file . . . and for a variety of subgroups defined by education, locale, sex, and political attitudes is ethnic antagonism—especially concerns about the political power and claims on government resources of immigrants, African Americans, and Latinos."[31]

The ethnic antagonism concept used by Bartels is based on questions similar to those used to measure White nationalism. Bartels writes "survey items tapping perceptions that immigrants, African Americans, Latinos and poor people have more than their share of government resources are powerful indicators of ethnic antagonism. . . . The single survey item with the highest average correlation with antidemocratic sentiments is . . . an item inviting respondents to agree that 'discrimination against whites is as big a problem as discrimination against blacks and other minorities.'"[32]

Because a majority of Republicans agree that violence might be necessary to protect their interests and American traditions does not mean they would use violence or even support its use by others. Yet since the late 1970s there has been a White militia movement in the United States, animated by anger about the US defeat in Vietnam, hostile to the social changes of the 1960s, and opposed to the power of the federal government.[33] These groups have in the recent past used violence against individuals and the political system—the January 6, 2021, storming of the Capitol is but the most recent and pertinent example. It is possible as the power of minorities, real and perceived, increases, White militia violence might also increase. Given the history of political violence in the United States, the prevalence and proliferation of weapons, and the level of support for the assault on the Capitol, the political system is not immune to this possibility.[34]

Notes

1. Stephen Skowronek, *The Politics Presidents Make: Leadership from John Adams to Bill Clinton* (Cambridge: Harvard University Press, 1997). For a succinct explanation of the theory and classifications of presidents, see his "The President in Political Order and Time in Presidential Studies," in James Pfiffner and Roger Davidson, eds., *Understanding the Presidency,* 6th ed. (New York: Longman, 2011).

2. That Trump may not be sui generis is the concern of Lara Brown in her historical-comparative study of character and the presidency. Focusing on presidents from Carter to Trump, she writes, "It seems important to ask one question: How is it that Trump's character (a celebrity real estate mogul with no political experience who has a highly volatile temperament, a scandalous personal background and a shady business history) is considered by a large minority of Americans to be more than sufficient to be President . . . and whether America's political system can endure the character and leadership of more presidents like Trump." See *Amateur Hour: Presidential Character and the Question of Leadership* (New York: Routledge, 2020): 7.

3. Charles Holden, Zach Messitte, and Jerald Podair, *Republican Populist: Spiro Agnew and the Origins of Donald Trump's America* (Charlottesville: University of Virginia Press, 2019); and Julian Zelizer, *Burning Down the House: Newt Gingrich and the Rise of the New Republican Party* (New York: Penguin Press, 2020).

4. The Gingrich quote is from Rick Perlstein, *Reaganland: America's Right Turn, 1976–1980* (New York: Simon & Schuster, 2020), 233. Buchanan wrote several of Agnew's incendiary speeches as a White House speechwriter.

Gingrich was one of Trump's strongest supporters writing panegyric books on the Trump presidency. See, for example, *Trump's America: The Truth About the Nation's Great Comeback* (New York: Center Street Publishing, 2019). Gingrich reportedly advised Trump in the development of a policy agenda for the 2022 elections and perhaps beyond, using as a template Gingrich's 1994 "Contract with America." See Meredith McGraw, "Trump Is Putting Together His Own Contract with America. And He's Teaming Up with Newt," *Politico,* May 26, 2021.

5. Theda Skocpol and Vanessa Williamson, *The Tea Party and the Remaking of the Republican Party* (New York: Oxford University Press, 2012), 11, 24. See also Christopher Parker and Matt Barreto, *Change They Can't Believe In: The Tea Party and Reactionary Politics in America* (Princeton: Princeton University Press, 2013).

6. Ibid., 56.

7. Alan Abramowitz, "Partisan Polarization and the Rise of the Tea Party Movement," paper presented at the annual meeting of the American Political Science Association, Seattle, September 2011, 18–19.

8. Ibid.

9. Reagan's 1980 campaign attempted to mobilize emergent White nationalist sentiments. That is, as Rick Perlstein writes, the campaign "target[ed] voters who felt victimized by government actions that cost them privileges their whiteness afforded them." See *Reaganland: America's Turn Right,* 675. In the early 1970s, Matthew Holden Jr. argued, "the chances are the Republican Party will [choose] to consolidate a national majority on an anti-black basis. . . . We may believe that the party would become the center of resistance born of a generalized unease about 'things going sour,' that this generalized unease is anti-reform and would under some circumstances be functionally equivalent to 'anti-black.' To capitalize upon such unease would simply become the most economical way for the party to take care of its own organizational interests." *The Politics of the Black Nation* (New York: Chandler, 1973), 139. See also Robert C. Smith, *Conservatism and Racism and Why in America They Are the Same* (Albany: SUNY Press, 2010), chaps. 6, 8.

10. Early postelection polls suggest Trump's base would likely embrace the lost-cause narrative. Eighty percent of Trump voters in the 2020 election accepted his contention that Biden had not "legitimately" won the election. Moreover, only 60 percent of all voters accepted the legitimacy of the election compared to 100 percent of Biden voters. Philip Bump, "More Than 8 in 10 Trump Voters Think Biden's Win Is Not Legitimate," *Washington Post,* November 11, 2020.

11. In a poll conducted shortly after Trump's impeachment, 60 percent of Republican respondents said party leaders "should follow Trump's lead in the future rather than go in a different direction." The 35 percent who said the party should move in a different direction tended to identify as moderates or liberals, to be college-educated, and were not White evangelical Christians. Scott Clement, Emily Guskin, and Dan Balz, "Poll Finds Opposition to Riot, Support to Bar Trump from Serving Again," *Washington Post,* January 15, 2021. For revealing interviews with local Republican party leaders still devoted to Trump after the second impeachment, see Lisa Lerer and Reid Epstein, "Abandon Trump? Deep in G.O.P. Ranks, the MAGA Mind-

Set Prevails," *New York Times,* January 15, 2021. See also Gary C. Jacobson, "Donald Trump's Big Lie and the Future of the Republican Party," *Presidential Studies Quarterly,* April 15, 2021, https://doi.org/10.1111/psq.12716. Jacobson argues Trump's "unshakeable" hold on Republican voters allows him to intimidate party leaders, and maintain control over them.

12. Shortly after the violent disorders at the Capitol, Trump's Twitter account was "permanently" suspended according to a statement issued by the company "due to the risk of further incitement of violence." If the suspension is indeed permanent, Trump would be deprived of what he views as his most important method of communicating with his followers. On the company's suspension of the account, see Christiano Lima, "Twitter Permanently Suspends Trump's Account," *Politico,* January 8, 2021.

13. Longitudinal survey data are not available—surveys of white identity or nationalist attitudes started with the ANES (American National Election Study) 2016 Pilot Study—so we cannot know with certainty if or to what extent there has been an increase in White nationalist sentiments since Reagan. Ashley Jardina in the survey of White identity or nationalist attitudes in 2016 for her book found between 30 and 40 percent of Whites were nationalist, exhibiting strong consciousness, identification, and support for perceived White interests and advantages. See *White Identity Politics* (New York: Cambridge University Press, 2019), 110–114.

14. Robert C. Smith, "Ronald Reagan, Donald Trump, and the Future of the Republican Party and Conservatism in America," *American Political Thought* 10 (2021): 283–289. Gwendoline Alphonso writes, "Donald Trump's campaign is not new or unprecedented." Instead, she argues, "it has built upon a long-standing hybrid strain of conservative ideology, termed here ascriptive neoliberalism, which has been integral to Republican ideology since the late 1960s," which was developed to bring "white southern Democrats into Republican ranks. . . . Trump's formulation builds on and retains the essence of this ideological strain, highlighting the link between racial identity and (market-based) liberalism that now constructs the political legitimacy of newer groups within the Republican fold such as working-class whites, while delegitimizing other groups, like Mexicans and Muslims." See "'One People, Under One God, Saluting One American Flag': Trump, the Republican Party, and the Construction of American Nationalism," in Zachary Callen and Philip Rocco, eds., *American Political Development and the Trump Presidency* (Philadelphia: University of Pennsylvania Press, 2020), 56. Alphonso traces the origins of these nationalist sentiments to the 1964 Goldwater campaign.

15. Julia Azari, "The Scrambled Cycle: Realignment, Political Time and the Trump Presidency," in Callen and Rocco, eds., *American Political Development and the Trump Presidency.*

16. Patrick Buchanan, *Suicide of a Superpower: Will America Survive to 2025?* (New York: Thomas Dunne, 2011), 349 (emphasis added). William Adler avers that even now Trump's politics should be viewed as disjunctive, "representing the end of the Reagan regime." In this respect, he writes, "Trump will quite likely be the last of this regime's presidents. His significant departure from previous norms of the presidency, while reminiscent in some ways of an unconventional president such as Teddy

Roosevelt, are fundamentally better understood as the last gasps of a dying regime, akin to the presidencies of Franklin Pierce, Herbert Hoover, or Jimmy Carter." See "Whose President? Donald Trump and the Reagan Regime," in Callen and Rocco, *American Political Development and the Trump Presidency*, 103, 109.

17. Rob Griffin, Ruy Teixeira, and William Frey, *America's Electoral Future: Demographic Shifts and the Future of the Trump Coalition* (Washington: Center for American Progress, 2020).

18. Hope Yen, "Hispanics Fuel U.S. White Population Growth," Associated Press, September 29, 2011. See also George Yancey, *Who Is White? Latinos, Asians, and the New Black/Non-Black Divide* (Boulder, CO: Lynne Rienner, 2003).

19. National Conference of Christians and Jews, *Taking America's Pulse: The Full Report of the National Survey on Inter-Group Relations* (New York: National Conference of Christians and Jews, 1994); and Paula McClain et al., "Racial Distancing in a Southern City: Immigrant Views of Black Americans," *Journal of Politics* 68 (2006): 541–584.

20. Lani Guinier and Gerald Torres, *The Miner's Canary: Enlisting Race, Resisting Power, Transforming Democracy* (Cambridge: Harvard University Press, 2002), 24.

21. Nate Cohn, "Why Rising Diversity Might Not Help Democrats as Much as They Hope," *New York Times*, May 4, 2021; and Richard Alba, "The Likely Persistence of a White Majority," *The American Prospect*, January 11, 2016.

22. Perlstein, *Reaganland*. See also Daniel Lucks, *Reconsidering Reagan: Racism, Republicans and the Road to Trump* (Boston: Beacon, 2020).

23. Robert P. Jones, *The End of White Christian America* (New York: Simon & Schuster, 2017). In the past decade, the percentage of Americans identifying as Christian declined by 12 percentage points to 65 percent. Pew Research Center, "In U.S., Decline of Christianity Continues at Rapid Pace," October 17, 2019. In the year of Trump's election 63 percent of Republican identifiers agreed to be "truly American" it was important to be a Christian. In 2020, those who agreed declined to 48 percent. Among Democrats, the comparable figures were 41 and 25 percent. See Aidan Connaughton, "In Both Parties Fewer Now Say Being Christian or Born in U.S. Is Important to Being 'Truly American,'" Pew Research, May 25, 2021. And the secularist segment of the population has grown and is likely to continue to grow. According to Pew data, in the 1960s secularists (persons with no religious affiliation) were 2 percent of the population. In 2018–2019 they constituted 26 percent, up from 17 percent in 2009.

24. Opinion tends to fluctuate on abortion but generally only about a third of the public favor a complete ban, while 77 percent of White evangelicals favor making all abortions illegal. Same-sex marriage is supported by nearly two-thirds of Americans including about a third of White evangelicals. See "Public Opinion on Abortion," Pew Research Center, Fact Sheet, August 29, 2019 and "Attitudes on Same-Sex Marriage," Pew Research Center, Fact Sheet, May 24, 2019.

25. Robert C. Smith and Richard Seltzer, *Polarization and the Presidency: From FDR to Barack Obama* (Boulder, CO: Lynne Rienner, 2015), 184–185.

26. Although the proportion of the White evangelical vote for Trump declined slightly between 2016 and 2020, it nevertheless constituted 40 percent of his voters. Although only 15 percent of the population (declining from 21 percent in 2008), their proportion of the electorate has remained steady or slightly increased. This suggests at least the short-term efficacy of Buchanan's strategy of mobilizing White Christians, which Trump effectively did during both campaigns. See Jason Husser, "Why Trump Is Reliant on White Evangelicals," Brookings Institution, April 6, 2020, http://www.brookings.edu/blog/fixgov/2020/04/06/why-trump-isreliant-on-white-evangelicals/. It should also be noted that there is a close relationship historically and today between White evangelicalism and racism. See Anthea Butler, *White Evangelical Racism: The Politics of Morality in America* (Chapel Hill: University of North Carolina Press, 2021). See also Robert Jones, *White Too Long: The Legacy of White Supremacy in American Christianity* (New York: Simon & Schuster, 2020).

27. The Senate by some calculations in a couple of decades will have approximately a third of the population living in disproportionately Republican states controlling about two-thirds of its seats. See one such calculation reported by Philip Bump, "By 2040, Two-Thirds of Americans Will Be Represented by 30 Percent of Senate," *Washington Post*, November 24. 2020. Unlike the electoral college, the Senate cannot be reformed by amending the Constitution to make it a more democratic, representative body because Article V provides "that no state, without its Consent, shall be deprived of its equal suffrage in the Senate."

28. Carol Anderson, *One Person, One Vote: How Voter Suppression Is Destroying Our Democracy* (New York: Bloomsbury, 2018); and Keith Bentele and Erin O'Brien, "Jim Crow 2.0? Why States Consider and Adopt Restrictive Voter Access Policies," *Perspectives on Politics* 11 (2013): 1088–1116. In 2021 Republican-controlled legislatures considered dozens of bills that could suppress the vote, including by limiting mail voting, early in-person voting, and election day voting; enhanced voter identification requirements; and narrower eligibility for absentee voting.

29. Larry Bartels, "Ethnic Antagonism Erodes Republicans' Commitment to Democracy," *Proceedings of the National Academy of Sciences* 117 (2020), https://www.pnas.org/content/117/37/22752, 3.

30. Ibid.

31. Ibid., 1.

32. Ibid., 5.

33. Kathleen Belew, *Bring the War Home: The White Power Movement and Paramilitary America* (Cambridge: Harvard University Press, 2019).

34. A CBS/PBS/Marist College poll found 21 percent of Republicans approved of the assault on the Capitol; 43 percent described it as patriotic, 50 percent as "defending freedom," and 47 percent agreed it was a "mostly legitimate protest." Overall, 26 percent of Republicans compared to 13 percent of Democrats agreed, "It can be acceptable for people to use force or violence to try to achieve goals, if necessary." Aaron Blake, "Many Republicans Sympathize with Those Who Stormed the Capitol," *Washington Post*, January 13, 2021.

Bibliography

Aberbach, Joel, and Bert Rockman. "Clashing Beliefs Within the Executive Branch: The Nixon Administration and the Bureaucracy." *American Political Science Review* 70 (1976): 406–468.

Abrajano, Marisa, and Zoltan Hajnal, *White Backlash: Immigration, Race, and American Politics.* Princeton: Princeton University Press, 2017.

Abramowitz, Alan. *The Disappearing Center: Engaged Citizens, Polarization, and American Democracy.* New Haven: Yale University Press, 2010.

———. *The Great Realignment: Race, Party Transformation, and the Rise of Donald Trump.* New Haven: Yale University Press, 2018.

Adler, William. "Whose President? Donald Trump and the Reagan Regime." In Zachary Callen and Philip Rocco, eds., *American Political Development and the Trump Presidency.* Philadelphia: University of Pennsylvania Press, 2020.

Alba, Richard. *Ethnic Identity: The Transformation of White America.* New Haven: Yale University Press, 1990.

———. "The Likely Persistence of a White Majority." *The American Prospect,* January 11, 2016.

Alberta, Tim. *American Carnage: On the Front Lines of the Republican Civil War and the Rise of Donald Trump.* New York: Harper Collins, 2019.

Alphonso, Gwendoline. "'One People, Under One God, Saluting One American Flag': Trump, the Republican Party, and the Construction of American Nationalism." In Zachary Callen and Philip Rocco, eds., *American Political Development and the Trump Presidency.* Philadelphia: University of Pennsylvania Press, 2020.

Alterman, Eric. *Lying in State: Why Presidents Lie and Why Trump Is Worse.* New York: Basic Books, 2020.

Anderson, Carol. *One Person, One Vote: How Voter Suppression Is Destroying Our Democracy.* New York: Bloomsbury, 2018.

Angelo, Nathan. *One America? Presidential Appeals to Racial Resentment from LBJ to Donald Trump.* Albany: SUNY Press, 2020.

Azari, Julia. "The Scrambled Cycle: Realignment, Political Time, and the Trump Presidency." In Zachary Callen and Philip Rocco, eds., *American Political Development and the Trump Presidency.* Philadelphia: University of Pennsylvania Press, 2020.

Barber, James David. "Adult Identity and Presidential Style." *Daedalus* 97 (1968): 938–968.

———. *The Lawmakers: Recruitment and Adaptation to Legislative Life.* New Haven: Yale University Press, 1967.

———. *The Presidential Character: Predicting Performance in the White House.* Englewood Cliffs, NJ: Prentice Hall, 1972.

———. "Strategies for Understanding Politicians." *American Journal of Political Science* 18 (1974): 443–467.

Bartels, Larry. "Ethnic Antagonisms Erode Republican Commitment to Democracy." *Proceedings of the National Academy of Sciences* 117 (2020). https://www.pnas.org/content/117/37/22752.

Belew, Kathleen. *Bring the War Home: The White Power Movement and Paramilitary America.* Cambridge: Harvard University Press, 2019.

Bergen, Peter. *Trump and His Generals: The Cost of Chaos.* New York: Penguin Books, 2019.

Bernhard, Michael, and Daniel O'Neil. "Trump: Causes and Consequences." *Perspectives on Politics* 17 (2019): 317–324.

Blair, Gwenda. *The Trumps: Three Generations That Built an Empire.* New York: Simon & Schuster, 2000.

Brown, Lara. *Amateur Hour: Presidential Character and the Question of Leadership.* New York: Routledge, 2020.

Buchanan, Patrick. *Day of Reckoning: How Hubris, Ideology, and Greed Are Tearing America Apart.* New York: St. Martin's, 2017.

———. *Suicide of a Superpower: Will America Survive to 2025?* New York: Thomas Dunne, 2011.

Bunyasi, Tehama Lopez. "The Role of Whiteness in the 2016 Presidential Primaries." *Perspectives on Politics* 17 (2019): 679–698.

Butler, Anthea. *White Evangelical Racism: The Politics of Morality in America.* Chapel Hill: University of North Carolina Press, 2021.

Callen, Zachary, and Philip Rocco, eds. *American Political Development and the Trump Presidency.* Philadelphia: University of Pennsylvania Press, 2020.

Ceaser, James. "Demagoguery, Statesmanship, and Presidential Politics." In Joseph Bessette and Jeffrey Tulis, eds. *The Constitutional Presidency.* Baltimore: Johns Hopkins University Press, 2009.

Clifford, Scott. "Reassessing the Structure of Presidential Character." *Electoral Studies* 54 (2018): 240–257.

Cohen, Marty, David Karol, and John Zaller. *The Party Decides: Presidential Nominations After Reform.* Chicago: University of Chicago Press, 2008.

Converse, Phillip. "The Nature of Belief Systems in Mass Publics." In David Apter, ed., *Ideology and Discontent.* New York: Free Press, 1964.

Cook, Corey. "White Nationalism, Black Interests, and Contemporary American Politics." In Robert C. Smith, Cedric Johnson, and Robert Newby, eds., *What Has This Got to Do with the Liberation of Black People: The Impact of Ronald W. Walters on African American Thought and Leadership.* Albany: SUNY Press, 2014.

Corwin, Edward. *The Presidency: Office and Powers.* New York: New York University Press, 1984.

D'Antonio, Michael. *Never Enough: Donald Trump and the Pursuit of Success.* New York: Thomas Dunne, 2015.

Dionne, E. J., Norman Ornstein, and Thomas Mann. *One Nation After Trump: A Guide to the Perplexed, the Disillusioned, the Desperate, and the Not-Yet Deported.* New York: St. Martin's, 2017.

Drezner, Daniel. "This Time Is Different: Why U.S. Foreign Policy Will Never Recover." *Foreign Affairs,* April 16, 2019. http://www.foreignaffairs.com/articles/2019-04-16/time-different/.

Edwards, George. "The Bully in the Pulpit: The Impact of Donald Trump's Public Discourse." Paper presented at the 2019 annual meeting of the American Political Science Association, Washington.

———. *Changing Their Minds: Donald Trump and Presidential Leadership.* Chicago: University of Chicago Press, 2021.

———. "No Deal: Donald Trump's Leadership of Congress." Paper presented at the 2017 annual meeting of the American Political Science Association, San Francisco.

———. *Why the Electoral College Is Bad for America.* New Haven: Yale University Press, 2005.

Fiorina, Morris, with Samuel Adams. *Disconnect: The Breakdown of Representation in American Politics.* Norman: University of Oklahoma Press, 2009.

Free, Lloyd, and Hadley Cantril. *The Political Beliefs of Americans: A Study of Public Opinion.* New Brunswick: Rutgers University Press, 1967.

Freeman, Jo. "The Political Culture of the Democratic and Republican Parties." *Political Science Quarterly* 101 (1986): 327–356.

Genovese, Michael. *How Trump Governs: An Assessment and Prognosis.* Amherst, NY: Cambria Press, 2017.

George, Alexander. "Assessing Presidential Character." *World Politics* 26 (1974): 234–282.

George, Alexander, and Juliette George. *Woodrow Wilson and Colonel House.* New York: John Day, 1956.

Glad, Betty. "Evaluating Presidential Character." *Presidential Studies Quarterly* 28 (1978): 861–872.

Graham, Jesse, et al. "Liberals and Conservatives Rely on Different Sets of Moral Foundations." *Journal of Personality and Psychology* 16 (2009): 1029–1046.

Green, Jon, and Sean McElwee. "The Differential Effects of Economic and Racial Attitudes on the Election of Donald Trump." *Perspectives on Politics* 17 (2018): 358–369.

Green, Joshua. *Devil's Bargain: Steve Bannon, Donald Trump, and the Storming of the Republican Party.* New York: Penguin, 2017.

Green, Steven. "The Role of Character Assessments in Presidential Approval." *American Politics* 29 (2001): 196–210.

Greenstein, Fred. *Personality and Politics: Problems of Evidence, Inference, and Conceptualization.* Chicago: Markham, 1969.

Griffin, Rob, William Frey, and Ruy Teixeira. *America's Electoral Future: Demographic Shifts and the Future of the Trump Coalition.* Washington: Center for American Progress, 2020.

Grossmann, Matt, and David Hopkins. *Asymmetric Politics: Ideological Republicans and Group Interest Democrats.* New York: Oxford University Press, 2016.

Haass, Richard. "Present at the Disruption: How Trump Unmade U.S. Foreign Policy*" Foreign Affairs,* August 11, 2020. http://www .foreignaffairs.com/articles/united-states/2020-08-11/presenr-disruption.

Hahl, Oliver, et al. "The Authentic Appeal of the Lying Demagogue: Proclaiming the Deeper Truth About Political Illegitimacy." *American Sociological Review* 83 (2018): 1–33.

Hanson, Victor Davis. *The Case for Trump.* New York: Basic Books, 2019.

Hargrove, Erwin. *Presidential Leadership: Personality and Style.* New York: Macmillan, 1966.

———. "Presidential Personality and Revisionist Views of the Presidency." *American Journal of Political Science* 17 (1973): 819–835.

Helderman, Rosalind, and Matt Zapotosky. *The Mueller Report.* New York: Scribner, 2019.

Hennessey, Susan, and Benjamin Wittes. *Unmaking the Presidency: Donald Trump's War on the World's Most Powerful Office.* New York: Farrar, Straus and Giroux, 2020.

Herbert, Jon, Trevor McCrisken, and Andrew Wroe. *The Ordinary Presidency of Donald Trump.* New York: Palgrave, 2019.

Hetherington, Marc, and Jonathan Weiler. *Authoritarianism and Polarization in American Politics.* New York: Cambridge University Press, 2009.

Holden, Charles, Zach Messitte, and Jerald Podair. *Republican Populist: Spiro Agnew and the Origins of Donald Trump.* Charlottesville: University of Virginia Press, 2019.

Hunter, James Davison. *Culture Wars: The Struggle to Define America.* New York: Basic Books, 1991.

Hutchings, Vincent, and Nicholas Valentino. "The Centrality of Race in American Politics." *Annual Review of Political Science* 7 (2004): 383–408.

Jacobson, Gary. "Donald Trump's Big Lie and the Future of the Republican Party." *Presidential Studies Quarterly.* April 15, 2021. https://doi.org /10.1111/psq.12716.

———. "Polarization, Gridlock, and Presidential Politics in 2016." *Annals of the American Academy of Political and Social Sciences* 667 (2017): 226–246.

Jamieson, Kathleen Hall, and Doron Taussig. "Disruption, Demonization, Deliverance, and Norm Destruction: The Rhetorical Signature of Donald Trump." *Political Science Quarterly* 132 (2017–2018): 619–650.

Jardina, Ashley. *White Identity Politics.* New York: Cambridge University Press, 2019.

Johnston, David Cay. *The Making of Donald Trump.* New York: Melville House, 2016.

Jones, Robert P. *The End of White Christian America.* New York: Simon & Schuster, 2017.

Karl, Jonathan. *Front Row at the Trump Show.* New York: Dutton, 2020.

Kernell, Samuel. *Going Public: New Strategies of Presidential Leadership.* Washington: Congressional Quarterly Press, 1997.

Kessler, Glenn, Salavador Rizzo, and Meg Kelly. *Donald Trump and His Assault on Truth.* New York: Scribner, 2020.

Kessler, Ronald. *The Trump White House: Changing the Rules of the Game.* New York: Crown Forum, 2018.

Kinder, Donald, and Nathan Kalmore. *Neither Liberal or Conservative: Ideological Innocence in the American Public.* Chicago: University of Chicago Press, 2017.

Kinder, Donald, and Lynn Sanders. *Divided by Color: Racial Politics and American Democracy.* Chicago: University of Chicago Press, 1996.

Kranish, Michael, and Marc Fisher. *Trump Revealed: An American Journey of Ambition, Ego, Money, and Power.* New York: Scribner, 2016.

———. *Trump Revealed: The Definitive Biography of the 45th President.* New York: Scribner, 2017.

Laderman, Charles, and Brendan Simms. *Donald Trump: The Making of a World View.* London: I. B. Tauris, 2017.

Lasswell, Harold. *Power and Personality.* New York: Norton, 1948.

Lee, Bandy, ed. *The Dangerous Case of Donald Trump.* New York: St. Martin's, 2017.

Leonhardt, David. "The Unique US Failure to Control the Virus." *New York Times,* August 9, 2020.

Levendusky, Matthew. *How Partisan Media Polarizes America.* Chicago: University of Chicago Press, 2013.

———. *The Partisan Sort: How Liberals Became Democrats and Conservatives Became Republicans.* Chicago: University of Chicago Press, 2009.

Levitsky, Steven, and Daniel Ziblatt. *How Democracies Die.* New York: Broadway, 2018.

Lim, Elvin. "Five Trends in Presidential Rhetoric: From George Washington to Bill Clinton." *Presidential Studies Quarterly* 32 (2002): 366–386.

Lucks, Daniel. *Reconsidering Reagan: Racism, Republicans, and the Road to Trump.* Boston: Beacon, 2020.

Lyons, Michael. "Presidential Character Revisited." *Political Psychology* 18 (1997): 791–805.

Mann, Thomas, and Norman Ornstein. *It's Worse Than It Looks: How the American Constitutional System Collided with the New Politics of Extremism.* New York: Basic Books, 2012.

Mansfield, Stephen. *Choosing Donald Trump: God, Anger, Hope, and Why Christian Conservatives Supported Him.* Grand Rapids, MI: Baker Books, 2017.

Martin, Jonathan, and Maggie Haberman. "Fear and Fealty: Trump Has Taken Control of the Republican Party with an Iron Grip and Retaliation." *New York Times,* December 12, 2019.

Mason, Lilliana. *Uncivil Agreement: How Politics Became Our Identity.* Chicago: University of Chicago Press, 2018.

Mayer, Jeffrey. "Two Presidents, Two Crises: Bush Wrestles with 9/11, Trump Fumbles Covid 19." *Presidential Studies Quarterly* 50 (2020): 629–649.

McAdams, Dan. *The Strange Case of Donald Trump: A Psychological Reckoning.* New York: Oxford University Press, 2020.

McClosky, Herbert. "Consensus and Ideology in American Politics." *American Political Science Review* 58 (1964): 361–382.

Medhurst, Martin. *The Prospects of Presidential Rhetoric.* College Station: Texas A & M University Press, 2018.

Mendelberg, Tali. *The Race Card: Campaign Strategy, Implicit Messages, and the Norm of Equality.* Princeton: Princeton University Press, 2001.

Mercieca, Jennifer. *Demagogue for President: The Rhetorical Genius of Donald Trump.* College Station: Texas A & M University Press, 2020.

Muir, William. "Ronald Reagan: The Primacy of Rhetoric." In Fred Greenstein, ed., *Leadership in the Modern Presidency.* Cambridge: Harvard University Press, 1988.

Mutz, Diana. "Status Threat, Not Economic Hardship, Explains 2016 Election." *Proceedings of the National Academy of Sciences* 115 (2018): 331–351.

Nelson, Michael. "The Psychological Presidency." In Nelson, ed., *The Presidency and the Political System.* Washington: Congressional Quarterly Press, 1998.

———. *Trump's First Year.* Charlottesville: University of Virginia Press, 2018.

Oliver, Eric, and Wendy Rahn. "The Rise of Trumpenvolk: Populism in the 2016 Election." *Annals of the American Academy of Political and Social Sciences* 667 (2016): 189–206.

Parker, Christopher, and Matt Barreto. *Change They Can't Believe In: The Tea Party and Reactionary Politics in America.* Princeton: Princeton University Press, 2013.

Patterson, Bradley. *The White House Staff: Inside the West Wing and Beyond.* Washington: Brookings Institution, 2001.

Perlstein, Rick. *Reaganland: America's Turn Right, 1976–1980.* New York: Simon & Schuster, 2020.

Pfiffner, James. *The Character Factor: How We Judge America's Presidents.* College Station: Texas A & M University Press, 2004.

———. "Donald Trump and the Norms of the Presidency." *Presidential Studies Quarterly* 51 (2021): 86–124.

———. "Judging Presidential Character." *Public Integrity* 5 (2002): 7–24.

———. "The Lies of Donald Trump: A Taxonomy." In Charles Lamb and Jacob Neiheisel, eds., *Presidential Leadership and the Trump Presidency: Executive Power and Democratic Governance.* New York: Palgrave Macmillan, 2020.

———. "Organizing the Trump Presidency." *Presidential Studies Quarterly* 48 (2018): 153–167.

Popkin, Samuel. *Crackup: The Republican Implosion and the Future of Presidential Politics.* New York: Oxford University Press, 2021.

Posner, Eric. *The Demagogue's Playbook: The Battle for American Democracy from the Founders to Trump.* New York: All Points Books, 2020.

Posner, Sarah. "White Evangelicals Think Trump Is Divinely Ordained." *Los Angeles Times,* June 14, 2020.

Prothro, James, and Charles Grigg. "Fundamental Principles of Democracy: Bases of Agreement and Disagreement." *Journal of Politics* 22 (1960): 276–294.

Qualls, James. "Barber's Typological Analysis of Political Leaders." *American Political Science Review* 71 (1977): 182–211.

Quirk, Paul. "Presidential Competence." In Michael Nelson, ed., *The Presidency and the Political System*. Washington: Congressional Quarterly Press, 1998.

Reedy, George. *The Twilight of the Presidency*. New York: World Publishing, 1970.

Renshon, Stanley. *The Psychological Assessment of Presidential Candidates*. New York: New York University Press, 1996.

————. *The Real Psychology of the Trump Presidency*. New York: Palgrave Macmillan, 2020.

Robinson, Donald. *Slavery in the Structure of American Politics, 1765–1820*. New York: Harcourt Brace Jovanovich, 1970.

————. *To the Best of My Ability: The Presidency and the Constitution*. New York: Norton, 1987.

Rossiter, Clinton. "The Powers of the Presidency." In Harry Bailey, ed., *Classics of the American Presidency*. Oak Park, IL: Moore, 1980.

Rottingham, Brandon, and Justin Vaughn. "Official Results of the 2018 Presidents and Executive Politics Presidential Greatness Survey." Washington: American Political Science Association, 2018.

Rucker, Philip, and Carol Leonnig. *A Very Stable Genius: Donald J. Trump's Testing of America*. New York: Penguin, 2020.

Schaefer, Todd. *Presidential Power Meets the Art of the Deal: Applying Neustadt to the Trump Presidency*. New York: Palgrave Pivot, 2021.

Schaffner, Brian, Matthew MacWilliams, and Tatishe Nteta. "Understanding White Polarization in the 2016 Vote for President: The Sobering Role of Racism and Sexism." *Political Science Quarterly* 133 (2018): 9–34.

Schwartz, Tony. "I Wrote *The Art of Deal* with Donald Trump." In Bandy Lee, ed., *The Dangerous Case of Donald Trump*. New York: St. Martin's, 2017.

Sides, John, Michael Tesler, and Lynn Vavreck, *Identity Crisis: The 2016 Presidential Campaign and the Battle for the Meaning of America*. Princeton: Princeton University Press, 2018.

Skocpol, Theda, and Vanessa Williamson. *The Tea Party and the Remaking of the Republican Party*. New York: Oxford University Press, 2012.

Skowronek, Stephen. *The Politics Presidents Make: Leadership from John Adams to Bill Clinton*. Cambridge: Harvard University Press, 1997.

Smith, Robert C. *Conservatism and Racism and Why in America They Are the Same*. Albany: SUNY Press, 2010.

Smith, Robert C., and Richard Seltzer. *Polarization and the Presidency: From FDR to Barack Obama*. Boulder, CO: Lynne Rienner, 2015.

————. "Ronald Reagan, Donald Trump, and the Future of the Republican Party and Conservatism in America." *American Political Thought* 10 (2021): 283–289.

————. "Understanding White Nationalism in America: The Contribution of Ronald Walters." *National Review of Black Politics* 2 (2021): 53–62.

Smith, Rogers, and Desmond King. "White Protectionism in America." *Perspectives on Politics* 19 (2021): 460–478.

Sniderman, Paul, et al. "The Fallacy of Democratic Elitism: Competition and Commitment to Civil Liberties." *British Journal of Political Science* 21 (1991): 349–370.

Stanley, Timothy. *The Crusader: The Life and Tumultuous Times of Pat Buchanan.* New York: Thomas Dunne, 2012.

Stuckey, Mary. "The Rhetoric of the Trump Administration." *Presidential Studies Quarterly* 51 (2021): 125–150.

Swain, Carol. *The New White Nationalism in America: Its Challenge to Integration.* New York: Cambridge University Press, 2004.

Teixeira, Ruy. *The Emerging Democratic Majority.* New York: Scribner, 2002.

Tesler, Michael. "The Return of Old-Fashioned Racism to White Americans' Partisan Preferences in the Early Obama Era." *Journal of Politics* 75 (2013): 110–123.

Thompson, Dennis. "Constitutional Character: Virtues and Vices in Presidential Leadership." *Presidential Studies Quarterly* 40 (2010): 23–37.

Trump, Donald. *Time to Get Tough: Make America Great Again.* Washington: Regnery, 2011.

Trump, Donald, with Tony Schwartz. *The Art of the Deal.* New York: Random House, 1987.

Trump, Donald, with Dave Shiflett. *The America We Deserve.* New York: Renaissance Books, 2000.

Tulis, Jeffrey. "On Presidential Character." In Bessette and Tulis, eds., *The Presidency in the Constitutional Order.* Baton Rouge: Louisiana State University Press, 1981.

———. *The Rhetorical Presidency.* Princeton: Princeton University Press, 1987.

Walker, Stephen. "The Psychology of Presidential Decision Making." In George Edwards and William Howell, eds., *Oxford Handbook of the Presidency.* New York: Oxford University Press, 2009.

Walters, Ronald. *White Nationalism, Black Interests: Conservative Public Policy and the Black Community.* Detroit: Wayne State University Press, 2003.

Whipple, Chris. *The Gatekeepers: How the White House Chiefs of Staff Define Every White House.* New York: Crown, 2017.

Willner, Ann Ruth. *The Spellbinders: Charismatic Political Leadership.* New Haven: Yale University Press, 1984.

Wilson, Carter. *Trumpism: Race, Class, Populism, and Public Policy.* Lanham, MD: Lexington Books, forthcoming.

Wilson, Robert. *Character Above All: Ten Presidents from FDR to George Bush.* New York: Simon & Schuster, 1996.

Wolff, Michael. *Fire and Fury: Inside the Trump White House.* New York: Henry Holt, 2018.

Woodward, Bob. *Fear: Trump in the White House.* New York: Simon & Schuster, 2018.

———. *Rage.* New York: Simon & Schuster, 2020.

Wright, Lauren. *Star Power: American Democracy in the Age of Celebrity Candidates.* New York: Routledge, 2020.

Zelizer, Julian. *Burning Down the House: Newt Gingrich and the Rise of the New Republican Party.* New York: Penguin Books, 2020.

Index

About the Book

CONVERSATIONS ABOUT DONALD TRUMP OFTEN BEGIN
with the question: how did he become president? In *Questions of Character*, Robert Smith provides some compelling answers based on his assessment of the role that personality and character played leading up to and during Trump's term in office.

Smith traces the impact of Trump's character on the conduct of domestic and foreign policy, the organization of the White House staff and decisionmaking processes, and the habitual use of inflammatory rhetoric to advance policies and rally and sustain the "Make America Great Again" constituency. He also looks at Trump's reaction to defeat in the 2020 election. The result is a comprehensive exploration of the consequences of Trump's character—personal, presidential, and democratic—during this contentious period in US presidential history.

Robert C. Smith is professor emeritus of political science at San Francisco State University. His numerous publications include *Polarization and the Presidency: From FDR to Barack Obama* (coauthored with Richard Seltzer) and *John F. Kennedy, Barack Obama, and the Politics of Ethnic Incorporation and Avoidance*.